**Alan Tomlinson** is Professor of Leisure Studies and Director of Research in the Centre for Sport Research, University of Brighton, UK. He is the author of *Sport and Leisure Cultures* and *A Dictionary of Sports Studies*.

**In the same series:**

'Unique and uniquely beautiful. . . . A single map here tells us
more about the world today than a dozen abstracts or scholarly tomes.'
*Los Angeles Times*

'A striking new approach to cartography. . . . No one wishing to keep a grip
on the reality of the world should be without these books.'
*International Herald Tribune*

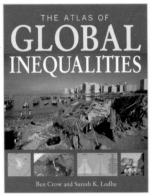

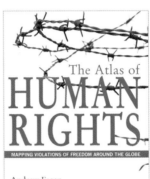

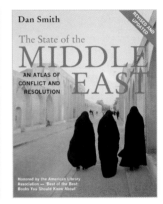

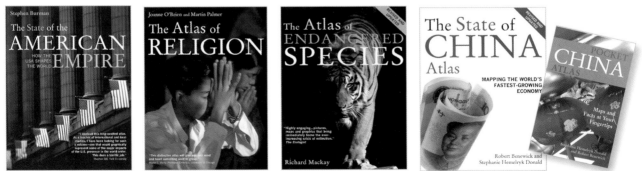

# THE ATLAS OF

## WHO PLAYS WHAT, WHERE, AND WHY

Alan Tomlinson

UNIVERSITY OF CALIFORNIA PRESS

*Berkeley  Los Angeles*

University of California Press, one of the most distinguished university presses in the United States, enriches lives around the world by advancing scholarship in the humanities, social sciences, and natural sciences. Its activities are supported by the UC Press Foundation and by philanthropic contributions from individuals and institutions. For more information, visit www.ucpress.edu.

University of California Press
Berkeley and Los Angeles, California

Library of Congress Control Number: 2010934245

ISBN: 978-0-520-26824-1 (pbk. : alk. paper)

Produced for the University of California Press by
**Myriad Editions Limited**
**Brighton, UK**
**www.MyriadEditions.com**

Edited and coordinated for Myriad Editions by
Jannet King and Candida Lacey
Design and graphics by Lisa Garner at Itonic Design
Maps created by Isabelle Lewis

Printed on paper produced from sustainable sources.
Printed and bound in Hong Kong through Lion Production
under the supervision of Bob Cassels, The Hanway Press, London.

15   14   13   12   11
10   9   8   7   6   5   4   3   2   1

# CONTENTS

## PART 3: THE ECONOMICS OF SPORTS     94

## PART 4: COUNTRY PROFILES     110

# INTRODUCTION

Sports have become one of the world's biggest cultural industries, and the highest profile events and contests attract the attention of increasing millions of people in homes, sports bars, and stadiums. Along with film and music, sports create superstars and celebrities. They offer dramatic diversions from the trials and routines of working or domestic living, as fans follow the fortunes of their favourite teams and players. They offer collective experiences in an individualized and fragmented world. Anyone who has been hugged by a stranger in a stadium knows the uncanny yet sustained capacity of sports to bring people together, and sports' ability to create temporary but real and passionately expressed bonds. They can also be practised individually and in isolation.

Magnificent trivia sports might be, but we have come to appreciate the importance of the everyday, vital for many people's well-being and balance. All agree that sports activity, or sports spectating, can enrich everyday living, and that sports also offer a lucrative route for talented and ambitious individual sportsmen and women to succeed. They contribute to national identity and pride, and international rivalries. Asking who plays what, where, and why takes us into fascinating areas of the global economy, international relations, consumer tastes, citizenship, and public culture; asking such questions directs us to extremes of extraordinary wealth and deprivation, exploitation and co-operation. Participating in a sport may still be just one available leisure option for some; for others it is a distant dream, or a matter of life and death. Whilst working on this atlas I spent time in Johannesburg, South Africa, during the 2010 men's Football World Cup Finals. A taxi-driver during one of my cross-city rides was expressing mild support for the national side. Tickets were beyond his means. I told him that I was going to Cape Town, and asked him whether he ever holidayed at the ocean. "Holiday", he sighed, "that for me is no more than a word in the dictionary."

## Who plays?

Psychologists, historians and anthropologists argue over the nature of what the great Dutch historian Johan Huizinga called the "play element in culture". Is play innate, a human universal? Are modern sports expressions of this core human characteristic? One very simple response to this is to see who plays our modern sports. And of course the answers are varied. People adapt their sporting choices to age and circumstances. But all available participation data confirm that if you did not play early in life through lack of opportunity (or inclination), you are unlikely to do so later in life. Many sports, therefore, continue to be characteristic of a particular social class grouping, or to be influenced disproportionately by the patriarchal, male-dominated values and attitudes that may have initially shaped them. Sports have empowered women in many ways, but inequality – in access, prize money, media coverage – continues to be the order of the sporting day.

## What is a sport?

Endless debates have failed to establish any simple or shared definition of a sport. Most agree that it is a human activity (a contest or performance) usually associated with a degree and combination of human exertion and skill, which in its modern form is conducive to measurement and the evaluation of individual and team performance. The degree of human exertion in sports such as darts or billiards is of course limited and, to some purists, laughable. But the sporting spirit, as competition, pervades even completely sedentary activities, and the International Olympic Committee (IOC) has given forms of recognition to games as diverse as chess and bridge.

Sociologists, though, like definitions, and for them further features of a sport include: its separateness from the hurly-burly of the workplace or the grinding routines of domestic life, its capacity to construct a world of its own with distinctive rules, schedules, and spaces, and the possibility of improvement of skill and performance through planned practice.

Sports therefore provide special kinds of experience that prove attractive to individuals and groups at particular times and in particular places. But, as any historically informed understanding of sports soon show, these times and places vary widely, and, recognizing this, many commentators have broadened their understanding to embrace a range of bodily practices that capture, but in widely varying ways, the key elements of the sporting experience. The IOC recognizes DanceSport and *Wushu* (traditional Chinese martial arts), and some contemporary surveys have identified more than 200 sports. Not all sports and body cultures are a matter of personal choice; some have been imposed, even forced, upon a population for political and ideological reasons. In awareness of this minefield of definitional problems, the atlas selects sports representing a range from the classic Greek legacy that has shaped much of modern track and field sports, to *les sports californienne*, as French social scientist Pierre Bourdieu dubbed the lifestyle sports that emerged as an accompaniment to the freedoms and promises of the hedonistic 1960s.

## Where?

In a time of new media, branding, rolling 24-hour news, and personalized portable internet devices and technologies, modern sports are omnipresent. When a particular story breaks – golfer Tiger Woods' serial sexual infidelities, soccer player Wayne Rooney's disillusionment with his employer Manchester United – it would be hard to remain unaware of this in the rhythm of any normal day, in the more developed and advantaged parts of the world in particular. But sports, in their separate worlds, still construct their own distinctive places. There is something special about the stadium, the bleachers, the journey or the walk to the match or game. The places where people play are part of the magic of the sports experience, now mediated anew by portable technologies and the internet. These contribute to new ways of consuming sports, and a constantly shifting economics of sports.

## Why?

We play and watch sports for fun, enjoyment, pleasure, excitement. But in some circumstances the fun soon fades. The great ice hockey player Eric Nesterenko recalled how much pleasure he got from playing as a child, but how the joy diminished the higher the stakes, and what was once play became routinized work. In the right balance, though, enjoyment and pleasure can come with the thrill of physical exhilaration, the tightness of the contest, the reaching for the "personal best". And in any contest or competitive encounter, sports provide ready-made dramatic narratives, with enigmas or questions posed along the way. Will s/he recover from that knock? Is s/he a choker? Does the head-to-head historical record matter? In a myriad of ways, sports theatricalize everyday life, bringing spectators into the dynamic of competition. Unlike in theatre, the opera or the classical concert, where hushed rows look on in awe at the performance, most sports draw in the crowd, encouraging participation and interactive response.

Some also play because they are spotted by talent scouts, and given a vision of the good life based upon potential success; or because the government of the day demands a particular kind of new citizen whose physical qualities represent the values of the political culture; or because policymakers equate physical activity and balanced exercise with a healthy life, and a cheaper health services bill. There is nothing new in much of this. The Roman satirist Juvenal noted that *mens sana in corpore sano* (a healthy mind in a healthy body) was something worth praying for, and that *panem et circences* (bread and races) became the focus of popular entertainment in times of declining political spirit. But what is always new is the contextual framing of a sport in time and place, which varies its meaning accordingly. People play sports or engage in bodily practices in modern affluent societies and the poorer countries of the world for reasons that may be very different to those of their predecessors; at the same time the nostalgia and sentiment that fuel sports fans claim historical connections and cultural continuity.

In this atlas we have embraced the everyday and the sublime, the mundane and the superlative. And at any of these levels, we know that sports produce marvellous human moments connecting the player and the onlooker. At the most elite levels, the athlete feels the emotions of the audience, and the onlooker is drawn into the production of the performance itself. This is what Hans Ulrich Gumbrecht calls "focused intensity", and, in the context of ball games, "beautiful plays" that can create moments of epiphany.

The individual, emotional pull of sports lies in their precious capacity to contribute to and make, not stand apart from, social contexts and meanings. Sports have the potential to transcend social cleavages of age, gender, class, status, and ethnicity; and in equal measure, an oft-proven capacity to deepen such cleavages. That is why sports are so serious a form of play, and deserving of the attentive curiosity of critical social scientists, imaginative mapmakers and graphic designers, as well as legions of worldwide fans and followers.

## Why sports matter

As this atlas was in the final stages of preparation, Tiger Woods was struggling for form and credibility, Germany's Sebastian Vettel became Formula 1 motor-racing's youngest-ever champion, and Europe had defeated the USA in a spine-tingling Ryder Cup thriller in a wet and chilly Wales. Some seasons were winding down, others were starting up again in the non-stop sporting calendar. For some, there could never be enough sports on our screens; for others, the cycles of the sporting calendar had long hit saturation point. But sports continue to matter. In their politicized and commercialized form they express the hopes of billions, and enrich beyond earlier imagination the talented and the entrepreneurial few.

The atlas is structured to represent these political and economic dimensions of sports. It is historically informed, and sensitive to the dynamics, influences, and legacies of the past, but concentrates on the contemporary world. The origins of numerous sports within 19th century Britain are described in individual case-studies, as are those of sports established in the rest of Europe, the Americas, and Asia. Part 1, though, focuses on the well-recognized political use of sports within societies, and in international sporting encounters. This includes the progressive cultural politics that are evident in sporting movements in the sphere of gay rights, peace and development initiatives, or disability. Part 3 looks at the key driving force of money and profit, at the deal-making in the world of international sports, and the contribution of sports to, for instance, merchandising and the gambling industry. Politics and money are at the heart of the expanding profile of sports in the contemporary world. Whilst these combine to provide astronomical rewards for a performing elite, and pleasure for countless millions across the world, there is little sign of any diminution of the profile of sports in the global economy and media marketplace.

Sports are politically convenient as a form of soft power, and economically seductive as a form of globalized commodity. Sandwiched between the politics and the money, we present an A to Z (or more accurately, an A to W) of selected sports, and, by telling their modern story and portraying their contemporary profile, we explore how this blend of the economic, the political, and the popular has sustained, and in many cases boosted, sports. This reveals the lurid as well as the laudable, the tragedy as well as the triumph. We see, in the mapping of resources and achievements, a picture of global sports in an increasingly unequal world.

The cultural profile and the global sports economy have massively increased, mainly through ever-expanding media coverage, and ever-larger international events, which transform cities, indeed countries, and boost their "brand". This has generated serious issues concerning the integrity of sports, as our coverage of gambling and the use of performance-enhancing drugs shows. The fans of sports from cycling to track and field, American Football to baseball, have had to accept that some of their sporting heroes are flawed champions. But outright cheating in sporting competition is rare, and the spirit of genuine competition – if not pure "fair-play", a term and ideal from a golden age of amateurism – appears overall to prevail. Sports continue to matter as long as the integrity of the competitive sporting spirit is upheld.

Sports also matter at the level of the individual and the community. For the individual they provide a source of identity, and a promise – if carefully managed – of a healthier life. For the group or the community, sports clubs and activities can be an expression of a buoyant civil society, a life between the market and the state, and lived in public rather than the privacy of the domestic setting. But in more advantaged societies the trend at the end of the last century – captured in Robert Putnam's *zeitgeist* phrase and metaphor "bowling alone" – was to move away from such collective activities, in societies characterized by decreasing social bonds and increasing forms of individualism. This tension – or balance – between the values of the traditional team-game and the more individualized, in some senses narcissistic, body cultures of our time is illuminated in the selected case-studies.

## Defying and defining the global trend

Whilst many of the sports covered in the atlas embody, and in turn reinforce, globalizing trends, we know how much sports are also a matter of local tradition, or of regional cultural affiliations and identities. In this opening part of the atlas, then, we follow this introduction with some coverage of sports that have little – or at least limited – aspiration to dominate the global sporting calendar. These are vignettes and colourful portraits of counter-currents, reminders of the idiosyncratic or distinctive nature of physical cultures and practices away from the mainstream.

For the most part, though, the sports selected for coverage tell a common story of the political significance of high-performance sports, the intensifying dependence of sports upon media-based income, and the rootedness of big sporting events in the affluent parts of the world. Brazil seeks to reverse this trend in staging the 2016 Olympic Games, but if the story of world sport continues in the ways depicted in this atlas, the main beneficiaries will continue to be the countries and the peoples of the already advantaged world.

**Alan Tomlinson**
Brighton, UK and Campillergues, L'Hérault, France
October 2010

# ACKNOWLEDGEMENTS

This has not been an easy story to tell. There is no world body to which we can refer for comparative credible figures on sports participation or the value of the sporting industry in a particular economy. We have therefore drawn upon a wide range of sources, from academic studies to commercial surveys, from government reports to industry overviews, from web and newspaper sources to personal observations throughout a third of a century of watching these trends and processes.

In making sense of what seemed at times an uncontrollable jumble of information and material, I am indebted to Candida Lacey and her team at Myriad Editions, in particular Jannet King, whose precise prose and semantic probings kept me on my mark; to Lisa Garner for her imaginative artistic and graphic skills, and Isabelle Lewis for her cartography; to Marcus Hunt for ferreting out much of the material that has found its way into maps and graphics in the atlas; to Bernadette Kirrane for locking me away in appropriate places to get on with the job, and then with a forensic eye spotting howlers and anomalies; to Steven Tomlinson for enthusiastic interest and supportive insights; to Lincoln Allison for sharing the writing of the Country Profiles, and to the University of Brighton for supporting me in a sabbatical period during which the research for and writing of the atlas was undertaken and completed.

**Alan Tomlinson**

# PHOTO CREDITS

The author and publishers would like to thank the following for the use of their photographs. Every effort has been made to identify and contact the copyright holders. The publisher shall be pleased to make appropriate acknowledgement in any future edition.

CC = Creative Commons License        iS = iStockphoto        Getty = Getty Images

5 Anita Ritenour / CC; 6 Jason R. William / CC; 7 Ben Blankenburg / iS; 9 Waverly Wyld / iS; 10 Adrian Dennis / Getty; 11 Alan Tomlinson; 12 Puma; 14 WorldWideImages / iS; CC; www.federationpeteca.com; Ciaran McGuiggan; Malouette; Focus on Nature / iS; 15 Pouria Lofti; jackol; Robert Murphy / Getty; 16 Alan Tomlinson; Les Cunliffe / iS; Mafue; 17 2009 jenswenzel-photography.com - all rights reserved; Right To Play; Jimmy Harris / CC; 18 Richard Giles; 21 Alan Tomlinson; 22 Commonwealth Games, Melbourne; 23 Commonwealth Games, Delhi; 24 Thomas Faivre-Duboz; Les Cunliffe / iS; 26 Mafue; Technogym; 27 Adysyady; 29 Courtesy Gay Games; 30 Puma; 2009 jenswenzel-photography.com - all rights reserved; 2009 jenswenzel-photography.com - all rights reserved; 31 Right To Play; 32 Gene Chutka / iS; Anita Ritenour / CC; Fabrizio Tarizzo / CC; 33 Courtesy Allison Fisher; jonethscone / CC; Pharaoh Hound / CC; 34 Ed Yourdon; National Football League; 35 Marcus Hunt; 38 Keith Allison; Ken Hackman / U.S. Air Force; 40 Claudio Gennari; 41 Tech. Sgt. Rick Sforza, U.S. Air Force.; 42 Gabriel Bouys / AFP / Getty; 44 Manan Vatsyayana / AFP / Getty; 46 Birgitte Magnus / iS; 47 Uzinusa / iS; Courtesy Allison Fisher; 48 Anita Ritenour / CC; 49 Fabrizio Tarizzo / CC; Neustockimages / iS; Union Cycliste Internationale; 50 Tsutomu Takasu / CC; Miriam Mannak; Yves Grau / iS; 51 JM Rosenfeld / CC; 52 Clive Mason / Getty; Andrew Yates/Stringer / AFP / Getty; 54 Denise Kappa / iS; 55 iShootPhotos, LLC / iS; 56 Keith Allison / CC; 57 Keith Allison / CC; 58 Angelika Schwarz / iS; John Dominis / Time & Life Pictures / Getty; 59 Alexei Mnogosmyslov / iS; FIG; 60 Armin Kuebelbeck / CC; International Handball Federation; 61 Steve Munday / Getty; 62 Tan Kian Khoon / iS; 63 Martin Rose / Bongarts / Getty; 64 Pharaoh Hound / CC; 65 IFHA; Goki / CC; 66 jonethscone / CC; 67 Robert Scoble / CC; Eric Feferberg / AFP / Getty; 68 Devon Stephens / iS; Giorgio Magini / iS; 69 Adrian Dennis / AFP / Getty; 70 Jeff Haynes / AFP / Getty; 71 SCC-RUNNING/Sailer; 72 Indrek Galetin / CC; 73 Chrkl / CC; Daniel Vaulot / CC; 74 Mark McArdle / CC; 75 Photo courtesy of U.S. Army, by Cameras in Action; Carey Akin / CC; 76 Jason R. William / US Navy ; 77 Steven Fruitsmaak / CC; Jeremy Teela / CC; 78 Stu Forster / Getty; 79 Jean-Pierre Muller / AFP / Getty; 80 Jonathan Fors / CC; Gilles Martin-Raget / BMW Oracle Racing; 81 Sculpies / iS; 82 Ben Blankenburg / iS; Michele Galli / iS; 83 technotr / iStocktphoto; Manuguf / CC; 84 Wolfgang Amri / CC; 85 Bryan Allison / CC; Tony Duffy / Getty ; 86 Justin Smith / CC; Justin Smith / CC; 88 André Zehetbauer / CC; 90 CC; 92 Ivan Burmistrov / iS; GameFace / iS; Jam Media / LatinContent Editorial / Getty; 93 J Mills / CC; 94 Ian Scott / iS; Sarah Holmstrom / iS; Leon Wilson / CC; 95 Bachpan Bachao Andolan; Alan Tomlinson; Alan Tomlinson; 96 Benoit Rousseau / iS; 99 Michiel Jelijs / CC; 100 Josh Hallet; Alan Tomlinson ; 102 Alan Tomlinson ; Daniel Padavona / iS; 103 Alija / iS; 105 Bachpan Bachao Andolan; Oxfam Australia; 107 UK National Lottery; 108 Carrie Bottomley / iS; Sarah Holmstrom / iS; 109 Matthew Dixon / iS; alle12 / iS; fotoVoyager / iS; bitbeerdealer / iS; Leon Wilson / CC; Danny Warren / iS; luoman / iS; Richard Rogers / iS; Ian Scott / iS; Vladimir Piskunov / iS; 110 Puma; Ed Yourdon / CC; Keith Allison / CC; 111 Alexei Mnogosmyslov / iS; Indrek Galetin / CC; technotr / iStocktphoto.

# NATIONAL SPORTS

In a world in which many sports aspire to achieve a global reach, and national associations and world championships are rampant, it is worth noting examples from around the globe of sports that are associated with specific countries or cultures, with no aspiration to take the global route. Some are preserved, revived, maybe even constructed, to encapsulate distinct national values. Others are nurtured as political symbols of minority groups.

**Basque Pelota – Basque country**
A game in which a small ball is hit against a wall or the side of a building. From the 1850s onwards, dedicated municipal and private *frontones* were built to accommodate spectators on banks of seats at the side of the court. The professional game is funded by a culture of bets and challenges rather leagues or knock-out competitions. The game is an emblem of regional nationalism.

**Gaelic Football – Ireland**
A 15-a-side game played between county teams across Eire and Northern Ireland that combines handling, passing, catching bouncing, carrying, and kicking the ball. Stimulated by the growth of the nationalist movement, the sport was codified in 1884 and transformed into a distinctive Irish cultural form. It has been successfully promoted to become one of the top spectator sports in Ireland.

**Pétanque – France**
A game widely played in France, where every settlement has enthusiasts and dedicated public areas. The Provence dialect gave the sport its name, which refers to how the thrower must keep the feet together when launching the ball. The national federation has 375,000 registered players, and millions of French people play the game casually, in vacations and on feast-days.

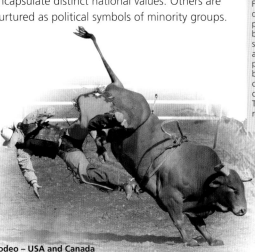

**Rodeo – USA and Canada**
A competitive exhibition of the skills of individual cowboys (or cattle-punchers) that originated in the southern and southwest states of the USA in the 1860s and 1870s. Its six classic events are calf-roping, bull-riding, team-roping, saddle-bronco riding, bareback bronco riding, and steer-wrestling. Animal rights activists have opposed rodeo, seeing it as a form of cruelty, and professional rodeo organizations have responded by introducing measures to protect the animals.

**Peteca – Brazil**
A game played with hand and shuttlecock on a court with a net. It existed in an elementary form among native Indians before the arrival of Portuguese explorers. The game was modernized in the 1940s, and moved from the streets, grass and sand to the courts. Its first national championship was held in 1987, presaging the growth of the game and the formation of a national confederation in 2001. Brazil has staged international matches with France, where a national federation was established in 1997.

**Pato – Argentina**
A sporting contest played on horseback by two teams of four, combining aspects of polo and basketball. The ball has handles, and players tug at it in the outstretched grip of rivals whilst standing in their stirrups; to score it must be thrown through a ring. It was particularly popular among the gauchos of Argentina, but with a live duck (a *pato*) rather than a ball. In the 1950s the country's president, Juan Perón, pronounced it the country's national game.

### Buzkashi – Afghanistan

A traditional game of the nomadic peoples of central Asia. In its modern form it involves hundreds of riders competing to get a headless goat's carcass into the opposition's goal. The sport is considered the Afghan (male's) national sport, and attracts crowds of thousands, justified by its practitioners and apologists as a means of teaching the riders not just equestrian skills, but principles of communication and teamwork.

### Dragon boat racing – China

An ancient Chinese sport combining competitive and aesthetic dimensions. Impromptu races developed, during the Tang dynasty (618–907), into major events commemorating public figures. Dragon boats are used in modern China as a form of cultural heritage, and by diasporic Chinese populations as an assertion of cultural identity.

### Sepak takraw – Thailand and Malaysia

A hybrid term derived from the Malay word for "kick", *sepak*, and the Thai word for "ball", *takraw*, to describe a three-a-side sport played on a badminton court. Known in Malaysia as *sepak raga*, it has been compared to volleyball, although no part of the hand can be used in keeping the ball up and propelling it over the net. Both men and women play the game, which is included in the Asian Games.

### Kabaddi – India

A traditional Indian team game usually played between two sides of 12 players, based on pursuit, with no equipment. Touch and movement are the basis of scoring. It is known as the "game of the masses", and has been linked to the notion of *Ahimsa*, which represents the separation of the self from violent acts and material possessions.

Promoted as an indigenous cultural practice and a form of resistance to colonial culture, it has been linked to militant Hindu politics. The sport's popularity has grown, and provides Indian women with a route to sports stardom.

### Rwandan high jump

Until the skill died out in the mid-20th century, Rwandan high jump – *Gusimbuka-Urukiramende* – was part of manly training, public celebration, and ritual. Heights were not measured, but a photograph from 1907 shows a man clearing a bar way above the heads of Europeans. Following the traumatic circumstances of the Rwandan genocide of 1994, attempts are being made by the organization Espérance, through a scheme called Jump Up! Rwanda, to revive high jumping as a source of indigenous and national pride.

### Australian Rules football – Australia

A fast and sometimes violent 18-a-side game played on an oval pitch of indeterminate size. The aim is to kick the oval ball between posts of different heights at the ends of the pitch. The ball may be moved by any part of the player's body, but must not be thrown. It was devised as a purely Australian game, though derived in part from Gaelic football played by Irish troops, gold diggers, and immigrants. It has prospered mostly in the southern and western states of Australia. It draws crowds of up to 120,000, of all ages, for its major tournaments.

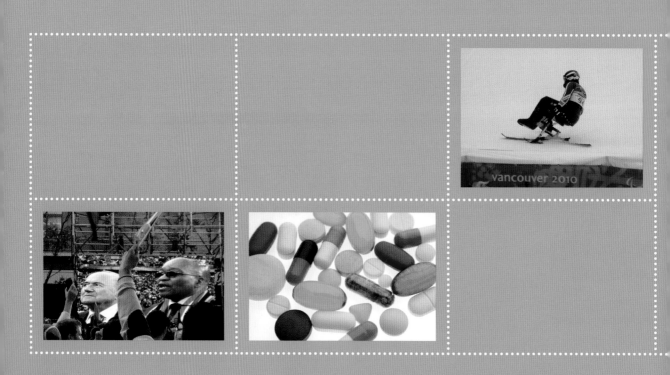

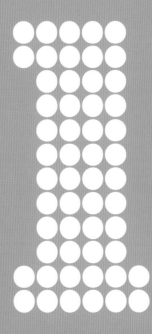

# INTERNATIONAL SPORTS POLITICS

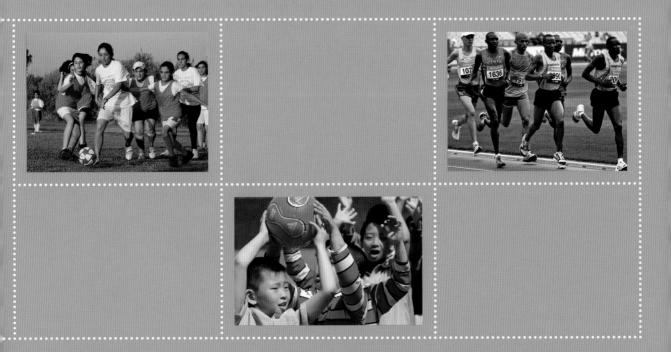

# THE OLYMPIC GAMES

The modern Olympic Games began in 1896, in Athens, Greece, the brainchild of French aristocrat Baron Pierre de Coubertin (1863–1937). The Summer Games have been held every four years since then, apart from when disrupted by two world wars. The first Winter Olympic Games was held in 1924. The Summer and Winter games were held in the same year up to 1992, after which the Lillehammer (Norway) 1994 Winter Games began a cycle that showcases the Olympics every two years. This keeps the Olympics "brand" to the fore, benefiting both broadcasters and corporate sponsors.

The Olympic Games has survived political and personal scandals and disasters, administrative corruption and economic crises, and continues to offer a spectacular mix of international sporting competition and national rivalries, claiming huge worldwide television audiences: 70 percent of the world's population for the 2008 Beijing Olympics. In the USA, the event attracted 27 million viewers each day and, with Michael Phelps winning eight gold medals in the pool, was the country's most viewed television event at the time.

The Olympics has often been used as a political platform, and as a way of asserting the qualities and characteristics of a particular social system. The 1936 Berlin Olympics was promoted by Nazi Germany as proof of Aryan superiority – though African American Jessie Owens' sprint victories put paid to that argument. Italian fascist Benito Mussolini aspired to stage an Olympics as a celebration of his ideology of the fascist New Man. The tit-for-tat boycotts in 1980 and 1984 echoed the rivalries of the Cold War.

At the same time, the USA was redefining the criteria for funding the Games. Commercializing the torch relay, and bringing in corporate sponsors and partners for Los Angeles 1984 produced a surplus of around $225 million, and an event supposedly in terminal decline was revitalized for the world's expanding media markets.

CANADA

USA

1976: Montreal

1932, 1984: Los Angeles

1904: St. Louis

1996: Atlanta

MEXICO

BAHAMAS

1968: Mexico City

CUBA

JAMAICA   HAITI   DOMINICAN REP.

GUATEMALA   BELIZE

HONDURAS

EL SALVADOR   NICARAGUA

COSTA RICA

PANAMA

VENEZUELA

GUYANA

SURINAME

FRENCH GUIANA

COLOMBIA

ECUADOR

PERU

BRAZIL

BOLIVIA

2008: Rio de Jane

CHILE   PARAGUAY

ARGENTINA

URUGUAY

Jamaican sprinter Usain Bolt in the Puma Complete Theseus II running shoes in which he dashed to three gold medals and a world record at the 2008 Beijing Olympics. Puma paid Bolt an annual endorsement fee of $1.5 million, and estimated his publicity value at €250 million in 2008.

## Cold War games

The Summer Olympics were dominated during the Cold War by the world's two superpowers, and in the 1976 and 1988 Games, before more rigorous drug-testing was implemented, the German Democratic Republic beat the USA into second place on the medals table, behind the USSR.

Russia continued the rivalry after the dissolution of the USSR, although China displaced Russia in second place in Athens 2004. In Beijing 2008, China's haul of gold medals took it to the top of the table.

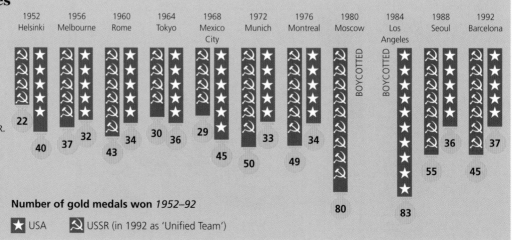

| | 1952 Helsinki | 1956 Melbourne | 1960 Rome | 1964 Tokyo | 1968 Mexico City | 1972 Munich | 1976 Montreal | 1980 Moscow | 1984 Los Angeles | 1988 Seoul | 1992 Barcelona |
|---|---|---|---|---|---|---|---|---|---|---|---|
| USSR | 22 | 37 | 43 | 34 | 29 | 50 | 49 | 80 | BOYCOTTED | 55 | 45 |
| USA | 40 | 32 | 36 | 30 | 45 | 33 | 34 | BOYCOTTED | 83 | 36 | 37 |

**Number of gold medals won** *1952–92*

★ USA    ☭ USSR (in 1992 as 'Unified Team')

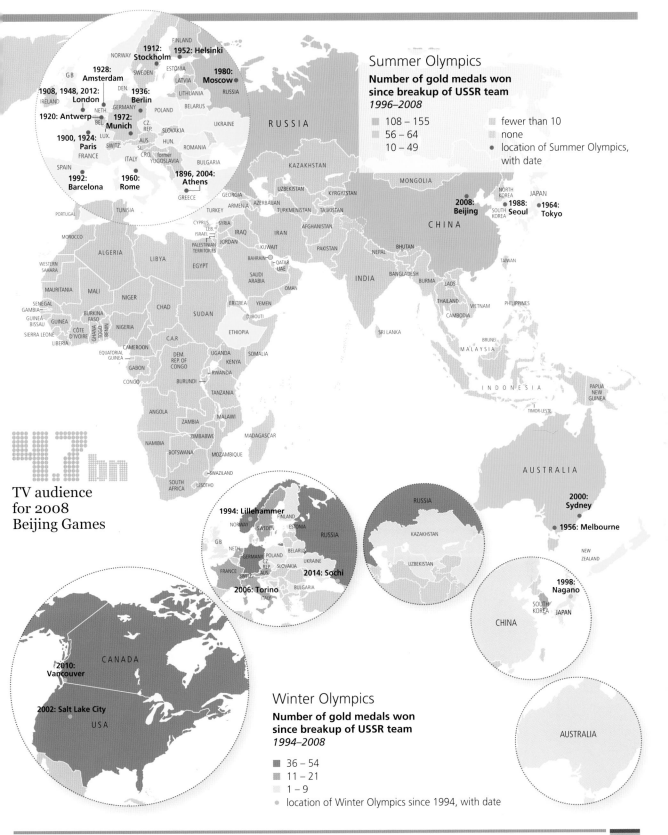

## Summer Olympics

**Number of gold medals won since breakup of USSR team**
*1996–2008*

- 108 – 155
- 56 – 64
- 10 – 49
- fewer than 10
- none
- location of Summer Olympics, with date

**1912: Stockholm**
**1952: Helsinki**
**1928: Amsterdam**
**1980: Moscow**
**1908, 1948, 2012: London**
**1936: Berlin**
**1920: Antwerp**
**1972: Munich**
**1900, 1924: Paris**
**1992: Barcelona**
**1960: Rome**
**1896, 2004: Athens**
**2008: Beijing**
**1988: Seoul**
**1964: Tokyo**
**2000: Sydney**
**1956: Melbourne**

TV audience
for 2008
Beijing Games

## Winter Olympics

**Number of gold medals won since breakup of USSR team**
*1994–2008*

- 36 – 54
- 11 – 21
- 1 – 9
- location of Winter Olympics since 1994, with date

**1994: Lillehammer**
**2014: Sochi**
**2006: Torino**
**1998: Nagano**
**2010: Vancouver**
**2002: Salt Lake City**

# THE FOOTBALL WORLD CUP

The men's World Cup is one of the most popular events in the sporting calendar. Staged every four years since 1930, barring 1942 and 1946, it is sought after by aspiring host nations, and attracts huge income from broadcasters and corporate sponsors. All 208 members of the Fédération Internationale de Football Association (FIFA) are eligible to participate in the qualifying rounds, which are organized within six confederations: Europe; South America; North, Central Americas, and Caribbean; Asia; Africa; and Oceania.

The World Cup was a relatively small-scale affair until 1982, but the victor in FIFA's 1974 presidential election – Dr João Havelange of Brazil – increased the number of finalists in 1982 and 1998, giving more places to Asia and Africa, and to the European confederation, which had grown in the 1990s following the collapse of the Soviet Union. Europe and South America have continued to provide the champions, but the party has expanded and, whoever wins, broadcasters and sponsors queue up to keep the FIFA accountants happy.

Escalating broadcasting and marketing rights for the World Cup have shaped a new financial framework for international sport. Six exclusive marketing partners were associated with South Africa 2010: Adidas, Coca-Cola, Emirates airlines, KiaMotors/Hyundai, Sony, and Visa. Each paid, on average, $24.75 million a year for the privilege, and FIFA's World Cup-related marketing income for 2009 totalled $277 million.

Organizers claimed record attendance at South Africa 2010, but on the dusty streets of the townships few flags were flying, and with FIFA controlling the prices, some matches had far from capacity crowds. Even though a special ticket category for South African residents offered low-grade seats for $18.15, that was beyond the reach of workers still paid in fruit and wine rather than cash, or for those with no work at all.

## Football playing nations

**FIFA points ranking**
*July 2010*

- 1,000 or more
- 750 – 999
- 500 – 749
- 250 – 499
- fewer than 250

World Cup winners
*1930–2010*

## Location of World Cup finals

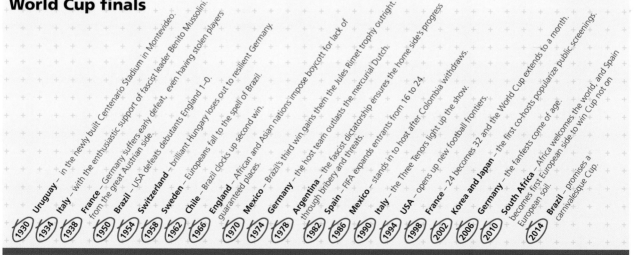

**Uruguay** – in the newly built Centenario Stadium in Montevideo. 1930

**Italy** – with the enthusiastic support of fascist leader Benito Mussolini. 1934

**France** – Germany suffers early defeat, even having stolen players from the great Austrian side. 1938

**Brazil** – USA defeats debutants England 1–0. 1950

**Switzerland** – brilliant Hungary loses out to resilient Germany. 1954

**Sweden** – Europeans fall to the spell of Brazil. 1958

**Chile** – Brazil clocks up second win. 1962

**England** – African and Asian nations impose boycott for lack of guaranteed places. 1966

**Mexico** – Brazil's third win gains them the Jules Rimet trophy outright. 1970

**Germany** – the host team outlasts the mercurial Dutch. 1974

**Argentina** – the fascist dictatorship ensures the home side's progress through bribery and threats. 1978

**Spain** – FIFA expands entrants from 16 to 24. 1982

**Mexico** – stands in to host after Colombia withdraws. 1986

**Italy** – the Three Tenors light up the show. 1990

**USA** – opens up new football frontiers. 1994

**France** – 24 becomes 32 and the World Cup extends to a month. 1998

**Korea and Japan** – the first co-hosts popularize public screenings. 2002

**Germany** – the fanfests come of age. 2006

**South Africa** – Africa welcomes the world, and Spain becomes first European side to win Cup not on European soil. 2010

**Brazil** – promises a carnivalesque Cup. 2014

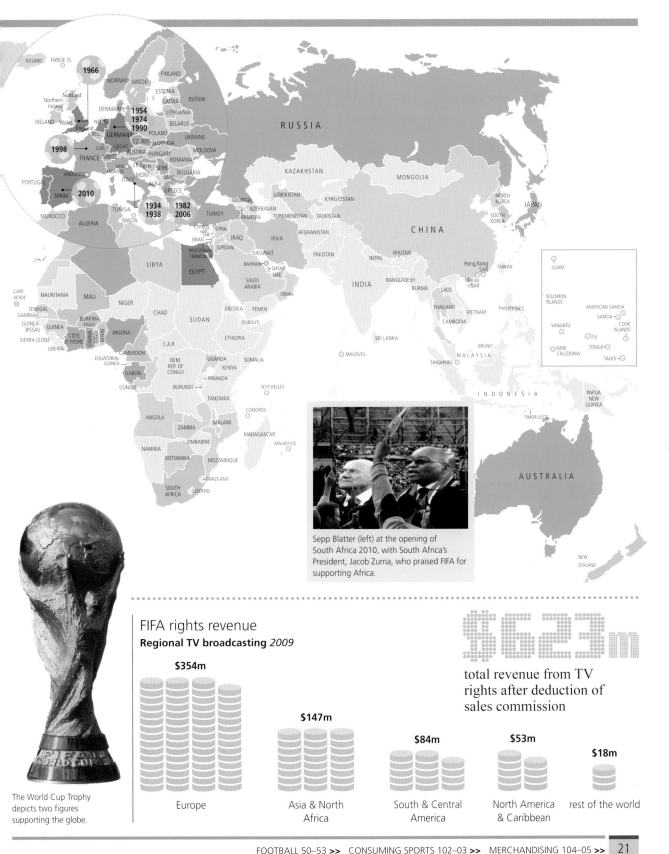

ICELAND | FAROE IS.

1966

NORWAY SWEDEN FINLAND

Northern Scotland DENMARK ESTONIA
Ireland LATVIA RUSSIA
IRELAND Wales LITHUANIA
England NETH. 1954 BELARUS
BEL. GERMANY 1974 POLAND
1998 LUX. 1990 UKRAINE
CZ. REP.
FRANCE SWITZ. AUSTRIA SLOVAKIA MOLDOVA
LIECHT. HUNGARY ROMANIA
SAN. SLOVENIA
PORTUGAL MARINO CRO B-H SERB. BULGARIA
ANDORRA ITALY MONT.
2010 ALB. MAC.
SPAIN GREECE
1934 1982 GEORGIA
TUNISIA 1938 2006 TURKEY AZERBAIJAN
MOROCCO MALTA CYPRUS ARMENIA
LEB. SYRIA
ALGERIA ISRAEL IRAQ IRAN
PALESTINIAN JORDAN
TERRITORIES KUWAIT

RUSSIA

KAZAKHSTAN

MONGOLIA

UZBEKISTAN
KYRGYZSTAN
TURKMENISTAN TAJIKISTAN
AFGHANISTAN
PAKISTAN

NORTH
KOREA JAPAN
SOUTH
KOREA

CHINA

NEPAL BHUTAN
Hong Kong TAIWAN
SAR
Macau
SAR

GUAM

SOLOMON
ISLANDS AMERICAN SAMOA
SAMOA
VANUATU COOK
ISLANDS
FIJI TONGA
NEW
CALEDONIA TAHITI

CAPE
VERDE MAURITANIA MALI
SENEGAL NIGER
GAMBIA CHAD
GUINEA- BURKINA
BISSAU GUINEA FASO
SIERRA LEONE CÔTE NIGERIA
LIBERIA D'IVOIRE GHANA BENIN
TOGO
EQUATORIAL CAMEROON
GUINEA
GABON C.A.R.
CONGO DEM.
REP. OF
CONGO

LIBYA EGYPT
SAUDI
ARABIA
OMAN
ERITREA YEMEN
SUDAN DJIBOUTI

ETHIOPIA

UGANDA
KENYA
SOMALIA

BAHRAIN
QATAR
UAE

INDIA

BANGLADESH
BURMA LAOS
THAILAND VIETNAM
CAMBODIA
PHILIPPINES

SRI LANKA

MALDIVES

BRUNEI
MALAYSIA
SINGAPORE

INDONESIA

RWANDA
BURUNDI
TANZANIA
SEYCHELLES
COMOROS

TIMOR-LESTE

PAPUA
NEW
GUINEA

ANGOLA
ZAMBIA MALAWI
MADAGASCAR
MAURITIUS
NAMIBIA ZIMBABWE
BOTSWANA MOZAMBIQUE
SWAZILAND
SOUTH LESOTHO
AFRICA

AUSTRALIA

NEW
ZEALAND

Sepp Blatter (left) at the opening of
South Africa 2010, with South Africa's
President, Jacob Zuma, who praised FIFA for
supporting Africa.

The World Cup Trophy
depicts two figures
supporting the globe.

## FIFA rights revenue
**Regional TV broadcasting** *2009*

**$354m**

**$147m**

**$84m**

**$53m**

**$18m**

Europe

Asia & North
Africa

South & Central
America

North America
& Caribbean

rest of the world

$623m

total revenue from TV
rights after deduction of
sales commission

# THE COMMONWEALTH GAMES

The Commonwealth Games, as a legacy of British imperial domination, might have been expected to go into a decline. Instead, against widespread expectation, it has survived, even though it is overshadowed in the international media by mega-events such as the Olympics.

Originally called the Empire Games (1930–50), then the British Empire and Commonwealth Games (1954–66) and the British Commonwealth Games (1970–74), the event was finally rid of its association with Britain and Empire at the 1978 Games in Edmonton, Canada. It seemed then to be ossifying in the post-colonial climate of suspensions and boycotts. In 1986, over half the member countries refused to come to Edinburgh, in protest at UK Prime Minister Margaret Thatcher's support for South African sporting relations during the apartheid era. However, since 1990, and in particular the 1994 reinstatement of a post-apartheid South Africa, the number of competing countries and participating athletes has increased. This has been aided by the admission to the Commonwealth Games Federation of former territories of imperial powers other than Britain – Mozambique, Cameroon, and Rwanda. And in 1998, the agenda was broadened beyond core athletics disciplines to include team games – field hockey, cricket, and rugby sevens.

The Commonwealth Games Federation seeks to "dynamically promote and celebrate a unique, friendly, world class Games," and offers an opportunity for many smaller countries to excel in the eyes of the world. Even the tiny Isle of Man has won three gold medals. With no US representation, and very little high-level European presence, African nations can send delegations with more realistic aspirations of victory than at an Olympics. Host cities that would never be considered a suitable Olympic venue can stage a global event. In Delhi, concern about low-quality facilities and substandard accommodation for competitors dominated early headlines – collapsing walkways and dirty bathrooms. But national pride was restored by India finishing fourth in the medal table.

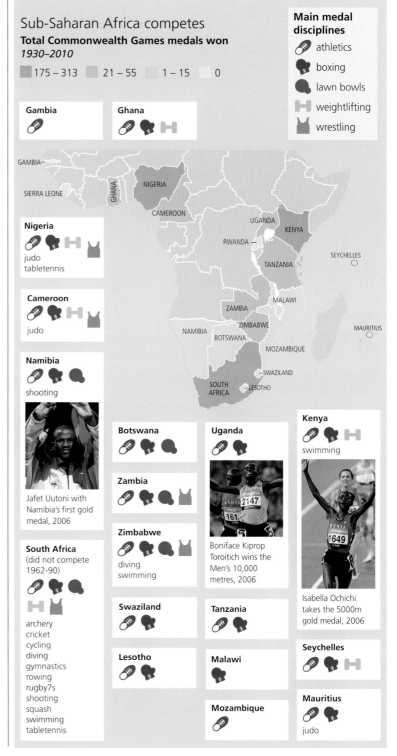

## Sub-Saharan Africa competes
**Total Commonwealth Games medals won**
*1930–2010*

175 – 313    21 – 55    1 – 15    0

**Main medal disciplines**
- athletics
- boxing
- lawn bowls
- weightlifting
- wrestling

**Gambia**

**Ghana**

**Nigeria**
judo
tabletennis

**Cameroon**
judo

**Namibia**
shooting

Jafet Uutoni with Namibia's first gold medal, 2006

**South Africa**
(did not compete 1962-90)
archery
cricket
cycling
diving
gymnastics
rowing
rugby7s
shooting
squash
swimming
tabletennis

**Botswana**

**Zambia**

**Zimbabwe**
diving
swimming

**Swaziland**

**Lesotho**

**Uganda**

Boniface Kiprop Toroitich wins the Men's 10,000 metres, 2006

**Tanzania**

**Malawi**

**Mozambique**

**Kenya**
swimming

Isabella Ochichi takes the 5000m gold medal, 2006

**Seychelles**

**Mauritius**
judo

GAMBIA
SIERRA LEONE
GHANA
NIGERIA
CAMEROON
RWANDA
UGANDA
KENYA
TANZANIA
SEYCHELLES
ZAMBIA
MALAWI
ZIMBABWE
NAMIBIA
BOTSWANA
MOZAMBIQUE
MAURITIUS
SWAZILAND
SOUTH AFRICA
LESOTHO

# Participating countries *2010*

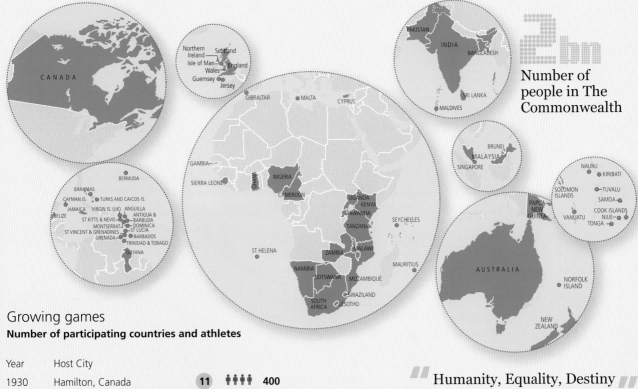

**2bn**
Number of
people in The
Commonwealth

## Growing games
**Number of participating countries and athletes**

| Year | Host City | Number of competing nations | Number of athletes |
|------|-----------|------|------|
| 1930 | Hamilton, Canada | 11 | 400 |
| 1934 | London, England | 16 | 500 |
| 1938 | Sydney, Australia | 15 | 464 |
| 1950 | Auckland, New Zealand | 12 | 590 |
| 1954 | Vancouver, Canada | 24 | 662 |
| 1958 | Cardiff, Wales | 35 | 1,122 |
| 1962 | Perth, Australia | 35 | 863 |
| 1966 | Kingston, Jamaica | 34 | 1,050 |
| 1970 | Edinburgh, Scotland | 42 | 1,383 |
| 1974 | Christchurch, New Zealand | 38 | 1,276 |
| 1978 | Edmonton, Canada | 46 | 1,474 |
| 1982 | Brisbane, Australia | 46 | 1,583 |
| 1986 | Edinburgh, Scotland | 26 | 1,662 |
| 1990 | Auckland, New Zealand | 55 | 2,073 |
| 1994 | Victoria, Canada | 63 | 2,557 |
| 1998 | Kuala Lumpur, Malaysia | 70 | 3,633 |
| 2002 | Manchester, England | 72 | 3,679 |
| 2006 | Melbourne, Australia | 71 | 4,049 |
| 2010 | Delhi, India | 71 | 4,345 |

**12** Number of competing nations

👤 Number of athletes

**"Humanity, Equality, Destiny"**
The Commonwealth motto

Athletes in the 1500m heat,
Delhi 2010

# DRUGS IN SPORTS

The use of performance-enhancing drugs in sports has been widespread. If all current prohibited substances and methods were banned retrospectively, record books would have to be rewritten. Thomas Hicks, US winner of the 1904 Olympic marathon, took strychnine and brandy during the race. Denmark's Knut Enemark died competing in the 1960 Olympic road cycling race, from the effects of amphetamines and nicotinyl tartrate.

Drug-detection began to be taken seriously in 1967, when the International Olympic Committee started to ban drugs, after which Soviet shot-put Olympic champion Tamara Press disappeared from international competition. Full-scale drug-testing began in 1972, initiating a central dynamic of modern competitive sports: the race between testers to detect abuse, and scientific and medical teams to mask uses of banned substances or suspend a drug programme prior to competition. Mandatory random testing was introduced in 1989.

China, in the 1990s, generated muscular women in the water. Events descended into farce as swimmers leapfrogged barriers to escape the testers, and stand-ins mounted the podium to pick up medals. China has done much to clean up its act, but its 2008 Olympic judo champion Tong Wen was suspended for two years in May 2010, and stripped of her 2009 world title.

The World Anti-Doping Agency, established in 1999, developed a World Anti-Doping Code, first applied at the 2004 Athens Olympics, and accredits 34 laboratories around the world. WADA has made an impact, yet its principles are far from universally accepted. Some sporting institutions remain reluctant to expose drug-use, as this could deprive their sports of some of its brightest stars, and also reduce the credibility of sports in the eyes of the paying public.

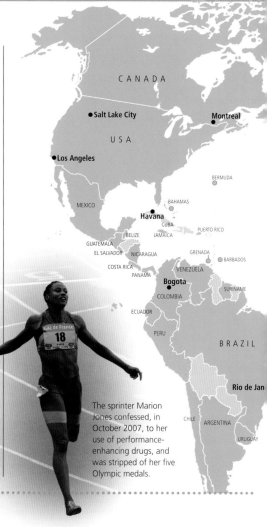

The sprinter Marion Jones confessed, in October 2007, to her use of performance-enhancing drugs, and was stripped of her five Olympic medals.

## Prohibited enhancements *2010*

| Both in and out of competition | In competition | Banned methods |
|---|---|---|
| **Anabolic agents** – including anabolic androgenic steroids, which build up tissue and bulk strength. | **Stimulants** – including cocaine and strychnine. | **Enhancement of oxygen transfer** – including blood doping. |
| **Peptide hormones** – which stimulate growth. | **Narcotics** – including heroin and morphine. | **Chemical and physical manipulation** – sample tampering, and non-medical intravenous intrusions. |
| **Beta-2 agonists** – which improve air intake, and therefore performance. | **Cannabinoids** – prohibited though not performance-enhancing. | **Gene doping** – the, as yet experimental, manipulation of genes to enhance performance. |
| **Hormone antagonists and modulators** – with anti-estrogenic capacity geared to increasing testosterone. | **Glucocorticosteroids** – which can improve the performance of the heart. | |
| **Masking agents** – such as diuretics with which athletes can rid themselves more rapidly of drug traces. | | |

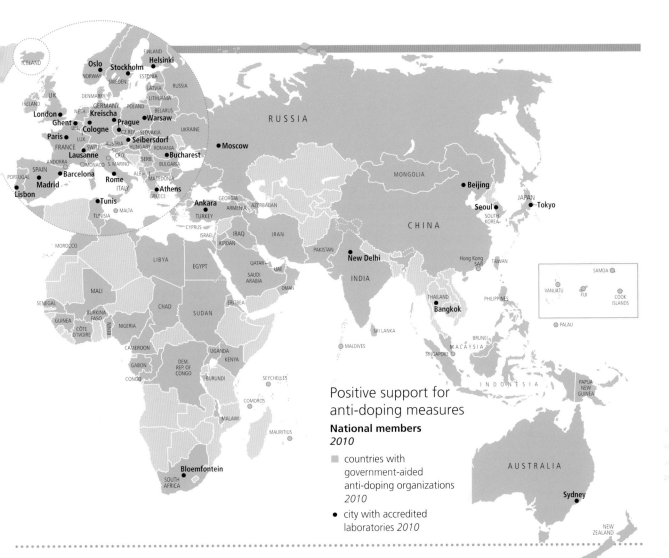

## Positive support for anti-doping measures

**National members**
*2010*

◾ countries with government-aided anti-doping organizations *2010*

● city with accredited laboratories *2010*

Map city labels: Iceland, Oslo, Norway, Stockholm, Sweden, Helsinki, Finland, Estonia, Latvia, Lithuania, Russia, London, UK, Ireland, Denmark, Germany, Kreischa, Poland, Belarus, Ghent, Neth., Bel., Cologne, Prague, Cz. Rep., Warsaw, Ukraine, Paris, France, Lux., Switz., Austria, Hungary, Slovakia, Seibersdorf, Slovenia, Romania, Moscow, Andorra, Monaco, S. Marino, Cro., Serb., Bucharest, Lausanne, Spain, Portugal, Barcelona, Rome, Italy, Alb., Macedonia, Bulgaria, Madrid, Lisbon, Tunis, Tunisia, Malta, Athens, Greece, Ankara, Turkey, Georgia, Armenia, Azerbaijan, Cyprus, Morocco, Israel, Jordan, Iraq, Iran, Pakistan, Libya, Egypt, Qatar, UAE, Saudi Arabia, Oman, New Delhi, India, Mali, Senegal, Burkina Faso, Chad, Sudan, Eritrea, Guinea, Benin, Nigeria, Côte D'Ivoire, Cameroon, Dem. Rep. of Congo, Uganda, Kenya, Gabon, Congo, Burundi, Seychelles, Comoros, Malawi, Mauritius, South Africa, Bloemfontein, Mongolia, China, Beijing, Japan, Seoul, South Korea, Tokyo, Hong Kong SAR, Taiwan, Thailand, Bangkok, Philippines, Sri Lanka, Maldives, Brunei, Malaysia, Singapore, Indonesia, Palau, Samoa, Vanuatu, Fiji, Cook Islands, Papua New Guinea, Australia, Sydney, New Zealand

## Out in the open

The investigation by the Canadian government following the shock of 100-metre champion Ben Johnson testing positive for stanozolol at Seoul 1988 revealed the problem to be endemic. In California, from 1984 until his lab was raided by the FBI in 2003, Victor Conte's Burlingame Bay Area Laboratory Co-operative (BALCO) was supplying athletes and some of the world's top sports stars with illegal steroids and growth hormones. Accounts from former Eastern European countries after the fall of Communism proved that such abuse crossed political ideologies and boundaries. Pre-pubescent girl swimmers in East Germany (GDR) were administered with steroids, regardless of the possible long-term health risks. Stricter testing from 1989 onwards caught out Bulgarian weightlifters and wrestlers. The International Weightlifting Federation has wiped out Olympic and world records (1992), and changed weight categories (1998) in attempts to cleanse the sport of steroid abuse.

**Number of Summer Olympic medals won by Bulgaria before and after mandatory testing**

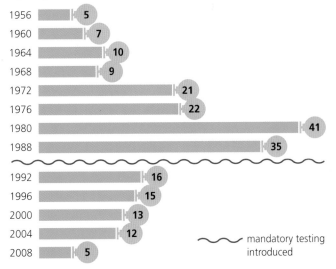

| Year | Medals |
|------|--------|
| 1956 | 5 |
| 1960 | 7 |
| 1964 | 10 |
| 1968 | 9 |
| 1972 | 21 |
| 1976 | 22 |
| 1980 | 41 |
| 1988 | 35 |
| 1992 | 16 |
| 1996 | 15 |
| 2000 | 13 |
| 2004 | 12 |
| 2008 | 5 |

〜 mandatory testing introduced

# TACKLING DISABILITY

Sports celebrate ideal or perfect (for the specified function) bodies, or construct the necessary body for the task, sometimes bordering on the freakish. Much of sporting achievement is based on the principle of the highly tuned human body as machine, able-bodiedness an unspoken premise of top-level performance. Since the middle of the 20th century, though, great progress has been made in the recognition of the importance of sports for people with disabilities, including its therapeutic and rehabilitative value. In parallel to this growing awareness has been the increasingly enhanced profile of the Paralympic Games.

Sporting competition in wheelchair basketball, archery, and table tennis for war veterans with disabilities was organized by neurologist Sir Ludwig Guttmann at Stoke Mandeville hospital from 1947, and in organized form on the same day as the opening of the 1948 London Olympics. Since the International Paralympic Committee (IPC) took over the staging of the Paralympic Games in 1993, the number of athletes involved has soared. Just a few hundred athletes with disability (from 23 countries) competed alongside the 1960 Rome Olympics, but there were more than 4,000 at Beijing 2008. Since Seoul 1988 and Albertville 1992, the Paralympics has been staged at the same venues as the Olympics. In 2001, the International Olympic Committee and the IPC agreed to stick to this principle for the foreseeable future.

The 20 sports at the Summer Paralympics include boccia, a ball and target game developed specifically for wheelchair-based players. But North American, European and Australian competitors have dominated the medal tables at both the Summer and the Winter Games, a reflection of the highly technical, and expensive, support and equipment the athletes require.

The Paralympics has had an important influence upon the public perception of disability, challenging stereotypes in the sphere of athletic achievement and physical performance. It has also generated controversies and ethical debates concerning the definition of disability, and the notion of eligibility for the able-bodied Games.

Talan Skeels-Piggins, Great Britain, in the Men's Slalom (sitting) at Vancouver 2010.

## Criteria for disability

Competitions for athletes are grouped into six main classes:

- amputee
- cerebral palsy
- visual impairment
- spinal cord injuries
- intellectual disability
- all others.

Constant debate takes place on the precise nature of these criteria. The classes are defined by each sport, and many individual sports identify sub-categories, seeking to ensure equitability of competition. A specialist science has developed to respond to the needs of disabled athletes in relation to training and improved performance.

An athlete at Beijing 2008, training in one of the dedicated gyms.

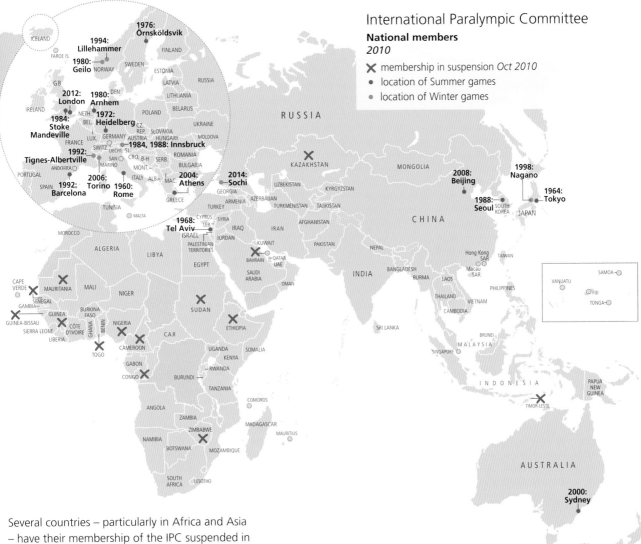

International Paralympic Committee
**National members**
*2010*

✕ membership in suspension *Oct 2010*
● location of Summer games
● location of Winter games

1976: Örnsköldsvik
1994: Lillehammer
1980: Geilo
2012: London
1980: Arnhem
1984: Stoke Mandeville
1972: Heidelberg
1984, 1988: Innsbruck
1992: Tignes-Albertville
2006: Torino
1960: Rome
1992: Barcelona
2004: Athens
2014: Sochi
1968: Tel Aviv
2008: Beijing
1998: Nagano
1964: Tokyo
1988: Seoul
2000: Sydney

ICELAND, FAROE IS., FINLAND, SWEDEN, NORWAY, ESTONIA, LATVIA, RUSSIA, LITHUANIA, GB, DEN., IRELAND, NETH., BEL., POLAND, BELARUS, UKRAINE, LUX., GERMANY, CZ., REP. SLOVAKIA, AUSTRIA HUNGARY, MOLDOVA, FRANCE, SWITZ., LIECHT. SL, RUSSIA, SAN MARINO, CRO., B-H, SERB., ROMANIA, ANDORRA, MONT., BULGARIA, PORTUGAL, SPAIN, ITALY, ALB., MAC., GREECE, GEORGIA, KAZAKHSTAN, MONGOLIA, UZBEKISTAN, KYRGYZSTAN, CHINA, TUNISIA, MALTA, ARMENIA, AZERBAIJAN, TURKMENISTAN, TAJIKISTAN, SOUTH KOREA, JAPAN, TURKEY, CYPRUS, LEB., SYRIA, IRAQ, IRAN, AFGHANISTAN, MOROCCO, ISRAEL, JORDAN, KUWAIT, QATAR, UAE, PAKISTAN, NEPAL, BANGLADESH, HONG KONG SAR, TAIWAN, ALGERIA, LIBYA, EGYPT, SAUDI ARABIA, OMAN, INDIA, BURMA, LAOS, MACAU SAR, PALESTINIAN TERRITORIES, BAHRAIN, CAPE VERDE, MAURITANIA, MALI, NIGER, SUDAN, THAILAND, VIETNAM, PHILIPPINES, SENEGAL, GAMBIA, GUINEA, BURKINA FASO, NIGERIA, ETHIOPIA, CAMBODIA, VANUATU, SAMOA, GUINEA-BISSAU, SIERRA LEONE, CÔTE D'IVOIRE, GHANA, BENIN, C.A.R, FIJI, TONGA, LIBERIA, TOGO, CAMEROON, UGANDA, KENYA, SOMALIA, SRI LANKA, BRUNEI, MALAYSIA, GABON, CONGO, BURUNDI, RWANDA, SINGAPORE, TANZANIA, COMOROS, INDONESIA, PAPUA NEW GUINEA, ANGOLA, ZAMBIA, ZIMBABWE, MADAGASCAR, MAURITIUS, NAMIBIA, BOTSWANA, MOZAMBIQUE, TIMOR-LESTE, SOUTH AFRICA, LESOTHO, AUSTRALIA, NEW ZEALAND

Several countries – particularly in Africa and Asia – have their membership of the IPC suspended in disputes over criteria and eligibility.

# Blade Runner

Oscar Pistorius has held world records and won gold medals for sprint events, competing at world championships, and the 2004 and 2008 Paralympics. He was born with no fibula in either of his legs, which at 11 months were amputated halfway between knee and ankle. Johannesburg-born, Pistorius was nevertheless an active schoolboy athlete, competing in rugby, tennis, water polo, and wrestling before taking up running. His attempts to be recognized as eligible to compete in the Olympic Games have fuelled debate and controversy. Would his carbon fibre artificial limbs be a danger to able-bodied rivals? Would they give him an unfair technical advantage? These questions will remain a matter for ethical debate as the boundaries between disability and able-bodiedness remain elastic.

# GAY GAMES

The idealization of heterosexuality within mainstream sporting culture has produced a marginalization of alternative sexualities, with few but the most established and strong-willed – tennis player Billie-Jean King for instance – able to declare their true sexuality. The sense of oppression and exclusion felt by gay athletes and sport enthusiasts was the driver behind the formation of the Gay Games, the founding principles of which are: "Participation, Inclusion, and Personal Best".

The founder of the Games, medical doctor and Olympic decathlete in 1968, Tom Waddell, sought to call the Games the Gay Olympics, but action by the United States Olympic Committee and the International Olympic Committee blocked his use of the word "Olympics", as much an act of brand protection as homophobia. But the second-choice title became its own brand. In 1994, New York was one of the host cities for the Football World Cup, but on the streets of Manhattan the sports posters that dominated were those for the fourth Gay Games.

Regular, large-scale and high-profile, and with affluent consumers at its heart, the Gay Games is seen as a lucrative opportunity by cities keen to host the event, as the Mayor of Cleveland recognized when celebrating

> **The City of Cleveland is prepared to roll out the welcome mat to the LGBT athletes, their families and spectators from around the world.**
> Mayor Frank G. Jackson, September 2009

the awarding of the 2014 Games to his city. Chicago attracted 12,000 participants in 2006, and over 9,000 men and women from 66 countries gathered in Cologne, Germany in 2010.

**$80m**

Estimated value to local economy of 2014 Cleveland games

Despite its alternative philosophy and mission, the success of the Gay Games is such that cities bid for it as an economic event just like any other, and as such it represents – however indirectly – a force for change in homophobic and residually prejudiced heterosexual communities.

CANADA

Vancouver 1990

San Francisco 1982, 1986

USA

Chicago 2006

New York 1994

Cleveland 2014

MEXICO

GUATEMALA
EL SALVADOR

JAMAICA

DOMINICAN REP.

PUERTO RICO

COLOMBIA

SURINAME

PERU

BRAZIL

CHILE

ARGENTINA

URUGUAY

## Too late for some

The Gay Games encourages athletes to reject the pressures of the heterosexual mainstream, which for some have been intense. Big Bill (William Tatem) Tilden (seen right) dominated tennis in the 1920s, turned professional in 1931, and mixed with the Hollywood stars. But a conviction in 1946 for criminal sexual acts with a teenage boy wrecked his reputation. Dunlop dropped its sponsorship, clubs were closed to him, and pupils warned off. He died in 1953, all but destitute.

Even today, homophobia is embedded in the culture of many sports. A number of players, including football (soccer) player Justin Fashanu (1961–98), who came out in 1990 and later committed suicide, and Welsh Rugby League player Gareth Thomas, who came out in 2010, have spoken of the compulsion they felt to hide their sexuality.

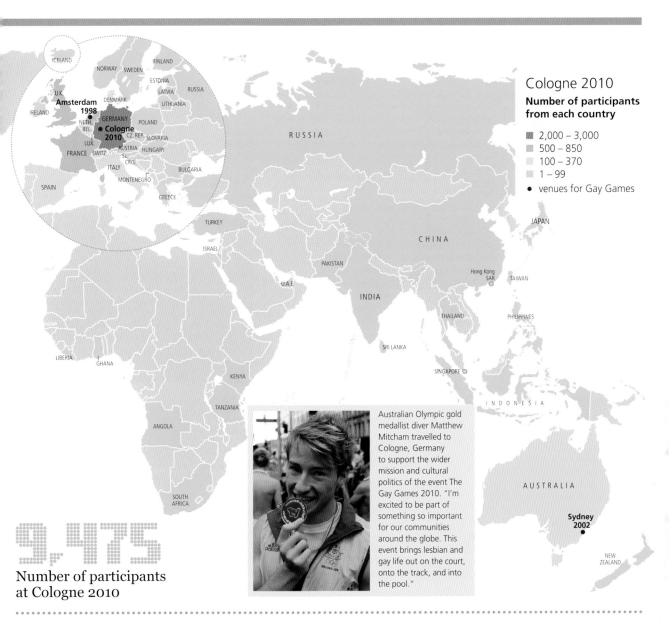

## Cologne 2010

**Number of participants from each country**

- ■ 2,000 – 3,000
- ■ 500 – 850
- ■ 100 – 370
- ▫ 1 – 99
- • venues for Gay Games

Australian Olympic gold medallist diver Matthew Mitcham travelled to Cologne, Germany to support the wider mission and cultural politics of the event The Gay Games 2010. "I'm excited to be part of something so important for our communities around the globe. This event brings lesbian and gay life out on the court, onto the track, and into the pool."

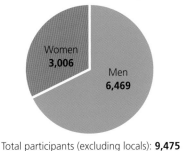

## Number of participants at Cologne 2010

---

## Cologne 2010

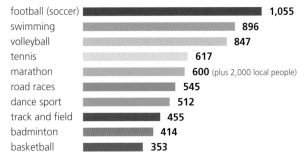

### Gender breakdown at Cologne *2010*

Women **3,006**

Men **6,469**

Total participants (excluding locals): **9,475**

### Sports with highest number of participants, Cologne *2010*

| Sport | Participants |
|---|---|
| football (soccer) | **1,055** |
| swimming | **896** |
| volleyball | **847** |
| tennis | **617** |
| marathon | **600** (plus 2,000 local people) |
| road races | **545** |
| dance sport | **512** |
| track and field | **455** |
| badminton | **414** |
| basketball | **353** |

Other events: band festival, beach volleyball, bodybuilding, bowling, bridge, cheerleading, chess, choir festival, cycling, diving, field hockey, figure skating, golf, handball, ice hockey, inline speed skating, martial arts, pool, power lifting, sailing, softball, sport climbing, sport shooting, squash, synchronized swimming, table tennis, triathlon, visual arts, water polo, wrestling.

# DEVELOPMENT AND PEACE

Sports are based upon rivalries and competition, but also bring people together, and have been used as a tool for conflict resolution, the cultivation of peaceful coexistence, health-awareness, and the promotion of humanitarian ideals. At its most positive, sports transcend social differences and national and geographical boundaries.

The Olympic movement was conceived as the "free trade of the future" by Baron Pierre de Coubertin, who saw in international sporting competition an antidote to war. On a smaller scale than the Olympics, sports-based initiatives have sought to bring disparate groups and populations together, and to convey messages about harmonious living and personal well-being. Sports development on the international level refers both to the generation of infrastructure to support the provision of sports, and to the wider benefits that participation might stimulate in relation to social issues such as HIV and intercultural conflict.

Sports development initiatives for the young seek to improve the lives of some of the poorest people on the planet, but can hardly hope to change the conditions that have created the inequalities experienced by those children. Similarly, interventions aimed at resolving conflict do not get rid of the causes of the conflict. Sports development initiatives can, then, be seen as the proverbial band-aid that only temporarily relieves a problem in need of radical surgery. Nevertheless, activists and critical social scientists continue to urge that doing something is better than doing nothing. L'Organisation pour la Paix par le Sport, for instance, established its "Peace and Sport" programme in 2007, operating in Haiti, Colombia, Côte d'Ivoire, Burundi, Israel–Palestine, and Timor-Leste. Sports development has also been taken up as a form of corporate responsibility by companies such as Puma, and world governing bodies such as FIFA.

## Puma programmes

Puma's sense of corporate responsibility reaches out to Africa. Its programmes – puma.safe (concerned with environmental and social issues) and puma.peace (supporting global peace) – have underpinned the company's initiatives.

The scheme One Day One Goal aims to stimulate football matches on 21 September in every one of the 192 member states of the United Nations and beyond. In 2008, 216 matches were played. Visibility, for Puma, was achieved by free T-shirts made of African cotton, and banners at African international professional games.

Participants in one of the football matches that took place to launch the One Day One Goal programme in 2008.

## Football4Peace

Sports-based programme F4P, a brainchild of private citizens, started as the World Sport Peace Project in 2001, and was developed by the University of Brighton, UK. The university, along with it partners, sends volunteer coaches and leaders to Israel, where they conduct coaching camps for children aged between 10 and 14 years from Jewish and Arab communities.

Its aims are not just to impart soccer skills, but to facilitate social contact across community boundaries, promote mutual understanding, and stimulate a commitment to peaceful co-existence.

The project has doubled in size year on year, and in 2010 involved over 1,000 children, from 24 mixed communities.

F4P also operates as a cross-border project in the Republic of Ireland and Northern Ireland, UK, run by local teachers and coaches, trained in the F4P methodology. It brings together children from both sides of the border, regardless of background and religion, stressing core values of neutrality, equity, inclusion, respect, trust, and responsibility.

# Right to Play

■ **places of operation,** *2010*

**Pakistan**
Since 2002, Right To Play has been working with Afghan child refugees in Pakistan, many of whom are affected by poverty, political uncertainty, discrimination, violence, trauma and limited access to education. Over 300 leaders organize regular activities for more than 15,000 children. A further programme works with children in the area affected by the 2005 earthquake, both in schools and through community projects.

**Peru**
In 2009 alone, Right To Play reached 33,000 children in Peru with its promotion of regular physical activity in schools, improving attendance and motivation, and reducing playground violence.

AZERBAIJAN
LEBANON
PALESTINIAN TERRITORIES
JORDAN
CHINA
PAKISTAN
MALI
THAILAND
GHANA
BENIN
LIBERIA
SUDAN
ETHIOPIA
UGANDA
SOMALIA
RWANDA
KENYA
BURUNDI
TANZANIA
ZAMBIA
BOTSWANA
MOZAMBIQUE
PERU

**China**
Right To Play works with the growing number of children in need of special care in China: street children, migrants, orphans, those affected by HIV, those with disabilities, and rural girls, who are often disadvantaged. It contributes to specific measures aimed at improving the children's physical, emotional and social well being.

## Values of Right To Play

Founded by Olympic medallist Johan Olav Kloss, Right to Play's mission is to improve the lives of children in some of the most disadvantaged areas of the world by using the power of sport and play for development, health and peace.

**C**o-operation
**H**ope
**I**ntegrity
**L**eadership
**D**edication
**R**espect
**E**nthusiasm
**N**urture

**Ethiopia**
Right To Play has worked in Ethiopia since 2005, and in 2009 used sporting activities to reach 16,400 children with messages about health issues and the importance of inclusion.

**Jordan**
By training teachers and staff of partner organizations to implement sport and play programs, Right To Play is able to help children in refugee camps and other disadvantaged communities.

## UNESCO programmes

UNESCO recognizes sport's disregard for geographical borders and social classes, and its potential to promote social integration and economic development, as an instrument for promoting peace.

**Sport for Peace in Central American countries** – uses sport to help prevent violence, delinquency and drug consumption.
**Sport for Peace in ECOWAS** – fosters greater cohesion and co-operation in the West Africa region.
**Sport for Health Awareness** – combats HIV and AIDS in Mozambique.
**Sport for a Culture of Peace** – brought together 500 people from 60 countries in France in 2001.

**$147m**

Amount FIFA allocated to African football associations 2006–09

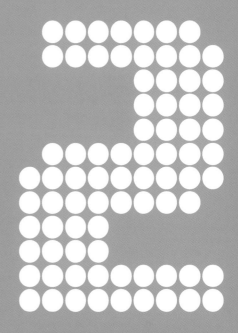

# AN A TO Z OF SPORTS

# AMERICAN FOOTBALL

## The gridiron game

### The gridiron camp

Early forms of football, including rugby style, were played by Canadian and US colleges and universities in the 1860s. A meeting at Princeton in 1876 formed the Intercollegiate Football Association in the USA, adopting the rugby code. Yale's representative at that meeting was Walter C. Camp (1859–1925), who began to change the form of the sport by introducing distinctive rules, preparation, strategy, and more developed tactics.

The number of players and the pitch dimensions were both reduced, and territorial space marked with white lines at five-yard intervals, in order to clarify the new system of "downs" that was introduced to vary possession. Looking like a gridiron, this gave the new sport its moniker.

Walter C. Camp at Yale.

American football or, in the USA, just "football", is becoming increasingly popular. It has a huge profile in the nation's universities, with college matches attracting capacity crowds and widespread media coverage. The college stars feed into the professional game via "the draft" – a system that recruits 224 college players each year, seven for each professional club. To ensure competitiveness, lowest-ranking professional teams get first pick of these players. Some college players forego their final year of study to enter the draft and seek lucrative contracts. Only some will eventually make the grade.

Unlike the other two big American sports, basketball and baseball, the number of children and adults playing informally is on the increase: from 5.7 million in 2000 to 6.8 million in 2007. The sport predominates in high schools, with over 1 million boy participants – more than twice that for either basketball or baseball.

Both the college and professional game have a large fan base, with over 7 percent of adults in the USA attending a match at least once a year. The average value of the 32 National Football League (NFL) teams in 2009 was a round billion, with the Dallas Cowboys coming in at $1.65 billion. The Super Bowl, started in 1967, brings together the top US teams in a contest to establish the national champion. The 2010 Super Bowl, described by the Wall Street Journal as "the most watched TV program ever" with 106.5 million US viewers and many more worldwide, vied with European soccer's UEFA Champions League Final for the top spot. Despite the economic crisis of 2008–10, the NFL continued to draw in the crowds, TV audiences, and corporate sponsors.

American football is the most specialized of team sports, with different players taking the field for attacking and defensive manoeuvres. NFL and college coaches have both

Footballers are larger-than-life figures, squeezed into their specialist uniforms at an average weight for defensive linesmen of 273 pounds (123.8 kg).

### Stacking

For decades there seemed to be one position for the white player, one for the black. The quarterback brains behind the brawn were usually white players – a stereotyping of player potential known as stacking. Several outstanding black quarterbacks have exposed the myth of such an ethnic-based division of labour in the game, but black stars such as Dwight Freeney and Julius Peppers do still gravitate towards specialist positions such as "running backs".

Doug Williams *(left)*, of Washington Redskins, was the first African American starting quarterback in a Super Bowl, in 1988. The Redskins won, and Williams got the Most Valuable Player award. This challenged racists who believed stacking to be part of the natural order, but in 2004 the successes of black quarterbacks were still novel enough to merit journalistic comment, and in 2010 none of those players was among the sport's top earners.

earned celebrity status. The Green Bay Packers' legendary coach Vince Lombardi is often credited with the comment "Winning isn't everything, it's the only thing", though this was actually coined by UCLA Bruins' coach Red Sanders in 1955.

# The American game

## On the grid
**Number of high-school boys per 1,000 in population playing in school leagues**
*2008/9*

- ■ 150 – 199
- ■ 100 – 150
- ■ 50 – 99
- ☐ fewer than 50

**Total: 1.1 million**

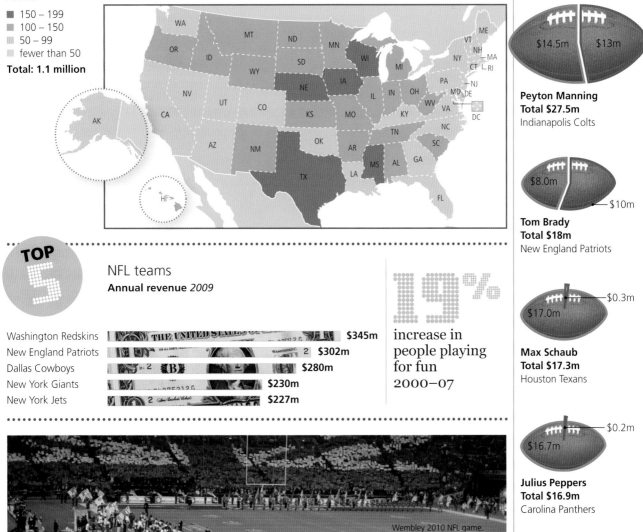

## Top NFL players

$14.5m   $13m
**Peyton Manning**
**Total $27.5m**
Indianapolis Colts

$8.0m   $10m
**Tom Brady**
**Total $18m**
New England Patriots

$17.0m   $0.3m
**Max Schaub**
**Total $17.3m**
Houston Texans

$16.7m   $0.2m
**Julius Peppers**
**Total $16.9m**
Carolina Panthers

$16.2m   $0.3m
**Dwight Freeney**
**Total $16.5m**
Indianapolis Colts

**Annual earnings** *2009*
▷ from endorsements
▷ in salary

## TOP 5

### NFL teams
**Annual revenue** *2009*

| Team | Revenue |
| --- | --- |
| Washington Redskins | $345m |
| New England Patriots | $302m |
| Dallas Cowboys | $280m |
| New York Giants | $230m |
| New York Jets | $227m |

**19%** increase in people playing for fun 2000–07

Wembley 2010 NFL game.

## Foreign fields

The NFL eyes the world as its potential market. In 2005, more than 103,000 people attended Arizona Cardinals versus San Francisco 49ers in Mexico City. In October 2007, the Miami Dolphins played the New York Giants at Wembley Stadium, London, in the first regular season NFL match to be played outside North or Central America. Sports editor of The Observer, Brian Oliver, wrote: "The future of sport starts today," referring to the global markets that such events were seeking to reach. The NFL has planned two games outside the country each season until at least 2012. Its commissioner, Roger Goodell, claims that "the international popularity" of the sport has no limits, as "the far corners of the world watch Super Bowl". But looking at the ritual and ceremony at the London fixture, the sport continues to stage a mass spectacle of Americana rather than a cosmopolitan cultural event.

# BASEBALL

## Diamonds are forever

### A reflection of the nation

Harvard students played a version of baseball in the 1820s. The game was codified in 1845, with the first competition held in the Elysian Fields, Hoboken, New Jersey. It was commercialized by the equipment manufacturer Albert C. Spalding, who stressed its American qualities by comparing it favourably with cricket's English traditions, and by 1900 baseball was the national game of both rural and urban America.

Baseball is the ideal backdrop for the exploration of American manhood, collective identity and community, and the game has continued to define continuity in a complex world. The prologue to Don Delillo's *Underworld* (1997) is set at a 1951 baseball game in New York, a "midcentury moment that enters the skin more lastingly than the vast shaping strategies of eminent leaders".

## 12% of US adults attend a game each year

Modern baseball, a hybrid of rounders and cricket, has become the USA's national game, and the batters and pitchers starring in the baseball diamond among the most enduring of the USA's sport legends. The sport is also a lucrative business. In 2010, the average value of the one Canadian and 29 US teams in Major League Baseball (MLB), whose play-off for the national title since 1903 has been confidently labelled the World Series, was $491 million.

The sport has also flourished in the Dominican Republic, Puerto Rico, and Venezuela, partly as a form of US "soft power". Fidel Castro's regime, on the other hand, promoted the game as part of its explicitly anti-US policy, and Cuba headed the Olympic medal haul (with three golds and two silvers) from 1992 to 2008.

The International Baseball Federation's World Cup – which typically draws upon rookies and veteran professionals for the US team – has seen Cuban domination challenged by consecutive US victories in 2007 and 2009. Asian strongholds include Japan, Taiwan,

and South Korea, which have been central to the marketing strategy of MLB's World Baseball Classic, inaugurated in 2006, and won by Japan in the San Diego final. In 2009, Japan's Daisuke Matsuzaka was voted the tournament's Most Valuable Player for his contribution to his country's successful defence of its title.

Major League Baseball in the USA remains the power base of the sport, and has given rise to some of America's greatest sporting heroes, including three New York Yankees players: Babe Ruth, Lou Gehrig, and Jo DiMaggio. Revelations of steroid use by top-earning Alex Rodriguez and others have disillusioned some. The number of "informal" players is thought to have declined, from 15.5 million in 1990 to 8 million in 2007, but the finances of the elite sport, and its organized base within schools, are stronger than ever. The global impact of the World Baseball Classic indicates a successful integrated marketing model, taking MLB to the world, and the world to MLB.

"Babe" Ruth, the "Sultan of Swing", whose record of 714 home runs held from 1935 until 1974.

## Breaking through the colour bar

On April 15, 1947, Jack Roosevelt ("Jackie") Robinson made his debut for the Brooklyn Dodgers. He was the first African American to play in top-level competitive baseball. African American players had been forced into separate leagues from the later 19th century, and the professional Negro National League (NNL) thrived in the Great Depression of the 1930s. Robinson's successful debut and high-profile impact attracted more and more African Americans to the major league, and the NNL collapsed.

Each year on April 15, players wear Robinson's number 42 jersey as a tribute to the historic breakthrough, although the proportion of African American players in top baseball teams has declined markedly since 1975.

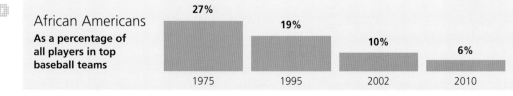

### African Americans
**As a percentage of all players in top baseball teams**

| | 1975 | 1995 | 2002 | 2010 |
|---|---|---|---|---|
| | 27% | 19% | 10% | 6% |

# The American game

## Ballpark figures

**Number of high-school boys per 1,000 in population playing in school leagues 2008/9**

- 105
- 50 – 99
- fewer than 50

**Total: 473,000**

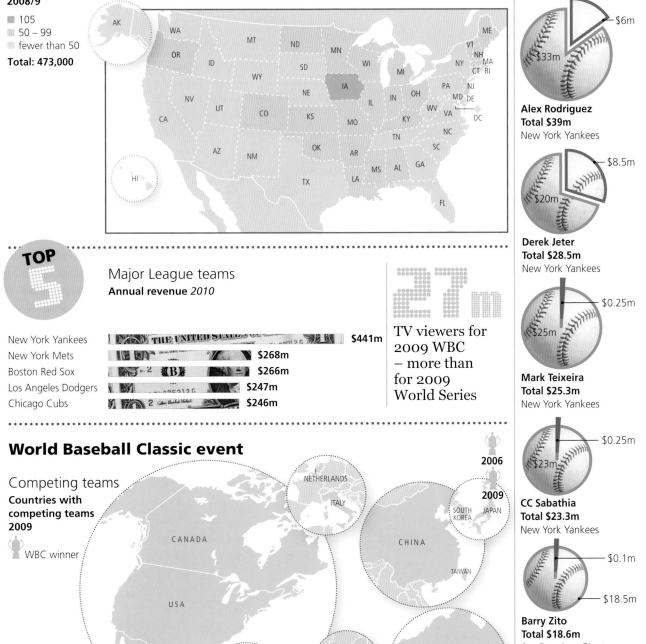

## Top Major League players

**Alex Rodriguez**
Total $39m
New York Yankees
$33m · $6m

**Derek Jeter**
Total $28.5m
New York Yankees
$20m · $8.5m

**Mark Teixeira**
Total $25.3m
New York Yankees
$25m · $0.25m

**CC Sabathia**
Total $23.3m
New York Yankees
$23m · $0.25m

**Barry Zito**
Total $18.6m
San Francisco Giants
$18.5m · $0.1m

**Annual earnings** *2009*
- from endorsements
- in salary

## TOP 5

### Major League teams
**Annual revenue** *2010*

| Team | Revenue |
|---|---|
| New York Yankees | $441m |
| New York Mets | $268m |
| Boston Red Sox | $266m |
| Los Angeles Dodgers | $247m |
| Chicago Cubs | $246m |

**27m**

TV viewers for 2009 WBC – more than for 2009 World Series

## World Baseball Classic event

### Competing teams
**Countries with competing teams 2009**

- WBC winner

2006
2009

---

# BASKETBALL

## Hoops and dreams

### Inventing the game

The origins of the sport lie in fitness initiatives in colleges and youth associations, and the desire to create a challenging and lively game of skill. In 1891 Canadian-born Dr James Naismith, YMCA instructor in Springfield, Massachusetts, adapted a peach basket for the point-accumulating target. His game was soon widely adopted in colleges across the USA, including at the elite women's institution Smith, Massachusetts, in 1892, where the students played in a converted gym with a net hung over a fireplace. The Young Women's Christian Association adapted the rules in 1895 to create netball.

James Naismith (1861–1939) is credited with having invented basketball.

Basketball lays claim to be one of the most popular sports in the world. Its accessibility and informality allow anyone to have a go. The basketball hoop on the garage or gable wall, or the confined space in a mid-Manhattan neighborhood, can attract people of all ages, sizes, and skills, including President Obama and his White House staff.

At the high-performance level, the sport is less accessible. The average height of the USA's National Basketball Association (NBA) male player in 2008 was almost 6 foot 7 inches (200.6 cm). Nearly 16 million people each year are drawn to a professional game that combines superb athleticism with manual dexterity, played at dazzling speed in a confined space, guaranteeing high-scores, achieved with considerable showmanship.

The US professional game is a product of the sports–media alliances that emerged when the Basketball Association of America and the National Basketball League merged to form the NBA in 1949. It has offered a route to riches and fame for players from African American backgrounds in particular, and promotes a street

Kobe Bryant, capturing the grace and skill of basketball, as he achieves a slamdunk – placing the ball into the basket rather than throwing it.

style that resonates with youth culture. As Nelson George has said: "Rapping, sermonizing, and soloing" in basketball moves expresses an "African American aesthetic".

This is typified by Michael Jordan, who inspired his team, the Chicago Bulls, to six championships in the 1990s. His profile and image underpinned the growth and expansion of Nike, who created the Air Jordan sports shoe, and generated an estimated $10 billion in revenue for the sport, and for its broadcast and corporate partners. His presence in an NBA Finals could boost a TV audience by as much as 9 million.

The total NBA League revenue for its 30 teams in the 2008/09 season was $3.2 billion, with media contracts through to 2015/16 worth $7.4 billion. Season 2009/10 listed 458 players on the NBA index, 83 of whom came from outside the USA – a proportion that is increasing. The sport has a strong club base in Europe, which feeds into the NBA.

### Olympic rivalries

Olympic basketball was dominated by the USA from 1936 onwards, but during the Cold War, the USSR team increasingly challenged the US team, and finally ended its streak of 62 Olympic match wins at the 1972 Munich Olympics. From 1989, professional players from the NBA were allowed to participate in the Olympics, and the so-called "Dream Team" of US professionals strolled to gold at Barcelona 1992. A hastily assembled US squad arrived at Athens 2004, professional stars having pulled out, but lost to Puerto Rico and Lithuania: Argentina took gold.

Women's basketball has been included at the Olympics since 1976, but has also been dominated by a USA–USSR rivalry. The USA had won six gold medals to the USSR/Russia's three by the end of the 2008 Games.

USA vs. USSR at the 1988 Olympics.

# The American game

## On the court
**Number of high-school boys per 1,000 in population playing in school leagues 2008/9**

- ■ 100 – 129
- ■ 50 – 99
- ■ fewer than 50

**Total boys: 545,000**
**Total girls: 445,000**

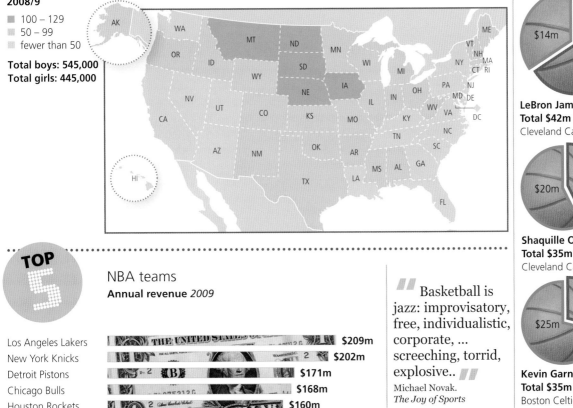

## Top NBA players

**LeBron James**
**Total $42m**
Cleveland Cavaliers
- $14m
- $28m

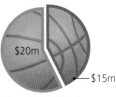

**Shaquille O'Neal**
**Total $35m**
Cleveland Cavaliers
- $20m
- $15m

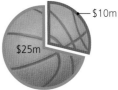

**Kevin Garnett**
**Total $35m**
Boston Celtics
- $10m
- $25m

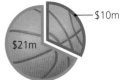

**Kobe Bryant**
**Total $31m**
Los Angeles Lakers
- $10m
- $21m

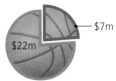

**Allen Iverson**
**Total $29m**
Philadelphia 76ers
- $7m
- $22m

**Annual earnings** *2009*
▷ from endorsements
▷ in salary

---

**TOP 5**

## NBA teams
**Annual revenue** *2009*

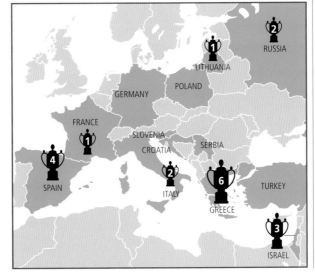

| | |
|---|---|
| Los Angeles Lakers | $209m |
| New York Knicks | $202m |
| Detroit Pistons | $171m |
| Chicago Bulls | $168m |
| Houston Rockets | $160m |

> Basketball is jazz: improvisatory, free, individualistic, corporate, ... screeching, torrid, explosive..
>
> Michael Novak.
> *The Joy of Sports*

---

# The European game

## Countries with clubs participating in Euroleague

🏆 **number of championship wins 1993–2010**

A men's club-based championship has been held in Europe since 1958, largely won by clubs from Mediterranean and East European countries. Panathinaikos, Greece, Maccabi Tel Aviv, and CSK Moscow predominated from 2000–09, but Regal FC Barcelona defeated Olympiakos Pireus of Greece in the 2010 final.

# BOXING – AMATEUR

## The noble art

### The Queensberry Rules

Bare-knuckle fighting has been a popular sport since classical times, but the introduction of the Queensberry Rules in 1867 introduced an element of restraint, bringing the sport into the modern age. The rules specify:
- the dimensions of the ring
- three-minute rounds, with a minute break
- the requirement to wear gloves
- the banning of spikes in footwear
- the prohibition of wrestling or hugging
- the banning of other people in the ring
- the conditions of a count and a knockout

The rules were actually codified by the Welsh sportsman John Graham Chambers, founder of England's Amateur Athletic Club, who named them after John Sholto Douglas, the 9th Marquess of Queensberry (below), a keen patron of the sport.

"There's no exercise in the world so good for the temper and for the muscles of the back and legs", as long as "you never have to use it in earnest", wrote Thomas Hughes of boxing in *Tom Brown's School-days* in 1857. A century and a half on, similar sentiments were shared by fictional boxing coach and reformed killer Dennis "Cutty" Wise in the third season of the TV classic *The Wire*. It is boxing's combined qualities of character-building, toughening-up, and fitness-building that have motivated organizers and enthusiasts of amateur boxing through the years.

It is obvious what attracts a fighter to the professional ranks: the one-to-one gladiatorial encounter, the baying of the crowd, the great riches that can be won. But the youth clubs, YMCAs, church halls, and small venues that stage the amateur bout stand for different values from those of the professional game. While the very best amateurs box at the Olympic Games, most pursue their sport in a different world, where few may be watching, and little is at stake.

Amateur boxing developed in the great metropolitan centres of newly urbanized and industrializing societies. In the USA as well as the UK, bare-knuckle fights were replaced by a more controlled amateur pugilism. Boxing was a foundation sport for the exclusive New York Athletic Club,

established in Manhattan in 1868, now located on the south edge of Central Park. In the UK, the sport was popularized and democratized when the Amateur Boxing Association, founded in 1880, began organizing annual indoor championship competitions. For generations of males, of all social classes, it would provide an appealing blend of physical skill and atavistic aggression.

Boxing is often seen as a way out of the ghetto. And, indeed, numerous fighters from deprived inner-city backgrounds have made successful professional careers. Learn to fight, and there opens before you a ladder of social mobility, the story goes. But very few do make it out of the ghetto, and sociologists have observed that the amateur boxing ring and club is more a provider of survival skills than of a passport to a new life.

Protective headgear is mandatory in amateur boxing.

## Boxing – the language of everyday life

Numerous phrases from the sport have made their way into the English language:

**Below the belt** – a foul punch that lands below the waist.
**Blow by blow** – scoring is based on blows that land on an opponent, and full descriptions of fights have been called "blow by blow accounts".
**Going the distance** – lasting the full schedule of rounds.
**Knock out** – when a boxer is knocked unconscious or fails to get to his/her feet before the referee has counted to 10.
**On the ropes** – a boxer under pressure often leans on, or is pinned against, the ropes.

**Out for the count** – the condition in which the boxer is unable to recover within a 10-second count by the referee, and so loses to a knockout.
**Ring rusty** – unprepared for sustained contest.
**Saved by the bell** – the bell signalling the end of a round saves the boxer from a knock out or further punishment.
**Sucker punch** – a punch that appears to carry little threat, but has a disproportionate effect.
**Throw in the towel** – the boxer's "second" or corner man does this to concede defeat.

Other phrases – **fight to the finish, toe to toe** – are applied to war, economic rivalries, and even everyday interpersonal relations.

## The politics of boxing

Cuban Teófilo Stevenson was tall, strong, handsome, and Olympic heavyweight gold medallist at the 1972 Munich Olympic Games. He was the product of a systematic nurturing of amateur boxing in Cuba after the revolution in 1959. If Stevenson could be persuaded to turn professional, a dream clash with Muhammad Ali would provide the boxing promoter's dream bout. He was offered $5 million to fight Ali, but replied with the rhetorical question: "What is 1 million US dollars compared to the love of 8 million Cubans?" He went on to win further Olympic gold medals at Montreal (1976) and Moscow (1980), representing socialist ideals against capitalist ideology.

For his sustained loyalty to his country, Stevenson received special privileges from the Cuban state, such as luxurious housing, and went on to coach the country's national boxing squad. Cuba's achievement in the Olympic boxing arena, second only to the USA, has been remarkable, with most of its medals won since 1970.

Olympic boxers, 2000

Boxing remains the only sport in the modern Olympics that excludes professionals, although many Olympians have gone on to have lucrative professional careers.

The Olympic format was changed in 2000, from three three-minute rounds to four two-minute rounds. Women's boxing makes its inaugural appearance on the Olympic programme at the London 2012 Games.

## TOP 10

## Olympic medals

**Total Olympic medals won for boxing** *1904–2008*

Gold
Silver
Bronze

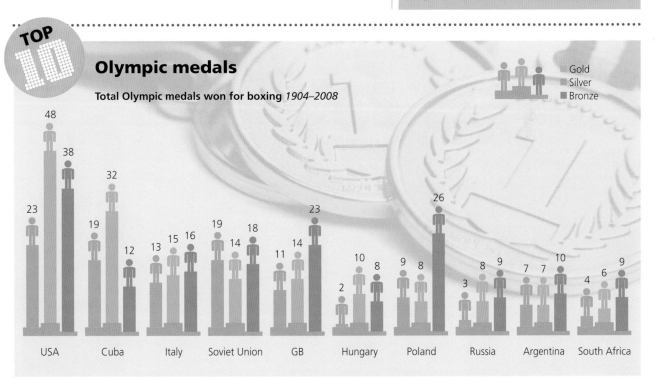

| | Gold | Silver | Bronze |
|---|---|---|---|
| USA | 48 | 38 | 23 |
| Cuba | 32 | 19 | 12 |
| Italy | 13 | 15 | 16 |
| Soviet Union | 19 | 14 | 18 |
| GB | 11 | 14 | 23 |
| Hungary | 10 | 8 | 2 |
| Poland | 26 | 9 | 8 |
| Russia | 3 | 8 | 9 |
| Argentina | 7 | 7 | 10 |
| South Africa | 4 | 6 | 9 |

# BOXING – PROFESSIONAL

## Masters of the ring

### Bare-knuckle fighting

Boxing prospered as bare-knuckle prize fighting from the late 18th century, and crowds flocked to fights with a transatlantic appeal. Englishman Tom Cribb fought freed black American slave Tom Molineaux in England in 1810 and 1811. The American was known as the "hurricane fighter", but lost to the "superior science" of the smaller Englishman. Cribb's trainer, "Captain" Robert Barclay, won £10,000 on the second fight – equivalent to £457,000 today. Cribb's protégé, Tom Spring, was also light on his feet, which stood him in good stead against the slower and heavier Irishman Jack Langan, whom he beat on two occasions before retiring in 1824.

In the USA, J.L. Sullivan (right) won over 450 fights as a bare-knuckle fighter before adopting the Queensberry Rules in 1883 and becoming the first world champion of gloved boxing.

The professional male heavyweight has always had the highest profile in the boxing world, for two reasons: the attraction of fights between larger-than-life males, and the national prestige attached to boxers as representatives of a nation or ethnic group. J.L. Sullivan was a national celebrity in the USA in the late 19th century, but was also lauded as an Irish American. In the 1960s, Muhammad Ali, previously Cassius Clay, symbolized civil rights and cultural and religious politics as much as physical and athletic prowess.

Professional boxing appealed to the working populations of growing cities. Poor boys, some as young as 12, were recruited to fight in local competitions and on regional circuits. Defensive skills were appreciated, but the influence of international promoters, and then radio and television broadcasting encouraged a more aggressive form of fighting. In the 1950s, support switched from local boxing heroes to national and international stars as professional boxing became part of the trend towards globalized consumerism.

The number of weight categories expanded, and rival organizations competed to represent the sport internationally, shifting the centre of organizational power from the east coast of the USA to Central America.

New heroes emerged across the weight ranges, such as Manny Pacquiao of the Philippines, challenging the hegemony of the heavyweights in the global marketplace.

The popularity of the sport, particularly among working-class men, has survived betting and match-fixing scandals, but questions are raised recurrently about the inherent violence of the professional form. Scandinavian countries have carried the moral conscience of the world. Professional boxing was banned by law in Iceland (1956), Sweden (1970) and Norway (1981), on what were mostly health and moral grounds. A more ideological rationale underlies the banning of professional boxing in communist North Korea and Cuba.

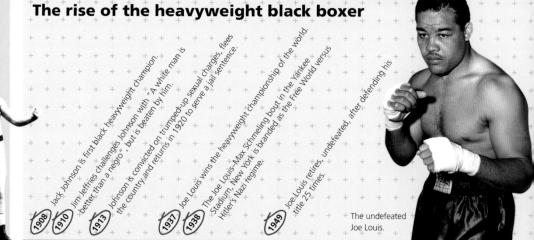

Ricky Hatton on the floor, after being knocked out by Manny Pacquiao, 2009.

## The rise of the heavyweight black boxer

**1908** Jack Johnson is first black heavyweight champion.

**1910** Jim Jeffries challenges Johnson with "A white man is better than a negro", but is beaten by him.

**1913** Johnson is convicted on trumped-up sexual charges, flees the country and returns in 1920 to serve a jail sentence.

**1937** Joe Louis wins the heavyweight championship of the world.

**1938** The Joe Louis–Max Schmeling bout in the Yankee Stadium, New York is branded as the Free World versus Hitler's Nazi regime.

**1949** Joe Louis retires, undefeated, after defending his title 25 times.

The undefeated Joe Louis.

# World organizations

## Breakups and mergers

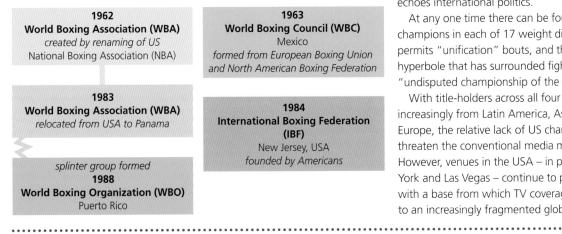

**1962**
**World Boxing Association (WBA)**
*created by renaming of US
National Boxing Association (NBA)*

**1963**
**World Boxing Council (WBC)**
Mexico
*formed from European Boxing Union
and North American Boxing Federation*

**1983**
**World Boxing Association (WBA)**
*relocated from USA to Panama*

**1984**
**International Boxing Federation
(IBF)**
New Jersey, USA
*founded by Americans*

*splinter group formed*
**1988**
**World Boxing Organization (WBO)**
Puerto Rico

As professional boxing generates increasingly lucrative markets, four bodies compete for control of the sport. The story of their mergers and rivalries echoes international politics.

At any one time there can be four world champions in each of 17 weight divisions. This permits "unification" bouts, and the marketing hyperbole that has surrounded fights for the "undisputed championship of the world".

With title-holders across all four bodies coming increasingly from Latin America, Asia and Eastern Europe, the relative lack of US champions could threaten the conventional media markets. However, venues in the USA – in particular in New York and Las Vegas – continue to provide the sport with a base from which TV coverage is transmitted to an increasingly fragmented global audience.

# The value of boxing

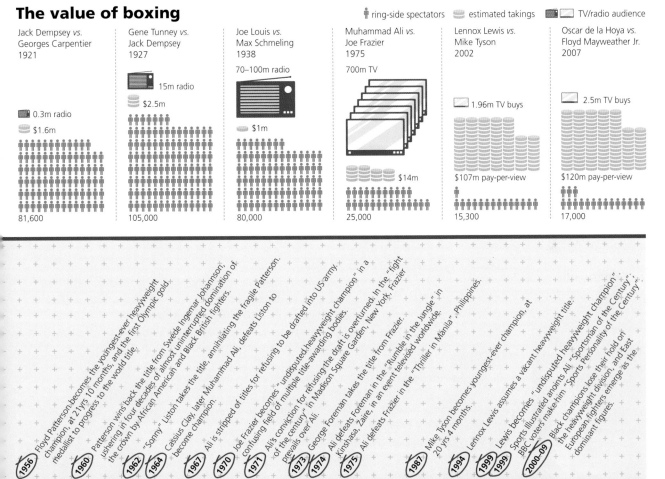

ring-side spectators    estimated takings    TV/radio audience

Jack Dempsey *vs.*
Georges Carpentier
1921

0.3m radio
$1.6m
81,600

Gene Tunney *vs.*
Jack Dempsey
1927

15m radio
$2.5m
105,000

Joe Louis *vs.*
Max Schmeling
1938

70–100m radio
$1m
80,000

Muhammad Ali *vs.*
Joe Frazier
1975

700m TV
$14m
25,000

Lennox Lewis *vs.*
Mike Tyson
2002

1.96m TV buys
$107m pay-per-view
15,300

Oscar de la Hoya *vs.*
Floyd Mayweather Jr.
2007

2.5m TV buys
$120m pay-per-view
17,000

# CRICKET

## The sound of leather on willow

### A sporting legend

W.G. Grace was England's first national sporting hero. He shot to prominence at the age of 15 in 1864, and dominated English and international cricket for 40 years. His batting and bowling achievements were unsurpassed, and he modernized stroke-making.

He was nominally an amateur, but he practised long, played hard, negotiated fees for captaining national tourist sides, and set up commercial deals with manufacturers and new consumer industries.

His rotund physique and beard were instantly recognizable, giving him an unprecedented profile in late-Victorian England, where his popularity straddled the class system.

Cricket has produced a vast literature, mixing nostalgia and analysis of performance, celebrating regional pride and national rivalries. Many see cricket as an expression of moral qualities – the spirit of fair play. The image of the willow bat striking the leather ball on sunny village greens in England or grounds around the world evokes an innocent, sportsmanlike past.

But cricket has produced intense international rivalries. The strongest national sides in the men's game comprise England and nine of its former colonies (who relish outplaying the England team). All but Zimbabwe participate in cycles of international encounters known as Test Matches, the first of which was held between England and Australia in 1877.

In its traditional form, in international Tests, a cricket match is a five-day (frequently weather-affected) encounter, which often ends in a draw (when one side fails to bowl the other side out twice). But, from the 1960s, other formats have been developed to suit the needs of broadcasters, including the one-day game in which each team has only one innings. In what the ICC hails as cricket's showpiece event, the men's Cricket World Cup that was first held in 1975, teams contest a one-day match of 50 overs (300 balls) per side. In the 20/20 World Cup, inaugurated in 2007, a mere 120 balls are bowled by each side.

The Indian subcontinent, where cricket stimulates more passion than perhaps anywhere else, now generates 70 percent of world cricketing revenues. A major recent initiative is the Indian Premier League (IPL), whose eight teams bid for the services of some of the world's top players. It was launched by the Indian Board of Control for Cricket in 2008, and after just six months had sold the broadcasting rights for $1 billion, and team franchises for over $700 million. It has succeeded despite being held in South Africa in 2009 because of security problems on the subcontinent, and the ongoing controversies concerning the business dealings of its organizers.

In April 2008, Sachin Tendulkar broke the record of aggregate runs in Test Matches, which West Indian Brian Lara had held for 19 years. In October 2010, he passed the symbolic figure of 14,000 runs in Test cricket. As former India captain Kapil Dev has observed: "Every kid wants to become Sachin Tendulkar. … The country needs heroes like him."

### The bodyline controversy

The England team touring Australia in 1932–33 used an intimidating tactic to unsettle Australian batsmen, in particular Don Bradman, who had dominated England in 1930. The fast bowler Harold Larwood was instructed by his captain Douglas Jardine to aim short deliveries at the batsman's legside, which would bounce early and rise towards the batsman's body and unprotected head. The Australian Cricket Board sent a telegram to the Marylebone Cricket Club (MCC), the England team's base, stating that the "bodyline" practice was "unsportsmanlike".

Political and economic relations between the countries were delicate, and the issue sparked diplomatic exchanges. Australia withdrew the allegation, and the series was completed, with England winning. But Jardine was not to captain England again against Australia, and Larwood, who refused to apologize, was never again selected for his country. Encouraged by former rivals in the bodyline series, he emigrated to Australia.

# International Cricket

The ICC relocated from London, England to Dubai, UAE in 2005, where it can combine tax-free privileges with proximity to the heartlands of the new cricketing monies.

## International Cricket Council
**Status of membership**
*2010*

★ ICC headquarters
■ full member
■ associate members
□ affiliate member

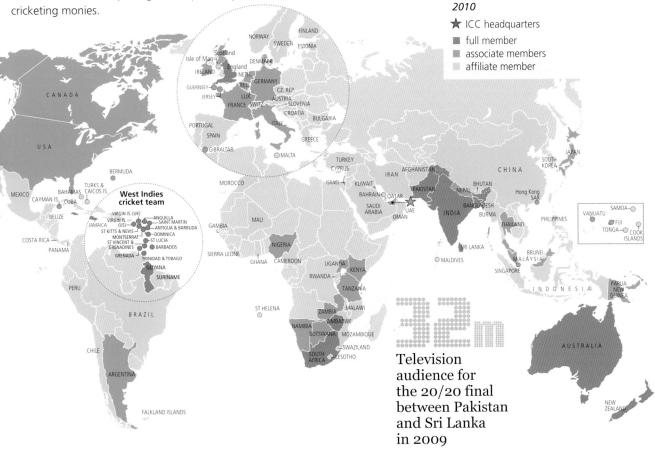

Television audience for the 20/20 final between Pakistan and Sri Lanka in 2009

32m

---

## ICC Cricket World Cup winners

Although a World Cup was established in women's cricket before men's, and has been dominated by Australia and England, it has had a relatively low cultural and media profile.

**Women's cup**

| 1973 England | 1978 Australia | 1982 Australia | 1988 Australia | 1993 England | 1997 Australia | 2000 New Zealand | 2005 Australia | 2009 England |

**Men's cup**

| 1975 West Indies | 1979 West Indies | 1983 India | 1987 Australia | 1992 Pakistan | 1996 Sri Lanka | 1999 Australia | 2003 Australia | 2007 Australia |

## Cricketing terms

**Clean bowled** – completely beaten by the bowler's delivery.

**It's not cricket** – not fair play.

**Out for a duck** – a batsman's no score, inspired by a duck's egg, the shape of a zero.

**Play a straight bat** – play defensively, showing dogged and determined qualities.

**Pull up the stumps** – stop play.

## Pocket money

Pool, carom, and snooker (known collectively as "billiard sports") are played by countless millions of people on a casual basis, but also have a niche in an entertainment industry that can support circuits of professional players.

The accessibility of the pool (pocket billiards) or carom billiards table in bars, clubs, and leisure centres can make almost anyone a participant. In the USA, 30 million children and adults play pool on a casual basis, making it the eleventh most played sport. In England, where there are only 98,000 regular pool players, snooker is the country's 25th most popular sport, with 163,500 players.

The popularity of cue sports has crossed social barriers. Pocket billiards was established in the UK, and entered the USA as a "gentleman's" game in the late 19h century, but in both countries it spread rapidly to the lower classes. Similarly, snooker, played on a larger table with more balls than the other cue sports, was developed by British military officers in India in the 19th century, but was soon played by British working men. Although it has a high profile in the UK, where the World Snooker Championship is held, it has less of a worldwide profile than either pool or carom.

Compared to champions and professionals in other sports, cue sport players are modest earners. The best earnings are to be had in snooker, where established sponsorship and television money secures funding and markets. In all cue-sports, however, players may earn well over the amount shown in official figures, as an informal – and sometimes corrupt – economy of gambling and hustling operates behind the public façade.

Worldwide organization of the sport is complex. The World Confederation of Billiard Sports was formed in 1992 with the aim of becoming an Olympic sport. Although it has gained recognition from the IOC, there is no immediate prospect of the inclusion of billiard sports in the Olympics.

### Cue sports

All are played with a wooden stick (a cue), which is used to strike a white ball against other coloured balls, on a rectangular table with green baize covering and cushioned sides. In pool (pocket billiards) and snooker the ball is potted into small baskets hanging from the table. In carom billiards there are no pockets.

## people play pool for fun in the USA

The most commonly played version of pool is 8-ball.

## A man's world

In the 1930s, the pool room and billiard hall were a major social institution of the American urban male working-class. Willie Mosconi (left) would play an exhibition match in front of 1,500 spectators. The pool room fostered a gambling culture, focused on the professional hustler, who would disguise his skills in setting up challenge matches on which many would bet. This was romanticized in the 1961 movie *The Hustler*, with Paul Newman playing the character Minnesota Fats.

A commemorative Mosconi Cup was established in 1994, in which the USA plays Europe in an annual 9-ball pool tournament modelled on golf's Ryder Cup. Players now qualify through tournament play during the year. The USA has dominated the event, with 12 wins to Europe's four.

# Structure of the WCBS

**World Confederation of Billiard Sports**
**WCBS**

**International Billiards and Snooker Federation** (non-professional snooker and English billiards)
**IBSF**
**94**

**Union Mondiale de Billiard** (representing carom)
**UMB**
**63**

**World Pool-Billiard Association** (representing pool)
**WPA**
**95**

## TOP 5

### Pool earners
**Life-time winnings** *2010*

**Men**

| | |
|---|---|
| Efren Reyes, Philippines | $1.77m |
| Mika Immonen, Finland | $1.02m |
| Francisco Bustamante. Germany | $892k |
| Johnny Archer, USA | $843k |
| Ralf Souquet, Germany | $837k |

**Women**

| | |
|---|---|
| Allison Fisher, UK | $814k |
| Karen Corr, Ireland | $728k |
| Jeanette Lee, USA | $346k |
| Ga-Young Kim, South Korea | $329k |
| Kelly Fisher, Ireland | $283k |

Allison Fisher, top UK woman snooker player, felt constrained by the limited support and exposure given to the women's professional game. Her move to the USA in 1995 to play the professional pool circuit made her the highest-earning woman in the sport, and one of the most competitive sportswomen, winning 41 major titles by 2009, and a Gold Medal representing England in the 2009 World Games.

## Professional snooker

Professional snooker grew in popularity in the UK in the 1960s, when broadcasts in colour first captured the drama of the 21-ball game for the television audience. Cigarette sponsors backed the sport, and an international circuit of professionals was established.

The 18.5 million people glued to the final of the 1985 World Snooker Championship between Irishman Dennis Taylor and England's Steve Davis represented the largest post-midnight audience in UK TV history. Always behind in the 35-frame match against the reigning champion, Taylor went ahead for the first time only on potting the final black to win the title.

## TOP 5

### Snooker earners
**Winnings in 2008/09 season**

| | |
|---|---|
| John Higgins, Scotland | £429k |
| Shaun Murphy, England | £268k |
| Ronnie O'Sullivan, England | £256k |
| Stephen Hendry, Scotland | £241k |
| Neil Robertson, Australia | £156k |

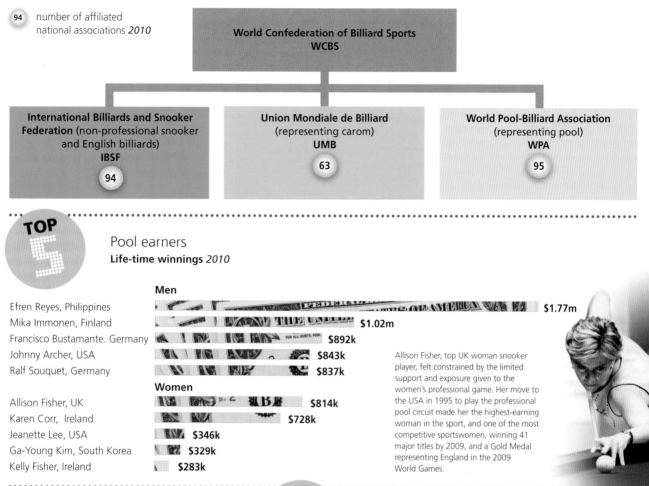

# CYCLING

## Deals on wheels

### Champion material

Frenchman Jacques Anquetil (1934–87), was the first to win the Tour de France, despite his smoking, drinking and playboy lifestyle. He was prepared to take anything necessary to gain a competitive advantage. French President de Gaulle was sanguine about Anquetil's methods, commenting that the most important thing was that he got the Marseillaise known around the world.

"It's not about the bike", Lance Armstrong entitled his autobiography. But to most cyclists it most certainly is. The bicycle oozed class distinction when it was invented, before mass production widened access for practical users and expanding leisure markets, and the bicycle market now offers a wide choice of specialist machines for work and play. It symbolizes the global marketplace, with China dominating production and the USA the leading importer.

Olympic track cycling favours short, sharp races on indoor purpose-built tracks (the vélodrome), in which minute detail in clothing and technology can affect the outcome. France and Italy have dominated the medal tables in road-racing and track at the Olympics, and in the newer mountain-biking event, with the USA fifth in the track and road events.

The greatest road races in the world are all in Western Europe: Tours of France, Italy and Spain. Champion cyclists have been produced by the combination of strong working-class masculinity, and regional and national pride. The Tour de France has attracted great American competitors, including Greg Le Monde and Lance Armstrong. The continuing attraction of road-race cycling lies in the empathy felt by the everyday cyclist with those who combine the latest in bike technology with heroic feats of human endurance and speed, and selfless teamwork with individual fearlessness.

Lance Armstrong, who battled cancer as well as the world's best road racers to ride to a record seven victories in the Tour de France. In August 2009, Armstrong used Twitter to invite Scottish fans out on a bike ride, giving hundreds of people the chance to ride with their hero.

## Tour de France

The Tour de France brings a major sports event to the people. Towns and villages through which it passes (in France and its neighbours) host a world-class event for which there is no charge for spectators. In addition, tens of millions of television viewers tune in to see some of the action. At different times in the Tour's history riders rode as individuals or as national teams. Now, teams are sponsored by companies. The team winner of the 2010 Tour was Radio Shack. Team Sky, with British Olympians transferring their track skills to the road, finished way down the field. Specialist bike manufacturers have supplied Tour winners: Trek (USA) 1995–2005, 2007 and 2009; Pinarello (Italy), 2006; and Cervélo (Canada), 2008.

**1903** First Tour de France, organized by L'Auto magazine.

**1910** Introduction of high-mountain stages.

**1919** Introduction of yellow jersey for overall Tour leader.

**1924** Produit Gibbs soap company provides money for stage winners.

**1930** Introduction of the caravane publicitaire, with companies paying to enter a vehicle in the procession preceding the riders, distributing gifts and samples to spectators.

**1948** L'Equipe takes over the Tour from the defunct L'Auto.

**1967** Death of English rider Tom Simpson while climbing Mont Ventoux, dosed up on stimulants.

**1998** Festina team vehicles raided by French police for evidence of drug-use.

**2005** Lance Armstrong (USA) wins his seventh title, a record.

**2006** Floyd Landis (USA) stripped of title after testing positive for banned drugs.

# Speed, endurance and artistry

**Road** | Individual road races and time trials for men and women. In trials, riders race against the clock over distances of 45–55 km. The road race is over 210–240 km on repeated circuits of a route.

| | |
|---|---|
| Italy | 9 |
| France | 8 |
| Netherlands | 7 |

**Track** | Individual and team sprints, indoors and outdoors, for men and women. These include complex point-scoring variants, such as the Madison (named after Madison Square Garden, Manhattan, where it was first raced) and the Keirin (based on a 1940s Japanese betting race), in which riders are paced for almost three-quarters of the distance by a motorbike before a sprint finish.

| | |
|---|---|
| France | 29 |
| Italy | 21 |
| Great Britain | 17 |

**Mountain bike** | First introduced at the Atlanta Olympics in 1996, a cross-country race of 40–50 km over gravel tracks, forest roads, rough earth, and fields. Tarred and paved roads must not make up more than 15% of the overall route.

| | |
|---|---|
| France | 3 |
| Italy | 2 |
| Norway | 1 |
| Germany | 1 |
| Netherlands | 1 |

**BMX** | BMX originated as a youth craze in California in the 1960s. A world championship was first held in 1982, and in 1995 the sport was a core event in the Extreme/X Games. BMX was introduced to the Olympic Games at Beijing 2008 as a race against the clock. It succeeded in adding drama to what many experience as the over-technical cycling events. The even more dramatic BMX freestyle has not been accepted into the Olympic programme.

| | |
|---|---|
| France | 1 |
| Latvia | 1 |

Cyclists fly off the bumps at the 2005 European BMX Championship.

**20m** bicycles were sold in Europe in 2008

**Cyclo-cross** | An event lasting about an hour over a hilly circuit of 2.5–3.5 km, in which riders often have to carry the bike.

**Trials** | A first World Championship was held in 1984. Cyclists must mount obstacles (rocks, shrubs, even furniture and cars). Penalties are incurred for foot contact with the ground, and the winner is the cyclist with fewest penalty points.

**Indoor cycling** | Artistic cycling – most popular in Germany – involves a 5-minute routine to music, and has held a world championship since 1956.

**Cycle-ball** | Cycle-ball is a male-only sport in which two team members use the wheels and their body to strike the ball into their opponents' goal. It is popular in some European countries, Russia and Japan.

Cycle-ball requires a fixed-wheel bicycle with adapted handle-bars.

The UK Cycling for All programme encourages as many people as possible to take up cycling in some form and at any level.

# FOOTBALL – INTERNATIONAL

## The beautiful game

### Football at the Olympics

International football competitions for men were held at the Olympic Games from 1900, with the exception of Los Angeles 1932. An amateur Great Britain side won three of the first four Olympics, but in the 1920s Uruguay won twice, and the fascist-backed Italian side won at the 1936 "Nazi Games".

Although Sweden won gold in 1948, the amateur ideology of the Olympics left the field open to state-socialist and communist teams until Spain's triumph in 1992. Nigeria and Cameroon heralded increased African expectations by winning gold in 1996 and 2000 respectively.

Women's football was introduced at the 1996 Olympics.

The secret of what Brazilian legend Pelé called "the beautiful game" lies in its accessibility and essential simplicity. Accounts abound of children playing the game with balls of many types, improvised balls, make-do goalposts, on surfaces of all kinds. No equipment is needed, and star players come in all sizes. The tiniest attacking player can bamboozle the giant defender.

Sir Stanley Rous, international referee, doyen of English football administration, architect of the streamlined laws of the game in the 1930s, and president of La Fédération Internationale de Football Association (FIFA) from 1961 to 1974, also pointed to the speed and the uncertainty of the game: "Football is a very fast game of quick and sudden improvisations, of situations which change with startling suddenness. Incident piles on incident so quickly, invariably in a highly charged atmosphere" so that the memory is strained, objectivity subjugated to personal opinion and bias. And all this in 1959, before any widespread live television coverage or replay technology.

Football has caught the imagination of fans and audiences across societies and cultures of all kinds, and made it indisputably the most popular sport in the world. The low-scoring ensures, in the main, an uncertainty of outcome. Team discipline has to be blended with individual flair. To some extent, all team

Didier Drogba, from the Côte d'Ivoire, playing for Premiership club Chelsea.

The opportunity for demonstrations of individual skill within the context of a team game makes football a popular sport with players and spectators alike.

games do this; but football does it more effectively. This accounts for its near-universal attraction.

International football is governed by FIFA, in association with six continental or regional federations, which stage their own championships, and contest FIFA's Confederations Cup. But although international football has escalated dramatically, the big leagues of Europe continue to attract players from around the world, leaving a pattern of uneven development in the domestic leagues of countries in Africa, Asia, and the Americas.

In its expansion of the international calendar FIFA has also emphasized youth development, women's football, and exploited alternative formats beyond the 11-a-side game.

## The universal language

A South African boy demonstrating his skill.

Football idols represent people's aspirations. As Ghana almost reached the last eight of the South Africa 2010 World Cup, Ghanaians in South London and Accra crammed into community and public spaces and felt at one with all of Africa.

Travel away from the big city, in any developing country, and makeshift football pitches can be seen everywhere: goalposts made from old piping, balls from rags and paper, or from banana leaves and fibres (shown here). But the simplicity and accessibility of the game has also enabled charities to get the basic equipment – a leather

ball – to kids in Africa's poorest areas, and to bring street kids together in Durban's Street Child World Cup.

The Zulu word *muti* means medicine, healing. Football *muti* is the power of the simplest game to enrapture people in the least promising of contexts and circumstances, and to provide a common language. In countries across Africa and beyond, the power of football transcends the deprivations of everyday life.

# The USA – football's final frontier

Frozen out by America's "Big Four", soccer has long seemed an unwelcome intruder. In fact, its national association was recognized by FIFA in 1914, and the USA got to the semi-final of the first FIFA men's World Cup in 1930. It made the last eight at the World Cup Finals in 2002, and the last 16 at South Africa 2010, where former president Bill Clinton gave his seal of approval.

The American women's game is a powerhouse of world football, achieving double Olympic gold with victories over Brazil in Athens 2004 and Beijing 2008; and two World Cup triumphs.

The North American Soccer League – even with soccer greats Pelé and Franz Beckenbauer – could not sustain its crowds and sponsors in the 1970s, but staging the 1994 men's World Cup was conditional upon re-establishing a national US league. The MLS (Major League Soccer) has developed new stadia, and attracted David Beckham in a bold marketing strategy.

Parents like soccer because the kit is cheap, the girls play too, and it's comparatively safe. Schools and colleges involve millions of young men and women in the game, and Latin Leagues are flourishing on the West Coast and in the South.

The television audience is taking off. Fox Soccer Channel is reaching more households, with the English Premier League the most watched European League on US television. Football may be conquering its final frontier, and the USA breaking out of its sporting exceptionalism to embrace the most popular sport on Earth.

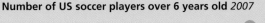

## Number of US soccer players over 6 years old *2007*

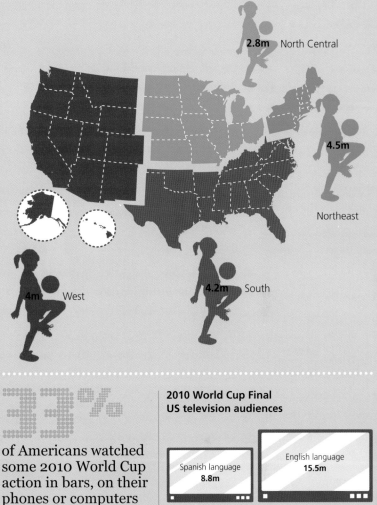

2.8m North Central

4.5m

Northeast

4m West

4.2m South

**33%**

of Americans watched some 2010 World Cup action in bars, on their phones or computers

### 2010 World Cup Final US television audiences

Spanish language
**8.8m**

English language
**15.5m**

# Women's football

Marta Vieira da Silva, one of the world's best-known women players.

Women's championships were introduced by the continental federations before FIFA introduced the Women's World Cup in 1991, and a women's Olympic event began in 1996. Women have had to counter prejudice and stereotyping, exemplified in the comment by FIFA president Sepp Blatter that women could "play in more feminine clothes like they do in volleyball" (2004). And although women's football is featuring more prominently in television schedules and the sporting press, it remains marginal to the mainstream media concentration on the men's game.

## Women's World Cup winners

| | | |
|---|---|---|
| **1991** | USA | (in China) |
| **1995** | Norway | (in Sweden) |
| **1999** | USA | (in USA) |
| **2003** | Germany | (in USA) |
| **2007** | Germany | (in China) |

# FOOTBALL – EUROPEAN

## The bountiful game

### Leagues of their own

Association football (or soccer) was developed in its modern form during the 19th century, taking shape in England's ancient universities and its expanding industrial cities. The FA (Football Association) Cup began in 1871, and a professional league was formed of 12 clubs in the industrial north and midlands in 1888.

By the turn of the century football was spreading to Europe and national leagues were established: Italy's Serie A in 1898 (restructured 1929), Spain's La Liga in 1929, France's Ligue 1 in 1932, and Germany's Bundesliga in 1963.

David Beckham, ex-Manchester United player, wearing a green and gold scarf, symbol of a fan-based movement opposed to the continuing ownership of the club by the American Glazer family, which brought with it a debt that stood at £1.1billion in 2010.

Europe has become the powerhouse of club football, drawing in top players from all over the world. The Big Five national leagues in Europe have been enriched by lucrative television contracts, although much of the money has been redistributed via a solipsistic cycle of inflated player salaries.

The most powerful clubs have threatened to break away from their national leagues, but the European football confederation UEFA (Union Européenne de Football Association) has satisfied some of their demands by expanding the premier European club competition, the Champions League. Initially a knock-out tournament for eight champion clubs, its extended format features 32 clubs, and dominates peak-time mid-week television throughout the season. Its exclusive corporate partners – MasterCard, Ford, Unicredit, Heineken, Sony, and (Sony) Playstation – and the income from television rights, have funded this expansion. UEFA has also restructured its other club competitions into an expanded Europa League, creating wider international opportunities for clubs from its extended constituency after the dissolution of the Soviet Union.

As a catalyst for the world's top talent, elite European clubs have both broadened the cultural and international base of their teams and professional staff, and, some argue, restricted opportunities for home-grown talent. The Italian club Internazionale won the Champions League in Madrid with a team containing no Italian players. In England, only about a third of players in the Premier League are eligible for the national side, and England's squad was the oldest at South Africa 2010. In Germany, though, a system implemented in 2002 has produced its youngest ever team. All 36 clubs in the two Bundesliga divisions must operate regulated academies, at least 12 players from each intake must be eligible to play for Germany, and no single entity can have a majority stake in the club, ensuring close club and national side co-operation. All 23 German players in South Africa had come through academies and, though relatively unknown, they outperformed global superstars from the English Premier League.

Argentinian, Lionel Messi, playing for FC Barcelona – one of four players in the 2009/10 European season who earned the equivalent of around $1 million a month.

## Finances of top clubs

Some of the richest clubs are saddled by debt. Reasons include takeovers by investors, based on huge loans, as in the case of Manchester United and Liverpool, or recruitment and remuneration strategies, such as at Real Madrid. Italian and German clubs appear less debt-ridden, but accounting practices may generate differences.

Barcelona and Real Madrid, both with membership models of ownership, represent the least and most debt-burdened clubs in Europe. New UEFA "financial fair play rules", coming into force from 2012/13, require clubs to avoid making persistent losses. Certain clubs will need to take urgent steps to reduce their expensive debts, and reign in salaries.

**Value of club** *2008/09*   ■ **debt as percentage of value**

| | 46% | 54% | 41% | | 14% | 47% | | 3% | 8% |
|---|---|---|---|---|---|---|---|---|---|
| $1,835m | $1,323m | $1,181m | $1,000m | $990m | $822m | $800m | $656m | $646m | $413m |
| Manchester United | Real Madrid | Arsenal | Barcelona | Bayern Munich | Liverpool | AC Milan | Juventus | Chelsea | Inter Milan |

# UEFA

**Member federations** *2010*

- ■ joined 1956–1991
- ■ joined 1992–2010

The breakup of the Soviet Union, the conflict in the Balkans, and the pragmatic politics of affiliation for several countries in Central Asia, boosted UEFA's membership by 17 from 1992 onwards. This was pivotal in the restructuring and then expansion of the old European Cup into the UEFA Champions League, and although winners of the trophy since then have all come from England, France, Germany, Italy, Netherlands, Portugal or Spain, the expansion has meant more money to go round.

## UEFA Champions League TV audience

Coverage of the UEFA Champions League is truly global. Its matches are beamed to satellite dishes in remote villages across the world. Fans in African countries, even the remotest of Ethiopian villages, and in Asian towns and communities, are as familiar with the stars of the Champions League as are their European counterparts. Knowledge of the game, and of its players and personalities has become a universal language for young and old, from all backgrounds. The sport provides a potential bond for cultural contact and friendship wherever you are in the world.

## €310m

The value to the European economy of Barcelona *vs.* Manchester United in May 2009

### European Cup/UCL winners *1956–2010*

| | |
|---|---|
| 9 | Real Madrid, Spain |
| 7 | Milan, Italy |
| 5 | Liverpool, England |
| 4 | Bayern Munich, Germany |
| 4 | Ajax Amsterdam, Netherlands |
| 3 | Barcelona, Spain |
| 3 | Internazionale, Italy |
| 3 | Manchester United, England |
| 2 | Benfica, Portugal |
| 2 | Juventus, Italy |
| 2 | Nottingham Forest, England |
| 2 | Porto, Portugal |
| 1 | Aston Villa, England |
| 1 | Borussia Dortmund, Germany |
| 1 | Red Star Belgrade, Yugoslavia |
| 1 | Feyernoord, Netherlands |
| 1 | Glasgow Celtic, Scotland |
| 1 | Hamburg, Germany |
| 1 | Marseille, France |
| 1 | PSV Eindhoven, Netherlands |
| 1 | Steaua Bucharest, Romania |

**Cumulative viewing figures** *2006/07 season*

- 299m — Americas
- 1,054m — Western Europe
- 567m — Eastern Europe
- 1,151m — Asia
- 142m — Middle-East
- 694m — Africa
- 43m — Oceania

...nothing unites the people of Europe like the UEFA Champions League

*Gazetto dello Sport* 2005

# GOLF – AMATEUR

## A good walk spoiled

### Origins of the modern game

Golf, in its modern form, originated in Scotland, with the Honourable Company of Edinburgh Golfers, established in 1744. England's first golf club was in Blackheath, London, in 1766. There were no more than a dozen courses in England by the 1870s, but a boom produced close to 1,200 clubs by 1914. Golf was established in the USA by the Saint Andrew's club in Yonkers, New York in 1888, and by the end of the 20th century the country provided more than half the world's courses.

### Golfing terms

**Bogey** – one shot more for a hole than the par score
**Bunker** – a designed obstruction on a golf course or links, usually a hollow part-filled with sand
**In the rough** – neither the fairway nor the green
**Make the cut** – the score needed to stay in a contest for the remaining rounds
**Par** – number of strokes a good player would be expected to take for a hole or a round
**19th hole** – the bar in the clubhouse at the end of an (18-hole) round

Around the world, 52 million people play golf, on 32,000 courses. It is a sport that has established a massive consumer base in the affluent markets of the Americas, Europe, South Africa and parts of Asia, particularly Japan.

In the UK, from its base in middle-class suburbs, golf expanded its reach through municipal and public provision in the later 20th century, though – despite a more egalitarian tradition in Scotland – the golf club has remained a bastion of exclusivity for more privileged social groups. Women and working-class males (or "artisans") were allowed to play only at restricted, off-peak times at early English clubs.

Across the USA and Europe the dominant profile of the golfer is male, white, early middle-aged or older, and of privileged social class and higher status. Tiger Woods stated in a famous late 1990s Nike advertisement that: "There are still some courses in the United States that I am not allowed to play on because of the colour of my skin." However, recent research shows that golfing is as popular amongst Asian-Americans as amongst non-Hispanic whites.

The number of people playing golf in the USA has grown steadily, although the recent economic climate has knocked it back slightly. In Japan, the number of golfers peaked at 14 million in 1994, declined to about 10 million, and is expected to fall further. A survey of the golf market in Europe, the Middle East, and Africa in 2009 reported a fall in revenue and profitability for almost half of the courses surveyed, with tourist destinations South Africa and Mauritius hit hardest. Nevertheless, more than half of the respondents looked positively into 2010 and beyond.

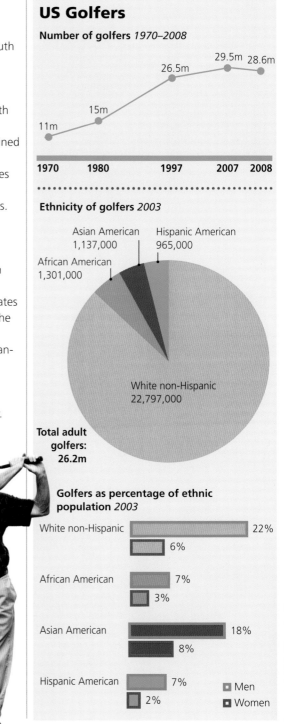

*Achieving the perfect swing is the aim of every golfer.*

## US Golfers

### Number of golfers 1970–2008

11m (1970) · 15m (1980) · 26.5m (1997) · 29.5m (2007) · 28.6m (2008)

1970  1980  1997  2007  2008

### Ethnicity of golfers 2003

Asian American 1,137,000
Hispanic American 965,000
African American 1,301,000
White non-Hispanic 22,797,000

**Total adult golfers: 26.2m**

### Golfers as percentage of ethnic population 2003

White non-Hispanic 22% / 6%
African American 7% / 3%
Asian American 18% / 8%
Hispanic American 7% / 2%

■ Men
■ Women

# The cost of golf

The golf business is, for the moment, fuelled by affluent retirees in wealthy countries, the association of sport with health promotion strategies, and the high profile of the professional game.

In Europe, the Middle East and Africa, golf has an annual economic value of €53 billion, linked to half a million jobs. Europe's 6,400 courses generate €7 billion a year in revenue, while those in the USA generate $28 billion. In Japan, $3 billion of equipment is sold every year.

Golf courses are costly to run, however, requiring regular irrigation, fertilizers, and other chemicals to keep the greens immaculate. Nor is the financial cost the only one being counted. The environmental impact of golf, and of golf tourism, has become a public issue, which has broadened the debate on the benefits of further expansion of the market.

## Golf in the USA

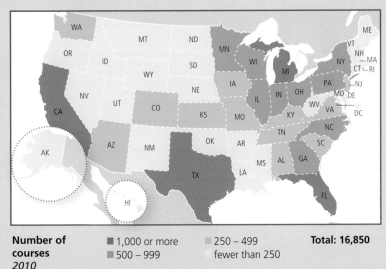

**Number of courses 2010**

- 1,000 or more
- 500 – 999
- 250 – 499
- fewer than 250

**Total: 16,850**

## Green fees

**Average weekend green fee for 18 holes** *2007/08*

- €90 or more
- €37 – €63
- €13 – €28

## Course upkeep

**Amount spent in USA on inputs** *2003*

Insecticides $124m

Irrigation equipment $125m

Herbicides $144m

Turf seed $153m

Water $511m

Fertilizer $380m

Fungicides $349m

**Total spend $1,785m**

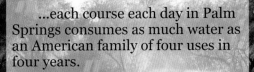

...each course each day in Palm Springs consumes as much water as an American family of four uses in four years.

Frank Deford, quoting figures from Audubon International on National Public Radio, 2008

# GOLF – PROFESSIONAL

## A walk with the wealthy

### The Tiger factor

Tiger Woods' professional career, which began in 1996, had a massive financial impact. The total prize money on the US PGA tour increased from $53 million to $135 million in just three years, and 40,000 more people attended each event, despite a hike in ticket prices. All players shared larger prize funds, and commanded higher sponsorship because of the larger TV audiences.

In December 2009, Woods's sexual indiscretions were revealed and he took time out of the game. Several of his sponsors dropped the 33-year-old, who had become the world's first billionaire athlete just weeks before. Woods' return to competitive golf in April 2010 was a relief to tournament investors, organizers, and players, who had feared a significant drop in takings without Tiger to draw the crowds.

The first golf professionals earned money through caddying and teaching amateur players. This became a route into professional competition. The modern club professional still offers lessons, along with merchandise and equipment from the club shop.

A second phase of the professional game was the commercialization of the international tournaments that have become the sport's flagship events, its "majors". The British Open (from 1860), the US Open (1895), the PGA (Professional Golfers Association) Championship (1916), and the Masters (1934) make up golf's Grand Slam.

The third phase ran parallel with the emergence of television markets. Colour television and entrepreneurs such as Mark McCormack, founder of pioneering marketing agency International Management Group (IMG), brought glamorous course locations and charismatic figures into the living rooms of committed players and curious viewers. Fans of IMG's superstar client Arnold Palmer established Arnie's Army, and with it golf as a major branch of celebrity culture and the entertainment business. This also included South African Gary Player, and American Jack Nicklaus.

The emergence of Tiger Woods dramatically increased the finance flowing into the professional game, catapulting the sport into its fourth phase. At the 2009 British Open, 156 players shared $6.86 million. Even those finishing only just in the top 40, pocketed almost $46,000. Lucrative year-round events such as this have created a grateful band of lower-ranked players. The Asian market hailed its first Asian-born winner of a major at the 2009 USA PGA Championship, when South Korean Yong-Eun Yang took the title. Women's tours have been established, but with much lower financial rewards.

The professional circuit is well established in the global marketplace. The 21 million television viewers of the final day of the US Masters put golf at eighth in a list of the top global TV audiences for sports events in 2009. The European Tour, defying geography, billed itself as The Race to Dubai, where the season's final event, with the highest prize money, was held.

## National pride

The biannual Ryder Cup, founded in 1927, is the main opportunity for golfers to compete for national prestige rather than individual prize money. It was, for decades, a competition between teams from the USA and Great Britain (plus Ireland 1973–77), but overwhelming US success in the post-war period led, in 1979, to a reformed opposition under a European banner. The match scheduled for September 2001 was postponed until 2002 following the events of 9/11, hence the switch from odd to even years.

The reinstatement of golf in the Olympic programme from the 2016 Rio de Janeiro Summer Olympics onwards will provide another opportunity for professionals to play for their country, rather than for personal reward.

| Number of Ryder Cup wins | | | |
|---|---|---|---|
| 1927-77 | | 1979-2010 | |
| USA | GB | USA | EUROPE |
| 18.5 | 3.5 | 7.5 | 8.5 |

## Professional tours

The PGA Tour and PGA European Tour are the largest of the tour organizations, and in recent years the PGA has responded to demand and expanded the circuits to include more international venues. Others tours include the PGA Tour of Australasia and the Asian Tour.

Three of the four major tournaments and the World Golf Championship are not organized by the PGA, but are integral to the PGA calendar, and have been included here in the total number of events and the average prize money.

Each event consists of four rounds, and players need a qualifying score ("the cut") to participate in the final two rounds. The total prize money for an event is divided among those who make the cut, according to their eventual placing. This system finances a large body of players, who tour the world, providing entertainment to enthusiastic spectators and TV audiences.

**Countries that hosted events in 2010 season**
- 🔴 number of events
- 💲 average total prize money per event

### USA PGA Tour

**47**

$6,000,000

### PGA European Tour

**45**

$3,570,000

### Ladies USA PGA Tour

**26**

$1,692,000

Despite limited on-course success, lucrative endorsements made Michelle Wie the highest-paid female golfer by the age of 20.

### Ladies European Tour

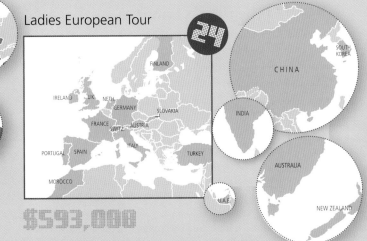

**24**

$593,000

# GYMNASTICS AND EXERCISE

## Balancing bodies and beams

### Politicized bodies

Rival models of gymnastics arose in the 19th century as pedagogic and political initiatives of pioneering thinkers. The fluent Swedish gymnastics of Per Henrik Ling were promoted in the physical education of women in England. Followers of Prussian Friedrich Jahn, who opposed organized team games, made gymnastics a nationalist project. This influenced Sokol, a collective form of physical exercise and gymnastics founded in Prague in 1862 by Miroslav Tyrš, who enthused about ancient Greek physical culture.

Gymnastics (alongside classic team games) is the foundation of much of the physical education curriculum of Western societies. It flourishes at the highest competitive level, in the schooling system, and at club and association level. It has also been used as a means of military fitness training. The British army formed an Army Gymnastic Staff as early as 1860.

It was in order to escape from the military emphasis on strength and discipline that more expressive and educational forms – artistic gymnastics – were devised in the later 19th century, and adopted by the modern Olympic movement. The sport was dominated by west European nations until the 1948 London Olympics, but was revolutionized by the Soviet Union, whose subsequent supremacy is attributed in part to the Russian tradition of *Spartakiad* – mass physical culture festivals that established a high level of gymnastic performance for future generations to emulate. At the 1952 Helsinki Olympics, Soviet gymnasts won five of the seven men's titles, and four out of six of the women's. Russia and other East European countries have continued to dominate events in the discipline, including in women's rhythmic gymnastics. The performance of Romanian women has been particularly notable, both before and after the tightening up on drug testing.

### The fitness boom

Since the 1970s, the fitness industry has been booming, as increasingly high-tech equipment has been developed to help people fine-tune their bodies. For those who prefer to do so in the privacy of their own homes, a succession of books, TV programmes, videos, DVDs and computer software has met their need. One of the earliest, a huge best-seller, was Jane Fonda's *Workout*, the video of which sold 17 million copies. From dancersize! to pilates, the fitness boom shows little sign of waning. In 2008, the market value of the fitness industry in the UK was put at £3.8 billion, and revenue in the USA in 2009 at $23.6 billion.

Individually tailored exercise regimes hold out the hope of achieving the ideal body shape.

### Elfins of the Bars: East to West

In Munich in 1972, Olga Korbut slipped from the bar and wept. ABC Sports focused in on the tiny Belarussian, the US television audience shuddered with empathy, and Korbut went on to win gold for floor exercise and balance beam. Thus, a little-known sport became one of the Olympics' main selling points, and gymnastics was never the same again.

In Montreal in 1976, Romania's Nadia Comăneci emerged to win three gold medals, scoring a first-ever perfect 10.0 in the discipline.

These two young women inspired countless girls across the world to join gym clubs, and have continued to be influential. Both now live in the USA. Korbut offers motivational speeches and warm-up (fitness) programmes; Comăneci combines sports-performance advice with skin-cream endorsement and international diplomacy.

Olga Korbut, Munich 1972, bringing a new level of expression to the floor exercise.

# Five gymnastic disciplines

As overseen by the Fédération Internationale de Gymnastique (FIG)

**Artistic gymnastics**
The men's competition comprises floor exercise, horizontal bar, parallel bars, pommel horse, rings, and vault; women compete on the beam, the floor, the uneven bars, and the vault. At the Olympics, medals are awarded in the team competition, in routines on individual apparatus, and in an individual all-around competition. A version of gymnastics has featured in every modern Olympic Games, though not for women until 1928.

**Rhythmic gymnastics**
This involves routines to music using hand-held apparatus: rope, hoop, ball, clubs, and ribbon, and is it is an event for women only at competitive levels, although men practise the sport in some countries, most notably Japan. It was introduced to the Olympics in 1984. Russia (where national championships were first held in 1942) dominates the medal table, along with Bulgaria. Spain, though, won the first-ever group gold at the 1996 Atlanta Olympics. Japan has produced two world champion teams.

**Trampoline**
Invented in the 1930s by George Nissen of the USA, the discipline had its first national championships there in 1948, and became an Olympic discipline in 2000. Russia, Ukraine, and China claimed the first three men's gold medals; Russia, Germany, and China the women's. In 2010 the top-ranked trampolinists were Russian, Chinese, and American.

**Aerobic gymnastics**
This includes dynamic moves accompanied by music on a floor area, and compulsory application of the seven basic aerobic steps: march, jog, skip, knee lift, kick, jack, and lunge. The first official championship was held in 1995. Brazil reports half a million practitioners.

**Acrobatic gymnastics**
In pairs, or groups of three (women) or four (men), gymnasts perform acrobatic routines such as pyramids. Sports acrobatics was incorporated into FIG in 1999. In competition, Russia is a powerhouse nation, challenged by China. France and Germany have also produced top performers.

## Gymnastics for All

FIG promotes gymnastics as an inclusive sport – a blend of entertainment with exercise, fitness with fun. The non-competitive World Gymnaestrada aims to attract 23,000 participants from all over the world to its 14th meeting, in Lausanne, Switzerland in 2011. Its official launch in October 2010 targeted children, with dazzling gymnastic performances and the introduction of a WG-2011 video game. The Gym for Life World Challenge, first held in 2009 (*see below*), is for gymnasts of all ages, and is next scheduled for Cape Town, South Africa, in 2013.

| USSR | USA | Japan | Romania | China | Switzerland | Hungary, Italy | Czechoslovakia, Germany | Unified Team | Russia, Finland | GDR | Yugoslavia, Sweden | Greece, Ukraine | France | Bulgaria, North Korea, Spain | Canada, Denmark, Latvia, Netherlands, Norway, Poland, Unified Team of Germany |
|---|---|---|---|---|---|---|---|---|---|---|---|---|---|---|---|
| 72 | 30 | 28 | 24 | 22 | 16 | 14 | 12 | 9 | 8 | 6 | 5 | 4 | 3 | 2 | 1 |

**Artistic gymnastics**
**Total Olympic gold medals awarded**
*1896–2008*

**9** The number of Olympic golds won by USSR's Larissa Latynina 1956–65

# HANDBALL

## Look no feet

### Konrad Koch

Handball was invented in the 1890s by schoolteacher Konrad Koch (below), who also organized the first football match in Germany, and wrote treatises on the moral value of sport and games. The sport was formalized, institutionalized in educational settings, and popularized in the 1920s. The International Amateur Handball Federation was established in 1928, with Avery Brundage (later president of the International Olympic Committee) of the USA as its first president. But, despite Brundage's commitment to the sport, it has scarcely prospered in his home country.

**1.5m**

The number of TV viewers who watched the 2009 men's European final

Although handball does not appear in any national survey of US sporting activity, and is played by fewer than 0.1 percent of English adults, it is well-established internationally. The men's and women's 2008 European championships were broadcast to more than 70 countries, and generated a total cumulative television audience of over 1.5 billion. In 2009, one list put the France–Croatia men's final as the 14th most watched television sports event.

Handball is based on throwing, catching and passing a ball, with the aim of getting it into the opponent's goal. When played on an indoor court, either five or seven players are involved on each side, with 11-a-side in the outdoor version of the game.

A goal-keeper preparing to defend a 7-metre penalty.

The sport emerged from the German gymnastics traditions and, once established in the 1920s, gained popularity across numerous countries. The seven-a-side indoor version was introduced into the Olympic Games (for men) in 1936, when the host city, Berlin, was allowed to add one sport to the Olympic programme. Men next contested it at an Olympics in 1972, again in Germany; a women's event followed at Montreal in 1976.

The international rankings are dominated by European nations, although Japan and China, as well as South Korea, have been strong, and the Mediterranean rim of northern Africa provides three nations in the top 30. In the Men's Indoor World Championships, France and Spain have broken the stranglehold of the east European, German, and Scandinavian nations.

The game is simple in conception and execution, and does not produce rich stars. In a world of economic excess in global sport, and the potential disillusionment of fans of mainstream sports, handball may well have a healthy future as the spectator and playing base continue to grow. Promoters claim it as the second largest sport in Europe, and put the number of participants at more than 15 million across 160 countries. It remains to be seen whether the presence of handball at the London 2012 Olympics leads to the British taking it to their hearts.

## Beach handball

A variant of handball for the beach was developed by Italians on the Isola di Ponza in southern Italy. Concerned at the lack of indoor halls on the island, two presidents of Italy's handball team adapted the sport and staged a floodlit tournament in 1992. A tournament in Rome in 1993 drew teams from Germany, Algeria, Taiwan, Russia, and Italy. The sport has become accepted as an official event in the programme of the World Games.

A member of the bronze-winning Brazilian women's team in 2010

Brazil won the men's event in Antalya, Turkey, in 2010. Norway took the women's gold.

# International handball

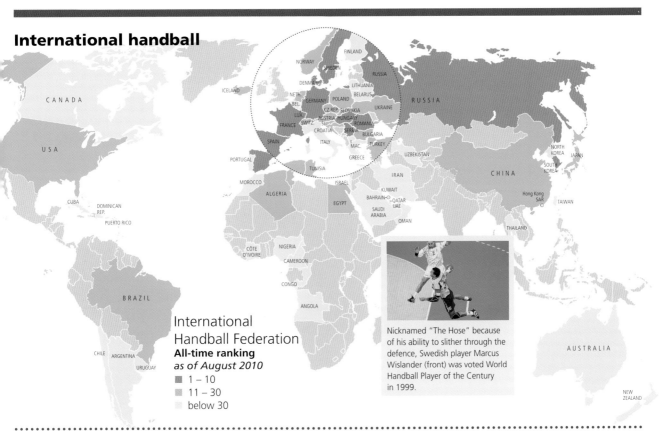

## International Handball Federation
**All-time ranking**
*as of August 2010*

- ◼ 1 – 10
- ◼ 11 – 30
- ◻ below 30

Nicknamed "The Hose" because of his ability to slither through the defence, Swedish player Marcus Wislander (front) was voted World Handball Player of the Century in 1999.

# Olympic handball

Until France's victory at Beijing 2008, men's handball at the Olympics since the 1970s had been dominated by eastern European nations, the USSR and Russia. Scandinavia and South Korea have provided the most prominent women's teams.

France's success is no accident. The accessibility and dynamism of the game encouraged the French to build a popular base and a development plan that enabled them to rise from the lowly level of international C-category matches, and a world ranking outside of the world's top 20 in the 1980s, to equal and then surpass the top nations.

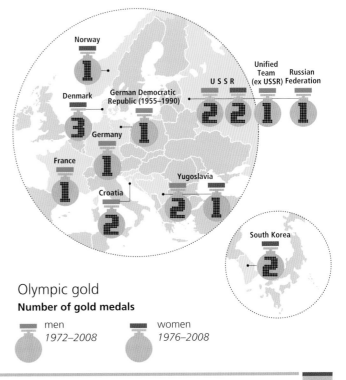

## Olympic gold
**Number of gold medals**

- 🏅 men *1972–2008*
- 🏅 women *1976–2008*

The winning French men's handball team on the podium at the 2008 Olympics.

# HOCKEY AND ICE HOCKEY

## Field and ice

Field hockey originated in England in the late 19th century, and quickly became established across Europe, including in the Austro-Hungarian Empire. However, it really took off in the British colony of India, with 11 of the first 15 Olympic men's gold medals being won either by India or Pakistan.

Hockey's subsequent growth reflected these colonial influences, and complementary developments in the informal empire of trade and business. The Asian Games introduced hockey in 1958, the Pan-American Games in 1967. In the women's championship in 2010, Argentina took the title, although the Netherlands, as current world and Olympic champions, retained number one spot in the rankings.

The Fédération Internationale de Hockey sur Gazon (FIH) was formed in Paris in 1924 to represent the sport's interests at future Olympics, and has 127 associated national members. The sport's global media profile remains relatively low, however. The speed of the ball, the association of the sport with privilege and exclusivity in some countries, and the relative inflexibility of playing positions and styles, have not appealed widely to television producers and viewers.

### Origins of field hockey

The modern game was invented as a winter alternative by a London cricket club in 1871, and became strongly established in British private schools. By 2006, however, it ranked a lowly 30th in England's list of most played sports.

Field hockey was initially played on grass, but international competitions are now played on all-weather pitches.

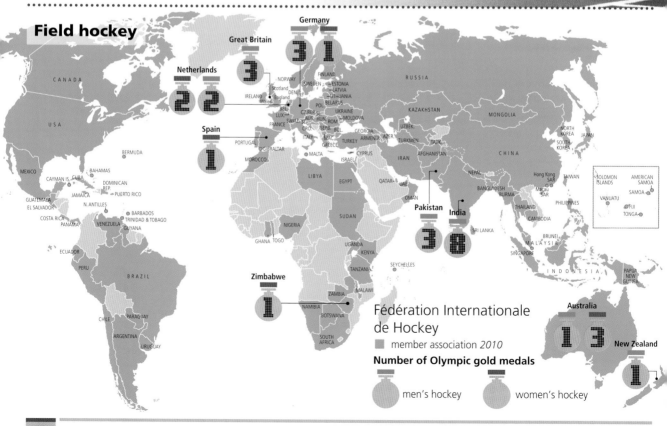

## Field hockey

Germany **31**

Great Britain **3**

Netherlands **22**

Spain **1**

Pakistan **3** India **8**

Zimbabwe **1**

Australia **13**

New Zealand **1**

### Fédération Internationale de Hockey

■ member association *2010*

**Number of Olympic gold medals**

men's hockey    women's hockey

# Ice hockey

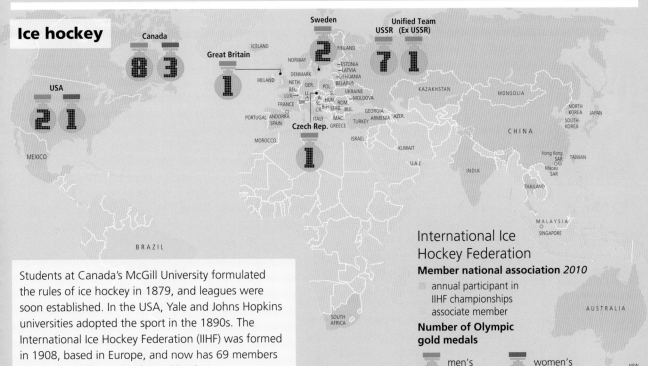

**Canada**
**8** **3**

**USA**
**2** **1**

**Great Britain**
**1**

**Sweden**
**2**

**Unified Team**
**USSR** **(Ex USSR)**
**7** **1**

**Czech Rep.**
**1**

Students at Canada's McGill University formulated the rules of ice hockey in 1879, and leagues were soon established. In the USA, Yale and Johns Hopkins universities adopted the sport in the 1890s. The International Ice Hockey Federation (IIHF) was formed in 1908, based in Europe, and now has 69 members involved at different levels worldwide.

## International Ice Hockey Federation

**Member national association** *2010*

annual participant in IIHF championships associate member

**Number of Olympic gold medals**

men's ice hockey    women's ice hockey

**TOP 10**

## NHL Teams

In North America, ice hockey is run largely by the National Hockey League (NHL). The game has a strong media profile, with highly valued teams and franchises in major US and Canadian cities. The pace, fluency, physical aggression and playful violent encounters between well-padded combatants, and the metropolitan and national pride underpinning top competition, continues to make the professional game a sustainable commodity.

Toronto Maple Leafs — $470m
New York Rangers — $416m
Montreal Canadiens — $339m
Detroit Red Wings — $337m
Philadelphia Flyers — $273m
Boston Bruins — $271m
Chicago Blackhawks — $258m
Dallas Stars — $246m
Vancouver Canucks — $239m
New Jersey Devils — $223m

**Most valuable** *2009*

★ US team    Canadian team

Politics and history are replayed on the ice as the Czech Republic (in white) beats Russia (in red) for the IIHF 2010 world championship. Czechoslovakia won the 1969 world championship the year after the Soviet invasion of the country, stimulating jubilant nationalist celebrations, though these prompted reprisals by the Soviet oppressor.

# HORSE RACING

## The sport of kings

### Seabiscuit

The exploits of the race horse Seabiscuit, initially considered physically and temperamentally unpromising, catapulted him to the centre of the new culture of sporting celebrity. When he began racing in 1935, only 66% of homes in the USA had radios; a couple of years later this was 90%, plus 8 million radios in cars. Seabiscuit's victories, problems, and comebacks captivated the new electronic sports media and its public.

He was coaxed to his potential in California by owner Charles Howard, trainer Tom Smith, and rider Red Pollard. In 1938, watched by 40,000 at Baltimore's Pimlico track, and followed by a radio audience of 40 million, he was ridden to a famous victory by Iceman George Woolf against the much taller bookies' favourite, East-coast-based War Admiral.

Red Pollard riding Seabiscuit.

The attraction of horse racing operates on several levels: the beauty of the beasts, the skill of the jockey, and the tension felt by the crowd as it follows the race. And fundamental to the punters' excitement is the outcome of their gambling.

The two main forms of horse racing are the "flat" and the "jumps". The first takes place on even terrain, the second involves man-made hurdles or fences. The latter, sometimes called the steeplechase, originated in the English countryside, where church steeples identified start and finish. Racing with mini-chariots has also been popular in some parts of the world, such as harness-racing in Australia and Canada.

Improved mobility and transportation helped horse racing attract huge crowds, for whom the excursion and the chance to gamble proved irresistible. In early 20th century Britain, prominent race-meetings were the backdrop to large country-house parties for royalty, aristocrats and politicians, but people of all backgrounds and social classes flocked to the races. In France, fashionable coastal resorts such as Deauville, Normandy, attracted the Parisian elite.

In the USA, particularly in the Depression years of the 1930s, horse racing provided spectacle, gambling thrills, and escapism. In 2008, a new course opened in England for the first time for 80 years, as the popularity of horse racing transcended the scandals concerning race-fixing and the ill-treatment of both horses and riders.

The USA's biggest events are flat races: the Belmont Stakes, (founded 1867), the Preakness Stakes (1873), the Kentucky Derby (1875), and the year-end Breeders Stakes, introduced in 1984. England's most famous race, the Derby, dates from 1780; the Grand National, over fences, began in 1839, and millions of people enjoy modest bets on its outcome. But two and a quarter centuries on from the first Derby day, the richest horse race in the world is run in Dubai, in the United Arab Emirates.

Horse racing at Churchill Downs, Louisville, Kentucky.

## Gambling

Billions are gambled throughout the world, much of this thrown at the industry by hopeful punters, often on the basis of scant knowledge of form or pedigree. Industry professionals such as owners and breeders gamble in more informed ways, as investment and livelihood.

**Largest turnovers from tote and bookmakers** *2008*

| | |
|---|---|
| Japan | €24.7bn |
| UK | €11.1bn |
| USA | €9.8bn |
| France | €9.5bn |
| Australia | €6.2bn |
| Hong Kong | €6.1bn |
| South Korea | €4.0bn |
| Ireland | €3.9bn |

### 15m
Number of British people who bet on the Grand National each year

# Racing purses

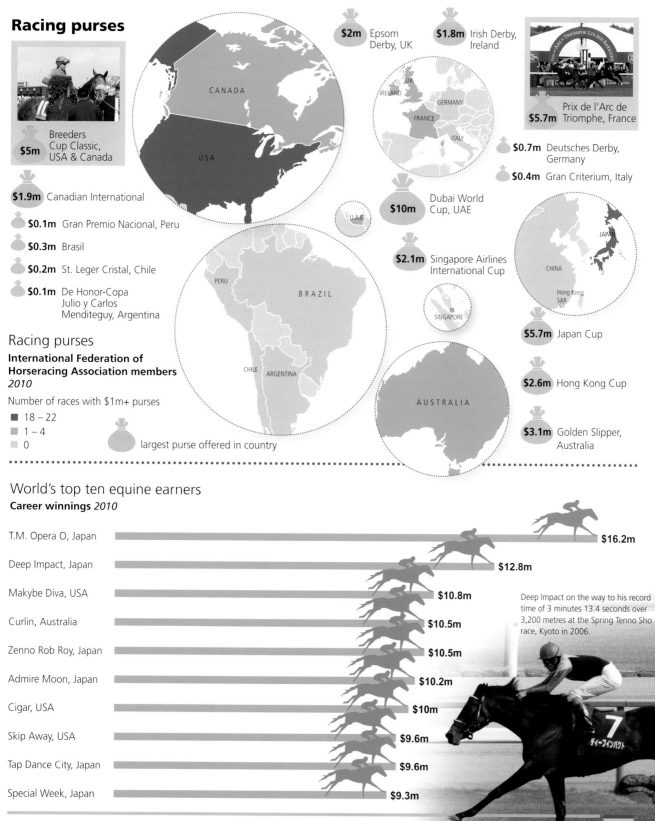

Breeders Cup Classic, USA & Canada
**$5m**

**$2m** Epsom Derby, UK

**$1.8m** Irish Derby, Ireland

Prix de l'Arc de Triomphe, France
**$5.7m**

**$1.9m** Canadian International

**$0.1m** Gran Premio Nacional, Peru

**$0.3m** Brasil

**$0.2m** St. Leger Cristal, Chile

**$0.1m** De Honor-Copa Julio y Carlos Menditeguy, Argentina

**$0.7m** Deutsches Derby, Germany

**$0.4m** Gran Criterium, Italy

**$10m** Dubai World Cup, UAE

**$2.1m** Singapore Airlines International Cup

**$5.7m** Japan Cup

**$2.6m** Hong Kong Cup

**$3.1m** Golden Slipper, Australia

## Racing purses
**International Federation of Horseracing Association members**
*2010*

Number of races with $1m+ purses
- ■ 18 – 22
- ■ 1 – 4
- ☐ 0

largest purse offered in country

## World's top ten equine earners
**Career winnings** *2010*

| | |
|---|---|
| T.M. Opera O, Japan | **$16.2m** |
| Deep Impact, Japan | **$12.8m** |
| Makybe Diva, USA | **$10.8m** |
| Curlin, Australia | **$10.5m** |
| Zenno Rob Roy, Japan | **$10.5m** |
| Admire Moon, Japan | **$10.2m** |
| Cigar, USA | **$10m** |
| Skip Away, USA | **$9.6m** |
| Tap Dance City, Japan | **$9.6m** |
| Special Week, Japan | **$9.3m** |

Deep Impact on the way to his record time of 3 minutes 13.4 seconds over 3,200 metres at the Spring Tenno Sho race, Kyoto in 2006.

# ICE SKATING

## Skates, speed and style

### Sonja Henie

A precocious figure skater, Henie competed at the 1924 inaugural Winter Olympics aged 11. Gold medals at subsequent Olympics and World Championships made her an international star. She introduced dramatic head gestures, faster movements, and spectacular leaps, and after turning professional in 1936 combined ice-revues with a lucrative Hollywood film career. She invested heavily in art, and at her death in 1969 her estate was worth $47m.

Ice-skating is a minority sport, but its main variants – figure skating with its aesthetic pretensions, and speed skating with its coiled-spring velocity – have captured the imaginations of generations. In 2007, there were still 11.5 million adults and children in the USA who had skated at some time, but this represented a fall of 38 percent over 17 years. In England, less than 1 percent of the adult population of the country skated. Yet, skating at the Winter Olympics, and in popular theatrical entertainments, continues to attract audiences and enthusiasts, and skating's international federation continues to expand the sport's competitive calendar.

Figure skating comprises competitions for individual men and women, mixed pairs, and ice dancing. Skaters are scored for both technical merit and artistic impression by a panel of nine judges. This inevitably raises questions of subjectivity and national bias, and the skating authorities have sought to make the scoring system as transparent and consistent as possible. What were seen as excesses of theatrical performance were countered after the 1992 Games. The Technical Committee on Dance forbade, for instance, the wearing by the man of tights not trousers, or the wearing by the woman of any alternative to a skirt.

Speed skating includes competitions for men and women over various distances, with competitors skating against the clock, in pairs, around a 400-metre oval. There is also a relay event. The more recent short-track version, in the Olympics from 1992, puts racers in groups of four on a track of only 111 metres. They skate the specified number of circuits before scrambling to be first across the finishing line. The speed skater, in tight-fitting body suit and crouched posture, personifies, in these explosive encounters, a focused competitiveness far removed from the grace and, as some would see it, the kitsch of the ice dancer and figure skater.

Short-track speed skaters battle it out to the finish.

## The expansion of ice skating

- **1889** First World Championships in Speed Skating, Amsterdam, Netherlands.
- **1892** International Skating Union (ISU) is formed.
- **1893** First World Championships in Speed Skating (men only) held under the auspices of the ISU, Amsterdam, Netherlands.
- **1896** World Figure Skating Championships (men only), St Petersburg, Russia.
- **1897** First World Championships in Speed Skating outside Europe, Montreal, Canada.
- **1906** First ISU Championships for Ladies Figure Skating, Davos, Switzerland.
- **1908** First ISU Championships for Pairs Figure Skating, St Petersburg, Russia.
- **1908** Figure Skating is the first winter sport to be included in the Olympic Games, London, UK.
- **1924** Speed Skating and Figure Skating is included in the first Olympic Winter Games, Chamonix, France.
- **1936** First Speed Skating World Championships for Ladies, Stockholm, Sweden.
- **1950** First international competition in ice dancing is held in London, UK.
- **1952** Ice Dancing World Championships along with World Figure Skating Championships, Paris, France.
- **1960** Women's speed skating is included in the Winter Olympics, Squaw Valley, USA.
- **1976** Ice Dancing is included in the Winter Olympics, Innsbruck, Austria.
- **1991** First World Short Track Speed Skating Team Championships, Seoul, South Korea.
- **1992** Short Track Speed Skating is included in Winter Olympics, Albertville, France.
- **1995/6** Grand Prix of Figure Skating series (Series and Final) is started.
- **1997** World Cup series in Short Track Speed Skating for Men and Ladies is launched.
- **2006** Team Pursuit Speed Skating is included in Winter Olympics, Torino, Italy.
- **2009** Inaugural ISU World Team Trophy 2009 is held in Tokyo, Japan.
- **2010** 100th Edition of ISU World Figure Skating Championships is held in Torino, Italy.

# Going for gold

The USA tops the Olympic table for figure skating, but has not won gold in the mixed pairs or ice dancing. The USSR, then the Unified Team, and Russia have dominated the pairs and ice dancing, but have failed to shine in the women's individual event. The German Democratic Republic produced the double Olympic champion Katarina Witt, who received 35,000 love letters after her first victory at Sarajevo in 1984.

Speed skating has long been dominated by a small group of countries, but the more recently developed short-track version has become the domain of a whole new set of countries, including South Korea and China.

Competitor in the Women's 5,000 meter finals at Vancouver 2010

**Total Olympic gold medals, top countries** *1908–2010*

### Figure skating – men and women

| Country | Gold |
|---|---|
| USA | 14 |
| Sweden | 5 |
| Austria | 5 |
| Russia | 4 |
| Great Britain | 4 |
| GDR (1955–90) | 3 |
| Norway | 3 |

### Speed skating – men

| Country | Gold |
|---|---|
| Norway | 24 |
| USA | 20 |
| Netherlands | 15 |
| USSR | 12 |
| Sweden | 7 |
| Finland | 6 |

### Speed skating – women

| Country | Gold |
|---|---|
| Netherlands | 12 |
| USSR | 12 |
| Germany | 11 |
| USA | 9 |
| GDR (1955–90) | 6 |
| Canada | 5 |

### Pairs and ice dancing

| Country | Gold |
|---|---|
| USSR | 10 |
| Russia | 7 |
| France | 3 |
| Germany | 3 |
| Canada | 3 |
| Austria | 2 |
| Unified Team (ex-USSR) | 2 |

### Short-track speed skating – men and women

| Country | Gold |
|---|---|
| South Korea | 19 |
| Canada | 7 |
| China | 7 |
| USA | 4 |
| Australia | 1 |
| Italy | 1 |
| Japan | 1 |

## Class wars on the ice

In early 1994, figure skater Tonya Harding's ex-husband and bodyguard hired a hitman to attack and injure fellow US Olympian Nancy Kerrigan. The assailant used a collapsible police baton to strike Kerrigan on the thigh, which was bruised but not broken. Harding won the national championship from which Kerrigan was forced to withdraw, and denied all knowledge of the plan.

Both skaters competed later that year in the Winter Olympics, at which Kerrigan won a silver medal. Harding, a distant eighth, was vilified in the national and international media as the worst kind of blue-collar, white-trash figure, a symbol of corrupted national values and moral ruin. She later had a short career (2002–04) as a professional boxer.

Harding (front) and Kerrigan warming up during the 1994 Lillehammer Winter Olympics.

# LIFESTYLE AND EXTREME SPORTS

## Play and display

A major trend in sports participation has been the individualization of the sporting experience, and the growing popularity of sports that have variously been dubbed action, adventure, alternative, trend, and extreme. "Risk" is another epithet that has long been attached to practices such as rock-climbing. "Lifestyle sports" is the term applied most widely to the various activities that add up to a new sporting movement. At its most commercially developed, by ESPN (Entertainment and Sports Programming Network), the Extreme Sports label has produced the "X Games".

These activities on land, water and in the air are associated with youth. Seen by many as an antidote to formal, organized team sports, they cover a wide range, from skateboarding in the shopping mall to hang-gliding from the hilltop, from surfing the ocean waves to cycling the mountain-track. All celebrate virtuoso individual performance, physical risk and, in some cases, remarkable acrobatics.

Lifestyle sports are significant minority activities, but the lifestyle sportsman/woman is an affluent consumer, and these sports have created a lucrative market for specialist equipment and merchandise.

Some of the countercultural values of lifestyle sports have been appropriated by

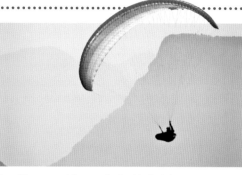

Paragliding – one of the more "unforgiving" of the extreme sports.

the international sporting establishment, and the consumer market. The success of the X Games stimulated the IOC to try and engage with the global youth market by bringing such sports into the Olympic programme. Many adherents of extreme sports oppose attempts to institutionalize them. In 2006, the IOC president Jacques Rogge, looking to keep in touch with trends in youth culture, requested help from the International Cycling Union to make skateboarding an Olympic event. Thousands of skateboarders mobilized online, one dedicated website telling the IOC president that: "Skateboarding is not a 'sport' and we do not want skateboarding exploited and transformed to fit into the Olympic program … [It] will change the face of skateboarding and its individuality and freedoms forever."

## Characteristics of lifestyle sports

**Encompasses both new and adapted activities**, such as windsurfing, ultimate frisbee, snowboarding, mountain-biking.
**Grassroots participation** is the driving motivation.
**Specialist equipment** such as boards, bikes, discs, gliders creates a strong consumer market.
**Heavy commitment** is required in terms of both time and money.
**Mainly western, white, middle-class** practitioners
**Individualism** is the predominant ethos.
**Hedonism** is one of the central drivers.
**Non-aggression** is one of its more appealing features.
**Unregulated outdoor spaces** worldwide are its venue.

Surfing is one of the oldest and most expressive lifestyle sports, in which the blend of body, board and surf creates a constantly remade individualist aesthetic.

## Pay for display

Tony Hawk last won a medal at an X Games in 1999, but has continued performing and earning millions from his brand and image. In a 2002 poll conducted by a US marketing firm specializing in "teens", Hawk was voted the "coolest big-time athlete" ahead of figures such as Michael Jordan and Tiger Woods. The charismatic Shaun White is ready to step into his shoes.

**TOP 10**

### Highest-earning action sports stars, *2008*
From sponsorship and related business activities

| | |
|---|---|
| Tony Hawk, skateboarding | $12m |
| Shaun White, skate/snowboarding | $9m |
| Ryan Sheckler, skateboarding | $5m |
| Travis Pastrana, freestyle motocross/rally | $3m |
| Kelly Slater, surfing | $3m |
| Laird Hamilton, surfing | $2.5m |
| Paul Rodriguez, skateboarding | $2m |
| Danny Kass, snowboarding | $1m |
| Dave Mirra, BMX | $1m |
| Travis Rice, snowboarding | $1m |

# X Games

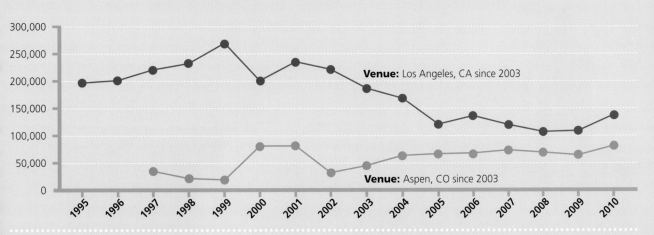

● **Attendance at X Games,** *1995–2010*    ● **Attendance at Winter X Games,** *1997–2010*

**Venue:** Los Angeles, CA since 2003

**Venue:** Aspen, CO since 2003

300,000
250,000
200,000
150,000
100,000
50,000
0

1995 1996 1997 1998 1999 2000 2001 2002 2003 2004 2005 2006 2007 2008 2009 2010

## Commercializing the counterculture

Specialist sports broadcaster ESPN first staged the X Games in the USA in 1995. Nine sports were featured: bungee jumping, eco-challenge, in-line skating, skateboarding, skysurfing, sport climbing, street luge, BMX (bicycle motocross), and water sports. Over the years, the range of sports has become more focused, with the 2010 X Games featuring only Moto X, skateboarding, BMX, and rallying, and the Winter X Games similarly narrowed down to the core sports of skiing, snowboarding and snowmobile.

Despite, or because of, this "specialization", television audiences and total prize money have risen steadily, although live attendance at the X Games has declined since the turn of the century. Attendance at the Winter X Games has bucked this trend, however, helped by the high profile of superstar snowboarder Shaun White.

While the Olympics TV viewing audience has aged, the X Games viewer has a median age of 20 years. Over 35 million people in the USA tuned in at some point for live and repeat telecasts. More than 282 million homes received the Games, across 175 countries or territories. Over the four days, ESPN swapped around 650,000 text messages with fans, who decided the medal winners for The Navy Best Whip competition (a mid-air somersault by a Moto X bike-rider coming off a steep ramp).

### Total Prize Money

**X Games**

| 1995 | 2009 |
| --- | --- |
| $375,150 | $1,650,000 |

**Winter X Games**

| 1997 | 2009 |
| --- | --- |
| $186,600 | $1,102,450 |

## Snowboard superstars

In February 2009, Shaun White's sponsor, Red Bull, built him a remote half-pipe in Colorado's Rocky Mountains and shuttled him to his practice sessions by helicopter. There, White invented his most daring move, the double McTwist 1260, for which he launched himself off a snow-packed embankment into an inverted aerial, then flipped head-over-heels twice as he simultaneously spun three-and-a-half times whilst holding his board.

At the 2010 Vancouver Winter Olympics, he showcased the move, taking gold in the Olympic snowboarding. The alternative snow sport was now the basis for wholesale commodification, its tousle-haired champion a global celebrity. Three other snowboarders – American women Hannah Teter, Lindsey Jacobellis, and Gretchen Bleiler – were in the Top 10 earners of those competing at the 2010 Vancouver Olympics.

Shaun White, pushing the sport of snowboarding to extremes.

**30m**

US viewers watched
Shaun White
win a gold medal
at the 2010 Olympics

# MARATHON

## The great suburban Everest

### Origins of the marathon

Phidippides, a soldier-messenger sent by the Athenians to raise troops to resist the invasion of the Persians, ran the 140 miles to Sparta in 36 hours – and back. A messenger – widely reported as Phidippedes – then ran from the Battle of Marathon (490 BC) to Athens, a mere 26 miles, to relay news of the Athenian triumph over the more numerous and powerful Persians; mission accomplished, he collapsed and died. In commemoration of this, the Greek hosts included the marathon event in the first modern Olympic Games at Athens 1896, when the victory of Spiridon Loues, peasant and water-carrier turned epic hero, was a highlight of the proceedings. The modern Olympic stadium constructed for the Athens Olympics of 2004 was named after him.

WMM jackpot shared equally by top man and woman every two years

The marathon is both an established elite track-and-field event, and a mass phenomenon. For years, long-distance runners who aspired to run a marathon were considered somewhat wacky. The event has a mystique around it. As Czech runner Emil Zatopek observed: "If you want to win something, run the 100 meters. If you want to experience something, run the marathon."

At 26 miles 385 yards, the marathon is the only elite track event not now contested in metric measures. The extra yardage – almost a lap of the stadium track – was added at the London 1906 Olympics to bring the finishing line in front of Queen Alexandra's royal box. That race was won by the USA's John Hayes, a Bloomingdales employee in New York. Italian Dorando Pietri, in a state of collapse, had finished first but was helped over the finishing line by the British race organizer and so disqualified. The resulting furore popularized the event and both Hayes and Pietri turned professional and earned big money around the world. Subsequent Olympic champions, men and women, have come from every continent, but Ethiopian and Kenyan men and women have dominated the professional circuit in the 21st century.

New York stages the world's largest marathon, which began in 1970 with just 127 runners. For the 2010 event there were 100,000 applicants, and applications for 2011 opened the day after the race. English Olympian and businessman Chris Brasher was inspired by the New York Marathon as "a vision of the human race happy and united, willing their fellow human beings to a pointless but wonderful victory over mental doubts and bodily frailty". He went on to establish the London Marathon in 1981, and saw the event as a "suburban Everest".

Five marathons now dominate the competitive calendar. Thousands run these races for a cause, or in memory of a close relative. London participants raised £47 million for charity in 2009; New York, $24 million. Millions of people turn out on the streets of these cities, to cheer on people like themselves who are aspiring to do what for so long was seen as undoable.

### In for the long run

For many years it was considered impossible (or inappropriate) for women to compete in long-distance races. In 1966, Bobbi Gibb ran the Boston Marathon unofficially, setting off from behind bushes and initially wearing a hooded sweatshirt to fool officials. The following year, despite the race director trying to bundle her off the course, Kathrine Switzer completed the course as a registered runner, and prejudice about women's physiological limitations was proven unfounded.

It was not, however, until 1984 that women were permitted to run a marathon at the Olympics, 88 years after the first men's event. Joan Benoit Samuelson of the USA, a Boston marathon record-holder, won that breakthrough event. More recently, American women have been eclipsed by Russian, African, and Japanese runners.

British runner Paula Radcliffe winning the marathon at the 2005 World Athletics Championships.

# World Marathon Majors (WMM)

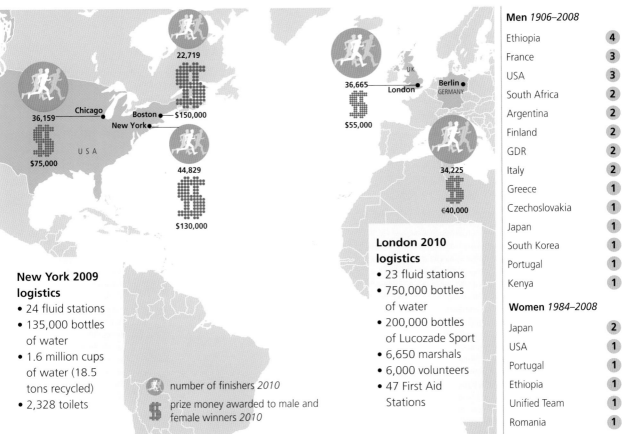

22,719

36,665 — London

Berlin •
GERMANY

$55,000

36,159 — Chicago •

Boston • — $150,000
New York •

$75,000

U S A

44,829

$130,000

34,225

€40,000

## New York 2009 logistics

- 24 fluid stations
- 135,000 bottles of water
- 1.6 million cups of water (18.5 tons recycled)
- 2,328 toilets

## London 2010 logistics

- 23 fluid stations
- 750,000 bottles of water
- 200,000 bottles of Lucozade Sport
- 6,650 marshals
- 6,000 volunteers
- 47 First Aid Stations

number of finishers *2010*

prize money awarded to male and female winners *2010*

# Olympic gold

**Men** *1906–2008*

| | |
|---|---|
| Ethiopia | 4 |
| France | 3 |
| USA | 3 |
| South Africa | 2 |
| Argentina | 2 |
| Finland | 2 |
| GDR | 2 |
| Italy | 2 |
| Greece | 1 |
| Czechoslovakia | 1 |
| Japan | 1 |
| South Korea | 1 |
| Portugal | 1 |
| Kenya | 1 |

**Women** *1984–2008*

| | |
|---|---|
| Japan | 2 |
| USA | 1 |
| Portugal | 1 |
| Ethiopia | 1 |
| Unified Team | 1 |
| Romania | 1 |

---

## Country of origin of winners of World Marathon Majors *2000–09*

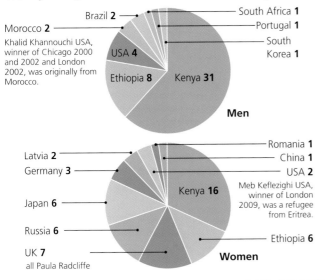

Brazil **2**

Morocco **2**

Khalid Khannouchi USA, winner of Chicago 2000 and 2002 and London 2002, was originally from Morocco.

South Africa **1**
Portugal **1**
South Korea **1**

USA **4**
Ethiopia **8**
Kenya **31**

**Men**

Romania **1**
China **1**
USA **2**

Latvia **2**
Germany **3**

Meb Keflezighi USA, winner of London 2009, was a refugee from Eritrea.

Japan **6**

Kenya **16**

Russia **6**

UK **7**
all Paula Radcliffe

Ethiopia **6**

**Women**

## African domination

At the Summer Olympics in Rome in 1960, Ethiopian shepherd Abebe Bikila became the first black African to win an Olympic gold medal, winning the marathon barefoot. He had been talent-spotted by a Swedish coach hired by the Ethiopian government to develop athletics. He defended his title (this time wearing shoes) in Tokyo in 1964. Bikila established a profile for Ethiopian and African runners. His successors, in Kenya as well as his own country, have dominated marathon running in the 21st century.

Ethiopian Haile Gebrselassie, one of the greatest long-distance runners, in the Berlin Marathon.

# MARTIAL ARTS

## Mind, body, and self-defence

### Principles for karate practitioners

1. Strengthening of mind and body through faithful training.
2. Willingness to endure rigorous training to achieve the goal.
3. Cultivation of a gentle heart even as strength increases.
4. Use of skill outside the dojo only in the most extreme circumstances.
5. Avoidance of infliction of injury on others, at all times.
6. Modesty about one's skill, and no malicious use of it.
7. Humility of spirit in training.

International Karate Federation

Men's karate heavyweight finalists, 2006

Martial arts, a sub-category of combat sports, includes numerous activities that share a concern with defensive and attacking strategies of individual fighters in, usually, unarmed physical combat. These are often linked to philosophical beliefs and ethical principles, sometimes derived from a military tradition or rationale.

Martial arts have largely emerged from traditional practices in societies across the world, most prominently and influentially the countries of the Far East: judo from Japan; karate an adaptation in 1930s Japan (Okinawa) of ancient Indian and even Chinese practices; and taekwondo, an ancient Korean practice established in its modern form in the 1950s.

There are many different forms of martial arts styles – 31 identified in the UK alone. A national survey in England in 2005/6 found 93,000 practitioners of karate, around 21,500 practitioners of taekwondo, and a further 141,250 adults practising one of the other martial arts. In the USA in 2007, the number of children and adults engaging in one or more of the martial arts at some level was 6 million, but judo featured at a competitive level in the school curriculum for only around 1,000 children, all but nine of whom were in Hawaii.

## Karate

Karate means "empty hand". Numerous national and international associations represent its 70 styles. The World Karate Federation claims 10 million members and 100 million supporters, and is said to be the most widely practised Oriental martial art.

Clubs have prospered in western countries, and classes for children are particularly popular, with many parents perhaps seeing karate as a controlled channel for excessive aggression. It teaches breathing as well as fighting techniques, and emphasizes silent meditation.

Shortlisted in 2009 for entry into the Olympics, it lost out to golf and rugby sevens, richer sports with superior lobbying power.

## Taekwondo

*Tae* means to kick with the foot; *kwon* means to destroy with the fist; and *do* is the art or method of the practice. Points are scored by striking an opponent with combinations of kicks (these can be jumping or flying kicks) and punches. Taekwondo, for both men and women, was introduced into the Olympic programme as a demonstration sport at Seoul 1988, and established fully within the Games at Sydney 2000. Koreans have dominated gold medal positions at the Olympics.

**Olympic gold medals, men and women**
*1988–2008*

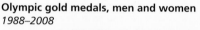

| Country | Medals |
|---|---|
| South Korea | 23 |
| Taiwan | 7 |
| USA | 7 |
| China | 4 |
| Spain | 4 |
| Mexico | 3 |
| Denmark | 2 |
| Iran | 2 |
| Australia | 1 |
| Cuba | 1 |
| Greece | 1 |
| Venezuela | 1 |

## How to make an Olympic event

South Korean Dr Kim Um Yong led the sport's rise, using it as a springboard to leadership of the international federations, the vice-presidency of the IOC, and runner-up to IOC President Jacques Rogge in the 2001 election for the presidency. In January 2004, Kim was suspended from all Olympic responsibilities, and in June was convicted in South Korea of embezzling more than $3 million from sports organizations, and accepting $700,000 in bribes, and sentenced to two years in prison.

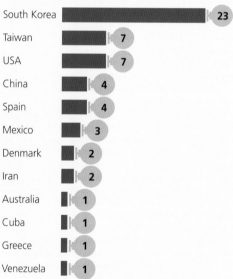

# Judo

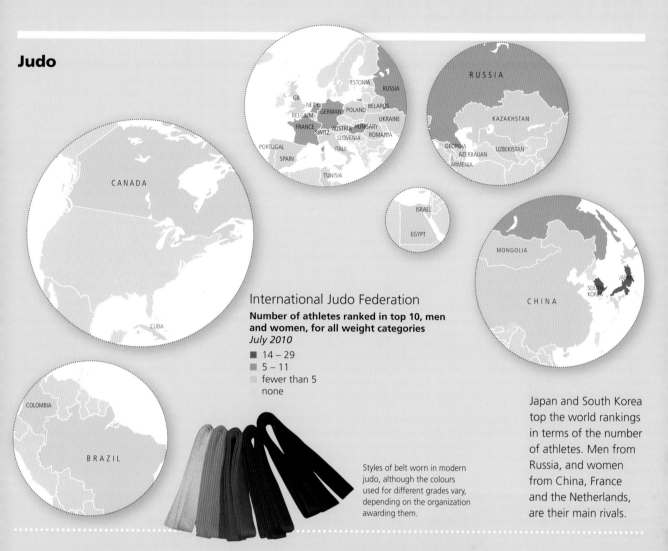

## International Judo Federation

**Number of athletes ranked in top 10, men and women, for all weight categories**
*July 2010*

- ■ 14 – 29
- ■ 5 – 11
- fewer than 5
- none

Styles of belt worn in modern judo, although the colours used for different grades vary, depending on the organization awarding them.

Japan and South Korea top the world rankings in terms of the number of athletes. Men from Russia, and women from China, France and the Netherlands, are their main rivals.

In Japanese, judo means "the easy way" or "the way of gentleness", and the object of the contest is to disable an opponent, or score an *ippon* – the equivalent of a knockout punch – by throwing, arm or neck locks, or holding him or her down. Punching and kicking are not permitted.

Judo is the longest-established martial art form in the Olympic programme. Men's events were introduced at Tokyo 1964, women's at Barcelona 1992. Japan is way ahead in the gold medal league table, but France has a particularly strong record compared with other European countries.

### Olympic gold medals, men and women *1964–2008*

| | |
|---|---|
| Japan | 36 |
| France | 10 |
| China, South Korea | 9 |
| Cuba | 5 |
| Netherlands, USSR | 5 |
| Germany | 4 |
| Belgium, Italy, Poland, Spain, | 3 |
| Austria, Brazil, Georgia, Great Britain, Unified Team (ex-USSR) | 2 |
| Australia, Azerbaijan, Belarus, GDR, Greece, Hungary, Mongolia, North Korea, Romania, Switzerland, Turkey | 1 |

Satoshi Ishii, with Yasuyuki Muneta in his grasp at the All-Japan Judo Championships, 2008.

# MOTOR RACING

## In the fast lane

### The Magic of Fangio

Timed trials for motor vehicles were held in France as early as the 1880s, and organized races staged in Chicago and the US East Coast in the 1890s. The Fédération Internationale de l'Automobile (FIA) was founded in Paris in 1904, and the first Grand Prix race was held at Le Mans in 1906. It was won by a car driven by the Renault's chief mechanic, but the sport really took off when the drivers emerged as stars.

Argentinian-born Juan-Manuel Fangio (1911–95) won five World Championships on the Grand Prix circuit in the 1950s. The son of Italian immigrants, his first racing car was a Model T Ford. Sponsored in Europe by the Argentinean government, he drove for Alfa Romeo, Mercedes, Maserati and Ferrari, personifying the glamour of a heady mix of celebrity, consumer dreams, and technological modernity.

The combination of human skill and technology means that the title of motor racing champion depends as much on the latest breakthrough in vehicle design as on the drivers' skill.

Formula 1, which grew out of the European Grand Prix circuit, becoming a World Championship in 1950, is powered by ruthless competitiveness, exemplified in blatant, yet thrilling, risk-taking on the track, all of which is shared almost first-hand by the spectator, thanks to onboard cameras. In fact, the sport's much improved safety record has actually reduced the level of risk considerably, and the sight of a driver walking away from a wrecked car is these days quite common. While 24 drivers died between 1954 and 1994, as of the end of the 2010 season, none had died since.

The global recession has undermined team sponsorship, which fell from $820 million in 2009 to $705 million in 2010. Honda quit in December 2008, followed by BMW and Toyota. Global financial services company ING, and the

Royal Bank of Scotland did not renew contracts. Bridgestone, Formula 1's exclusive tyre supplier, declared that as its final year. The sport has also been sullied by race-fixing and dubious team tactics and ethics. Nevertheless, motor racing in general has appeared to retain its core market. In 2009, Formula 1 and NASCAR provided two of the 20 most watched sports events in the world on one list of major broadcasts.

A winning formula of speed, glamour, and celebrity has continued to deliver for those teams and sponsors that stayed in the race. Drivers continue to be walking billboards, cars whirlwinds of corporate branding. New sponsors have emerged, with online currency firm FX-Pro replacing the beleaguered traditional banking sector. And, despite strict anti-tobacco legislation banning overt on-car branding, cigarette company Marlboro continues to support the Formula 1 Ferrari team – to the tune of $100 million in 2009 – and to be included in the team name.

A Ferrari car sporting Marlboro subliminal advertising. The cigarette giant has invested $1.4 billion in its 37-year partnership with Ferrari.

## TOP 10

### Formula 1 driver salaries *2009*

|  |  |
|---|---|
| Kimi Räikkönen – Ferrari | $37m |
| Fernando Alonso – Renault | $20m |
| Lewis Hamilton – McLaren | $20m |
| Felipe Massa – Ferrari | $14m |
| Jarno Trulli – Toyota | $12m |
| Jenson Button – Brawn | $9m |
| Robert Kubica – BMW Sauber | $8m |
| Sebastian Vettel – Red Bull Racing | $8m |
| Mark Webber – Red Bull Racing | $6m |
| Heikki Kovalainen – McLaren | $5m |

$4.6bn

the total revenue of Formula 1 2009 races

## Racing USA

Although the USA is a listed member of the Fédération Internationale de l'Automobile (FIA), with a club/committee representing the country in Formula 1, American motor racing is largely homegrown.

The National Hot Rod Association promotes a professional sport in which drivers such as Tony Schumacher (national champion 2004–08) have surpassed 330 miles an hour.

NASCAR features drivers circuiting oval tracks in excess of 200 miles an hour, and claims 75 million fiercely partisan fans. NASCAR's Daytona 500 celebrated its 60th anniversary in 2009, and was, according to one listing, the 15th most watched television event in the world that year.

The Indianapolis 500, first held in 1911, offered prize money of $13.6 million in 2010, the winner taking more than $2.75 million. Brazilian Helio Castroneves, three-time winner, had Indy500 career winnings of over $9 million by the time of his 2009 victory.

Indy has accepted women drivers, and Danica Patrick has earned millions in the sport since 2005. As the first woman NASCAR driver she has no shortage of sponsors. Of her modelling for *FHM* and *Sports Illustrated* she said: "Number 1 priority is on the track, this stuff comes after it", but, of her glamorous image: "It's my brand. It's who I am."

NASCAR is considered the USA's premier blue-collar sport.

Helio Castroneves, one of the most successful Indy drivers, practising for the 2007 Indianapolis 500.

## Formula 1

Fédération Internationale de l'Automobile

- Members *2010*
- Formula 1 venues

# MULTI-SPORTS

## All-rounders

### The greatest athlete

Jim Thorpe, born to an Irish–Native American father and French–Native American mother, was a phenomenally fast American Football player. In 1911, he scored all 18 points when his government-run Indian school, Carlisle, beat Harvard. In the 1912 Olympics, he romped to victories in the pentathlon and the decathlon, and was given a ticker-tape parade in New York City. But his triumphs were struck from the official records, and his medals returned when his amateur status was challenged because he had earlier been paid to play minor league baseball. Only in 1983 were his medals given back to his family, 30 years after he died all but penniless.

Jim Thorpe ready to play for his school.

As the rewards for individual success have multiplied, and the obsession with national prestige has intensified, modern sports have become increasingly specialized, producing highly tuned skills: specialists with the bat, or the ball, offensive or defensive players, those better suited to a particular surface. In this context, the sporting all-rounder is over-looked. The "athlons" preserve a different model of sporting excellence, in which the runner can jump and throw, the horse rider or cross-country skier can shoot, and the cyclist can swim. It is a model of the amateur all-rounder, the victor ludorum of school sports.

The medallists at the inaugural women's Modern Pentathlon in 2000 embodied the all-round amateur. As athlete–scholars (gold medallist Stephanie Cook was a medical doctor) they personified the values of the mind–body balance. A survey conducted at Sydney 2000 showed that spectators admired the contestants' multiple talents, and saw a higher level of fair play and less concern with financial reward in the event than in any other sport. But even pentathletes need financial backing to enable them to train and compete. The British women were aided by funding through the UK National Lottery, allowing them to take what were essentially sabbaticals from their professions to concentrate on the Olympics.

Multi-sports may lack the large number of participants of the single disciplines, but an expanding body of committed participants is participating in individual and team competitions. Mixed-gender team-based triathlons have been developed, in which Swiss men and women have excelled in international competition. At grassroots level, the triathlon is the contest most likely to prosper, its components being among the most popular sporting activities in the world, and easily adapted to mini-formats and lower levels of performance.

The start of the 2005 World Military Triathlon

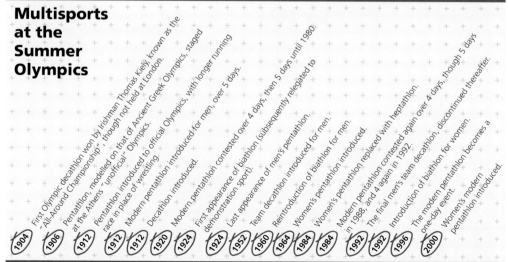

## Multisports at the Summer Olympics

|  |  |
| --- | --- |
| 1904 | First Olympic decathlon won by Irishman Thomas Kiely, known as the "All-Around Championship", though not held at London. |
| 1906 | Pentathlon, modelled on that of Ancient Greek Olympics, staged at the Athens "unofficial" Olympics. |
| 1912 | Pentathlon introduced to official Olympics. |
| 1912 | Modern pentathlon introduced for men, over 5 days. |
| 1920 | Decathlon introduced, with longer running race in place of wrestling. |
| 1924 | Modern pentathlon introduced. |
| 1924 | First appearance of biathlon (subsequently relegated to demonstration sport). |
| 1952 | Last appearance of men's pentathlon. |
| 1960 | Team decathlon introduced for men. |
| 1964 | Reintroduction of biathlon for men. |
| 1984 | Women's pentathlon introduced. |
| 1984 | Women's pentathlon replaced with heptathlon. |
| 1992 | Modern pentathlon contested over 4 days, then 5 days until 1980. Modern pentathlon contested again over 4 days, though 5 days in 1988, and 4 again in 1992. |
| 1992 | The final men's team decathlon, discontinued thereafter. |
| 1996 | Introduction of biathlon for women. |
| 2000 | The modern pentathlon becomes a one-day event. Women's modern pentathlon introduced. |

# Main events

SKIING 82-83 >> SWIMMING 84-85 >>

## Olympic gold medals

### Decathlon – men
Day 1: 100 m,
long jump, shot put,
high jump, 400 m
Day 2: 100-m hurdles,
discus, pole vault,
javelin, 1,500 m

The decathlon has been part of the Olympic programme since 1912. Decathlete champions from the USA, seen as athletic supermen, have been recruited into the movies, from Jim Thorpe appearing as an extra in Westerns, to Glen Morris's single appearance as Tarzan in the 1930s. Bob Matthias, 1948 champion, and at 17 years old the youngest winner of a men's track-and-field gold in Olympic history, acted with Jayne Mansfield in *It Happened in Athens*.

| | |
|---|---|
| USA | 12 |
| Great Britain | 3 |
| Czechoslovakia , Czech Republic, Estonia, Finland, GDR, Norway, Sweden, United Team, USSR | 1 |

### Modern pentathlon – men and women
1 day: shooting, fencing,
200-m swim,
show jumping,
3,000-m run

This event is the brainchild of the founder of the modern Olympics, Baron Pierre de Coubertin, who imagined a soldier on a mission, shooting his way out of a difficult situation, fencing with a challenger, swimming across a river, riding an unfamiliar horse, and completing his mission on foot. Many early champions were military men. Modern pentathlon thrives away from the Olympics, with 90 national federations affiliated to the international union, which oversees a world championship and world cup, and provides regularly updated world rankings. East Europeans dominated the men's rankings in 2010.

| | |
|---|---|
| Sweden | 10 |
| Hungary | 9 |
| USSR | 5 |
| Poland, Russian Federation | 3 |
| Germany, Great Britain, Italy | 2 |
| Kazakhstan | 1 |

### Heptathlon – women
Day 1: 100-m hurdles,
high jump, shot put,
200-m run
Day 2: long jump,
javelin, 800-m run

The event replaced the pentathlon for women in the Olympics in 1984, adding the 200 metres run and the javelin. Syria's first Olympic champion, Ghada Shouaa, won at Atlanta 1996, after defending double-Olympic champion Jacqueline Joyner-Kersee of the USA withdrew through injury. Great Britain has also produced two champions: Mary Peters from Belfast in the 1972 pentathlon that preceded this event, and Denise Lewis at Sydney 2000.

| | |
|---|---|
| USA | 2 |
| Australia, Great Britain, Sweden, Syria, Ukraine | 1 |

### Triathlon – men and women
Performed consecutively,
with no break.
Olympic distances:
1500-m swim (often in
open water),
40-km road cycle ride,
10-km run

Although the race is a test of overall strength and endurance, it is often the better runners who finish in the winning position. The triathlon is an international discipline, with federations in every continent, affiliated to the International Triathlon Union. The distances covered in each leg can vary, but an important component of the race is the speed with which the contestants make the transition from one discipline to the next.

| | |
|---|---|
| Australia, Austria, Canada, Germany, New Zealand, Switzerland | 1 |

Competitors in the middle section of the 2007 International Weiswampach Triathlon.

### Biathlon – men and women
cross-country skiing
and rifle shooting over
various distances

Originally called "military patrol", this winter sport combines cross-country skiing and rifle-shooting, over a range of distances, in both individual and team events.

| | |
|---|---|
| Germany | 15 |
| Norway | 9 |
| USSR | 9 |
| Russia | 7 |
| France, GDR | 3 |
| Canada, Sweden, | 2 |
| Unified Team, Bulgaria, Switzerland | 1 |

Jeremy Teela, USA, Winter Olympics 2002. The biathlon involves extreme exertion followed by intense focus.

# RUGBY

## A hooligan's game played by gentlemen

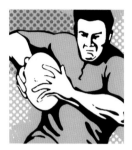

### Rugby sevens

The seven-a-side format has been promoted by Dubai, UAE, with an annual international tournament involving 16 countries. In 2009, the International Olympic Committee granted men's and women's Rugby Sevens a place in the starting line-up of the Summer Olympics from Rio 2016, won over by the International Rugby Board's case that this scaled-down sport could be played in the centre of the athletics stadium and would therefore not require additional expenditure. This was also the basis of a successful debut of the format at the 2010 Commonwealth Games.

**20 lbs**

Extra weight professional rugby union players carry compared with amateurs

Rugby football exists in three different forms. The game was originally devised by the English upper-classes in the early 19th century, and its first international match – between England and Scotland – was in 1871. This 15-a-side game of rugby union maintained an almost exclusively amateur status until 1995, when players were finally allowed to turn professional. In this they were following the 13-a-side professional game of rugby league, which had been established 100 years earlier as a predominantly working-class sport. Both branches of the game, along with the smaller and faster seven-a-side version, have been successfully developing national and international championships, with the lucrative TV deals these entail.

Olympic gold-medal US team in 1924 – the last time the 15-a-side game was included in the Games.

Rugby union is played, at club level, in over 100 countries. Canadian and US universities played each other in the late 19th century, but the sport became marginalized by American Football. It has thrived at elite level in former British colonies, which have dominated the Rugby (Union) World Cup. In Europe, the British-based Home International Championship, established in 1883, became the Six Nations Championship in 2000.

A professionalized rugby union league was formed in England in 1997, becoming, in 2005/6, the Guinness Premiership. European Club Rugby (ERC) formed the Heineken Cup to realize "the potential of European club rugby, by … creating matches of unique drama", as stated by ERC boss Jean-Pierre Lux in 1999. The World Cup, inaugurated in 1987, expanded in this professionalized and commercialized climate. Its worldwide partners for 2011 – MasterCard, Emirates Airline, and Heineken – matched the financial, travel, and drinking needs of the modern rugby fan.

The sixth Women's Rugby World Cup (England 2010) included teams from former British Commonwealth countries and from Kazakhstan, the USA, France, Ireland, and Sweden.

## The class divide

Rugby football is a team game named after the English public school where it was first played – with 120 players on each side. The game was taken on to England's ancient universities, where it developed into the 15-a-side rugby union format, dominated by an educated elite and a strict amateur code.

Rugby league broke from the union game in 1895, when 21 clubs met in Huddersfield, Yorkshire, and formed the Northern Union. It was played by professionals, and watched by paying spectators in the industrial heartlands of northern England. The league game involves 13 team members, and is faster paced than rugby union. In recent years, a super league has been formed of clubs from England, Wales and France. And in the southern hemisphere, teams from the conurbations of Australia and New Zealand, with names such as Broncos, Dragons, Sharks, Titans and Warriors, contest their own Premiership.

Rugby Union player, c.1920

When Rupert Murdoch decided to buy the rights to broadcast southern hemisphere rugby for $550 million in 1995, it was largely on the strength of the magnificent Jonah Lomu. "He just wanted Jonah on his television screen" said a BSkyB executive.

# International Rugby Board

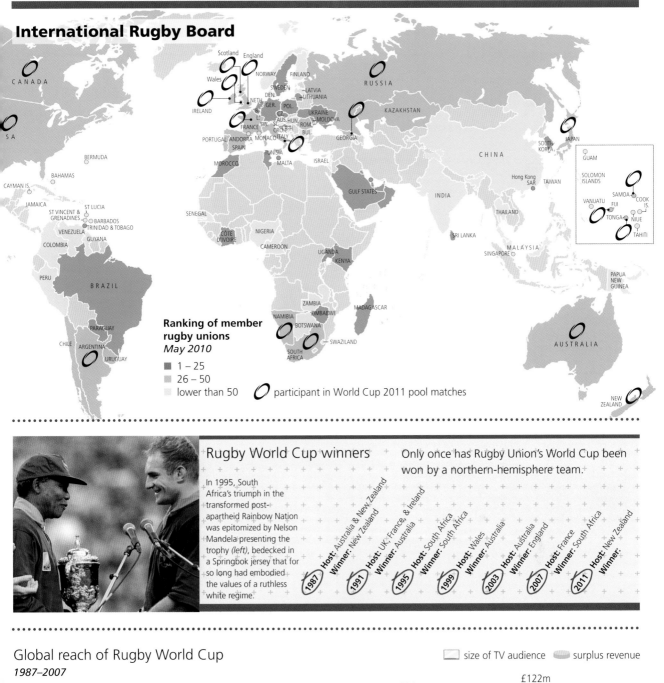

CANADA
USA
BERMUDA
BAHAMAS
CAYMAN IS.
JAMAICA
ST VINCENT & GRENADINES
ST LUCIA
BARBADOS
TRINIDAD & TOBAGO
VENEZUELA
GUYANA
COLOMBIA
PERU
BRAZIL
PARAGUAY
CHILE
ARGENTINA
URUGUAY

Scotland England
Wales
IRELAND
NORWAY FINLAND
SWEDEN
DEN.
NETH.
GER. POL.
FRANCE
CZ.
AUS. HUN.
SW.
SL. CRO. B-H.
ITALY
ROM.
BUL.
PORTUGAL ANDORRA MONACO
SPAIN
TUNISIA
MALTA
MOROCCO
ISRAEL
LATVIA
LITHUANIA
UKRAINE
MOLDOVA
GEORGIA
RUSSIA
KAZAKHSTAN
CHINA
SOUTH KOREA
JAPAN
Hong Kong SAR
TAIWAN
INDIA
THAILAND
SRI LANKA
MALAYSIA
SINGAPORE
PAPUA NEW GUINEA
AUSTRALIA
NEW ZEALAND

SENEGAL
CÔTE D'IVOIRE
NIGERIA
CAMEROON
GULF STATES
UGANDA
KENYA
ZAMBIA
ZIMBABWE
MADAGASCAR
NAMIBIA
BOTSWANA
SWAZILAND
SOUTH AFRICA

GUAM
SOLOMON ISLANDS
VANUATU
SAMOA
COOK IS.
FIJI
TONGA
NIUE
TAHITI

## Ranking of member rugby unions
*May 2010*

- ■ 1 – 25
- ■ 26 – 50
- □ lower than 50
- ○ participant in World Cup 2011 pool matches

## Rugby World Cup winners

In 1995, South Africa's triumph in the transformed post-apartheid Rainbow Nation was epitomized by Nelson Mandela presenting the trophy (*left*), bedecked in a Springbok jersey that for so long had embodied the values of a ruthless white regime.

Only once has Rugby Union's World Cup been won by a northern-hemisphere team.

**1987** Host: Australia & New Zealand — Winner: New Zealand
**1991** Host: UK, France, & Ireland — Winner: Australia
**1995** Host: South Africa — Winner: South Africa
**1999** Host: Wales — Winner: Australia
**2003** Host: Australia — Winner: England
**2007** Host: France — Winner: South Africa
**2011** Host: New Zealand — Winner:

## Global reach of Rugby World Cup
*1987–2007*

size of TV audience    surplus revenue

| 1987 | 1991 | 1995 | 1999 | 2003 | 2007 |
|------|------|------|------|------|------|
| £1m | £4.1m | £17.6m | £47m | £64m | £122m |
| 230m | 1.4bn | 2.3bn | 3.1bn | 3.4bn | 4.2bn |

# SAILING

## Haves and have-yachts

**Peter Blake
1948–2001**

The man who won the Whitbread Round the World Race in 1990, set a record of under 75 days for circumnavigating the world in 1995, and led New Zealand to two successive America's Cup victories, was murdered by Brazilian pirates on an expedition concerning environmental exploration – a tragic reminder that the oceans are more than the adventure playgrounds of the rich.

Sports are, in many respects, based on the premise of equality of opportunity, and their outcomes seen as meritocratic. But, as the competitive stakes increase, in terms of both status and reward, sports need more than just raw talent and basic equipment. People are often influenced in their choice of sport by their socio-economic background, and sailing is an example of a sport's capacity to reflect and reproduce privilege and status. As the rich city workers of London, Manhattan, and Zurich put it: if you really have it, flaunt it – join the have-yachts.

At the other end of the scale, enthusiastic amateur sailors launch their dinghies and wind surfboards off lake shores, jetties, beaches, and muddy estuaries, and participate in yacht club regattas, or just enjoy the exhilaration of being propelled through the water by the power of the wind.

International competitive sailing includes a wide range of events, from regattas on coastal waters for 90 different classes of windsurf board, dinghy, and yacht, to endurance events involving highly engineered ocean-going yachts. The first Whitbread round-the-world race was held in 1973–74, and has taken place every three years since, changing to the Volvo Ocean Race in 2000. It lasts more than 9 months, with teams racing between ports on five continents, and participating in races within the ports in order to maximize media coverage.

The greatest test of endurance is the quadrennial Vendée Globe, in which individuals sail single-handed, non-stop from the English Channel down to the South Atlantic, and then head eastwards through the Southern Ocean, eventually rounding Cape Horn and racing northwards back up to the French coast. Of the 118 sailors who have started the race, only half have reached the finish line.

Many sailors start at a young age.

BMW Oracle and Alinghi competing in the 33rd America's Cup.

## The America's Cup

This event began as a transatlantic challenge between rich Americans and the British establishment, but has developed into a multi-national battle of technology, backed by multi-millionaires. The schooner America defeated British yachts in a race at the Isle of Wight, England in 1851. A commemorative cup was donated to the New York Yacht Club in 1857, and of the 33 challenges up to 2010, US-based teams have beaten off all but five.

From 1970, eliminating rounds established which challenger would face the holder in a one-to-one race. The US grip on the trophy was first broken in 1983 by Australia, and New Zealand has won it on two occasions. A Swiss-based challenger, Alinghi, backed by pharmaceutical billionaire Ernesto Bertarelli, took the title in 2003 – a first for Europe. In February 2010, software mogul Larry Ellison returned the trophy to the US for the first time since 1992, and President Barack Obama granted a White House reception to the victorious BMW Oracle team.

# International sailing

## International Sailing Federation

■ member association *2010*

The ISAF defines the rules that govern competitive sailing, oversees qualification for the Olympic and Paralympic sailing events, and co-ordinates an annual circuit of regattas, the ISAF World Cup, at which Olympic class sailors from 65 countries hone their skills.

## First world first

The UK and the USA have dominated Olympic sailing disciplines, although Spain – stimulated by success in home waters and helped by familiar tides and winds at the 1992 Barcelona Olympics – has emerged strongly in the last few Games. Regardless of the class of event, Olympic sailing has been dominated by the wealthiest nations.

| Great Britain | USA | Norway | Denmark | France | Spain | Sweden | Australia | New Zealand | Brazil |
|---|---|---|---|---|---|---|---|---|---|
| 25 | 19 | 17 | 12 | 11 | 11 | 9 | 7 | 7 | 6 |

**Olympic gold medals for sailing** *1900–2008*

## Windsurfing

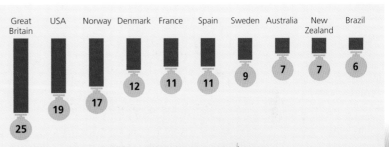

Windsurfing first boomed on the beaches of southern California, associated with counter-cultural currents of the 1960s, and expressing a lack of deference for mainstream sports. It was somewhat ironic, therefore, that it made its first appearance on the Olympic programme at the 1984 Los Angeles games. Olympic champions have come from a wide range of countries – European, Oceanic and East Asian – but none from the USA. This reflects a tension between the Olympic discipline and a more expressive variant involving slalom racing, wave acrobatics, and tricky freestyle manoeuvres, promoted and administered by the Professional World Windsurfing Association.

# SKIING AND SNOWBOARDING

## Boardwars

### Piste pioneer

In 1894, Arthur Conan Doyle climbed up to the Maienfelder Furka pass above Davos in the French Alps, carrying the latest in ski technology: 8-ft long "Norwegian snowshoes". Having reached the pass, he and his guide set off to ski down to Arosa on the other side.

"In that great untrodden waste ... it was glorious to whizz along. It seemed that we had only to stand on our skis and let them carry us ... I believe I may be the first, save only two Switzers, to do any mountain work, but I am certain I will not, by many thousands, be the last."

The ski-slopes have always been the playgrounds of the rich, and when boot and ski technology, however rudimentary, opened up the mountain tracks and the slopes, ski clubs mushroomed from Norway to the Alps, and from California to Turkey. The British upper-classes and aspiring upper-middle classes became active in the Alps, following in the footsteps of the scientists and Romantic intellectuals for whom the mountains had offered a glimpse of the sublime. Skiing became a fashionable winter sport of the cosmopolitan European elite, encouraged by entrepreneurs such as Sir Henry Lunn, founder of Lunn Poly, whose son, Sir Arnold Henry Moore Lunn, founded the Alpine Ski Club, and invented the modern slalom in 1922.

Cheap travel opened up the resorts to new markets of affluent consumers, and international competition such as the Winter Olympics glamourized the ski-slopes and their scenic settings. Young, affluent skiers embraced the pleasures of *après ski,* and by the mid-1990s up to 70 million people were estimated to be enjoying the sport (15 million from the USA; 14 million from Japan). Most stick to the piste – areas of carefully prepared (and often artificially manufactured) snow, linked by mechanical methods for getting the skiers to the tops of

Recreational skiing provides enormous pleasure to those able to afford it.

the slopes. But skiers and snowboarders are increasingly attracted by the more risky off-piste sport, which can involve a helicopter ride to a remote area, followed by the pleasures of fresh powder.

At the level of elite performance, Alpine sports continue to produce stars from the established nations, with the USA and Norway topping the Olympic skiing and snowboarding medal tables at Vancouver in 2010. And while the Olympic Freestyle events are providing opportunities for other nations – some of them not known for their mountains – to find success, the Vancouver medal winners, with the exception of China's silver and bronze medals, confirm the status of skiing as a sport of the affluent West.

Snowboarders have brought an anarchic presence to the slopes, subverting the conventions of the downhill establishment.

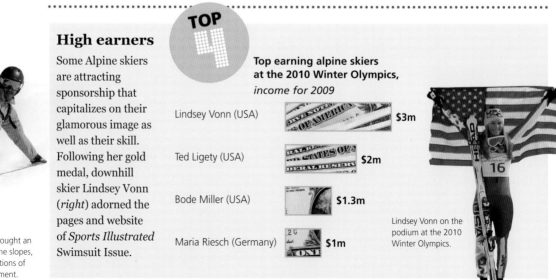

### High earners

Some Alpine skiers are attracting sponsorship that capitalizes on their glamorous image as well as their skill. Following her gold medal, downhill skier Lindsey Vonn (*right*) adorned the pages and website of *Sports Illustrated* Swimsuit Issue.

**TOP 4**

**Top earning alpine skiers at the 2010 Winter Olympics,** *income for 2009*

| | |
|---|---|
| Lindsey Vonn (USA) | $3m |
| Ted Ligety (USA) | $2m |
| Bode Miller (USA) | $1.3m |
| Maria Riesch (Germany) | $1m |

Lindsey Vonn on the podium at the 2010 Winter Olympics.

# Ski disciplines and boarder tensions

| | |
|---|---|
| Austria | 31 |
| Switzerland | 18 |
| France | 15 |
| USA | 14 |
| Italy | 13 |
| Germany | 11 |
| Norway | 9 |
| Sweden | 7 |
| Canada, Croatia | 4 |

**Alpine**

Although this is the kind of skiing most people do on their holidays, few reach the level of expertise displayed in competition. The downhill, super giant slalom, giant slalom, slalom and combined (downhill and slalom) all require strength, flexibility, split-second reactions and, above all, courage, but in subtly different combinations that create specialist practitioners (and equipment) for each event. Although the European Alpine nations head the medal table, the USA has been increasingly successful in recent years.

**Ski-jumping**

This highly specialist sport requires a huge ramp from which to leap and an optimally designed landing area. The IOC is showing signs of opening up this male-only Olympic competition to women, "looking favourably" on its inclusion in 2014.

The closest a skier comes to flying.

| | |
|---|---|
| Finland | 10 |
| Norway | 9 |
| Austria | 6 |
| Switzerland | 4 |
| Germany, Japan | 3 |

**Cross-country**

Developed from the practical use to which cross-country skiing was traditionally put in Norway, it was included as a men's event in the first Winter Olympics in 1924, and as a women's event since 1952. It incorporates classic and freestyle races against the clock over distances ranging from 1.2 km to 50 km.

| | |
|---|---|
| Norway | 35 |
| Sweden | 27 |
| USSR | 25 |
| Finland | 19 |
| Russia | 13 |

**Nordic combined**

This event, for men only, comprises a ski-jump and a cross-country race. It has been held at the Olympics for individuals since 1924 and for teams since 1988.

| | |
|---|---|
| Norway | 11 |
| Finland | 4 |

**Freestyle**

The mogul, in the Olympics from 1992, takes the downhill skier over bumps and ramps. Aerials, introduced at the 1994 Olympics, demand mid-air spins and twists. Ski cross, introduced in Vancouver in 2010, pits skiers alongside each other in a manner not seen in the Alpine disciplines, providing a level of drama and unpredictability as skiers clash and fall.

Racers in the Ski Cross 2010 World Cup at Les Contamines-Montjoie.

| | |
|---|---|
| Canada, Switzerland, USA | 5 |
| Australia | 3 |
| France, Norway | 2 |
| Belarus, China, Czech Republic, Finland, Japan, Uzbekistan | 1 |

**Snowboard events**

Snowboarding was developed in the USA from the 1960s onwards, and the first World Cup was held in Austria in 1985. The International Snowboard Federation (ISF), founded in 1989, standardized competition regulations, but in 2002 control of boarding was taken on by the International Ski Federation (FIS). The sport made its Olympic debut in 1998 at Nagano, Japan. The increasing popularity of the sport, and the "alternative" image of the snowboarders, initially created tensions on the slopes, and many recreational skiers are still wary of the freestyle approach of the, often younger, boarders.

| | |
|---|---|
| USA | 7 |
| Switzerland | 5 |
| Canada | 3 |
| France | 2 |
| Australia, Germany, Netherlands | 1 |

# SWIMMING AND DIVING

## Four strokes and a board

### Ahead of the game

Seeking to gain a competitive edge, swimmers have experimented with different techniques, and at the 1956 Olympics Japanese swimmer Masaru Furukawa won the 200-metre breaststroke swimming underwater for three-quarters of the race. His technique was quickly banned. Beijing 2008 Olympic champions Michael Phelps (USA) and Rebecca Adlington (UK) were among users of Speedo's LZR Racer polyurethane swimsuit, developed in association with NASA and launched early in 2008. 90 percent of all available medals were won by swimmers wearing the suit, and 23 world records broken. The hi-tech bodysuit was banned from the beginning of 2010.

Rebecca Adlington in hi-tech bodysuit, 2008.

Recreational swimming is second only to exercise walking or aerobic exercise as a mass participation activity in wealthy countries. In the UK, 13 percent of adults say they swim once a month, and in the USA, where children are included in the figure, it is as high as 19 percent. Beyond those who swim regularly, millions take casual dips on occasional holidays, or swim for recuperative or therapeutic reasons.

Most people swim primarily for pleasure, as well as for the perceived health benefits. Only a tiny minority of swimmers has experienced competitive swimming. However, the combination of performance and competition in water can draw large audiences.

Competitive swimming is framed by Olympic standards, in 50-metre pools of eight lanes, though the first Olympic contests were held in 1896 in open water at the port of Piraeus on the edge of Athens. The 100-metre freestyle champion, Hungarian Arnold Guttmann, had to battle 3.5-metre (12-ft) waves and 13°C (55°F) water, and he recalled that "the icy water almost cut into our stomachs". Women's events were introduced at the 1912 Stockholm Olympics.

The Fédération Internationale de Natation Amateur (FINA) was founded in 1908, and administers and regulates international competition. The four main swimming strokes are: freestyle, in the form of front crawl; backstroke; the traditional breaststroke; and, from 1952, butterfly. As well as straightforward racing, FINA oversees water polo, diving, and synchronized swimming.

In September 2010, FINA executive director Cornel Marculescu referred to the spectacular appeal of cliff diving, and the prospect of it being added to the Olympic programme: "Aquatics will be left behind and marginalized," he said, if it did not innovate. IOC sports director Christophe Dubi remained sceptical about cliff diving, but conceded that the inclusion of mixed relay teams in the inaugural Youth Olympics in Singapore earlier in the year had "created a buzz", and that they warranted consideration for inclusion in future Olympics.

## Channel swimming

The first person to swim between England and France was Matthew (Captain) Webb (1848–83), an English merchant seaman. Although he was accorded the status of a hero, he was subsequently forced to perform exhibitions and endurance feats to survive, and perished in the waters of the Niagara Falls when attempting to swim downriver.

The Channel challenge could be big international news. When American Gertrude Ederle (1905–2003), triple Olympic medallist in 1924, announced her intention to became the first woman to swim the Channel (from France to England) in 1926 she met with ridicule and outright opposition. In her support, W.W. McGeehan wrote in The *New York Herald Tribune*: "If there is one woman who can make the swim, it is this girl, with the shoulders and back of Jack Dempsey and the frankest and bravest pair of eyes that ever looked into a face." She not only succeeded, but broke the men's record by two hours.

Captain Webb, who, in 1875, was the first person to swim the English Channel.

Gertrude Ederle, who, in 1926, was the first woman to swim the English Channel.

Synchronized swimming is mocked for its emphasis on appearance, but it requires immense body strength and breath-control to perform these aquatic gymnastics.

# Olympic success

US male and female swimmers dominate the Olympics gold medal tables, although Australia has provided strong competition. At Sydney 2000, Australian Ian Thorpe and his freestyle relay team-mates beat the USA to gold and, responding to the pre-race boast of the American Gary Hall Jr that his team would "smash" the Australians "like guitars", celebrated by miming guitar playing.

Michael Phelps (below) managed to break his countryman Mark Spitz's 1972 record by winning eight gold medals at the 2008 Beijing Olympics, but his projected billion-dollar career was threatened in 2009 by allegations of marijuana-smoking that led to a three-month suspension and Kellog ending its sponsorship deal with him. Phelps apologized to fans and sponsors, but some of his aura was gone, and in the 100% textile fabric waist-to-knee jammers that have replaced the banned polyurethane bodysuits, his dominance in the water could no longer be taken for granted.

**Swimming gold medals** *1896–2008*

**Men**

| | |
|---|---|
| USA | 127 |
| Australia | 31 |
| Japan | 16 |
| Hungary | 13 |
| Germany | 9 |
| Great Britain | 9 |
| USSR | 9 |

**Women**

| | |
|---|---|
| USA | 99 |
| GDR | 37 |
| Australia | 25 |
| Netherlands | 17 |
| Hungary | 14 |

# Diving for China

Although the USA has dominated diving in the past, China is the new force. At Beijing 2008, Chinese women won all four available gold medals, and Chinese men won three of the four.

Back in 1992, Fu Mingxia won gold at Barcelona just before her 14th birthday. She had been training on the diving board from earliest childhood, in specialist camps and institutions. Her brilliant diving was a product of child cruelty as well as dedicated commitment. To cope with pain she had been forced as a child to sit with her legs outstretched whilst an adult sat on her swelling knees. Her precocious achievements led to a minimum age being set for Olympic diving competitors.

**Diving gold medals** *1904–2008*

**Men**

| | |
|---|---|
| USA | 28 |
| China | 11 |

**Women**

| | |
|---|---|
| USA | 20 |
| China | 16 |

Fu Mingxia winning Olympic gold in 1992, aged 13.

# TENNIS

## Net profits

### A sporting gem

The first lawn tennis club was founded in 1872 by Major Harry Gem, in Leamington Spa, UK. The following year, Major Walter Wingfield developed clearer rules for the game, patenting these in 1874, although the name *spharistiké* (Greek for "ball games") did not stick.

The All England Croquet Club persevered with the sport, further formalized the rules, and staged the first Wimbledon men's lawn tennis championship in 1877.

The new sport spread rapidly, not least in the USA, where tennis captivated less academic students at Harvard, including Dwight Davis, founder of the Davis Cup.

In 2009, the final of the Wimbledon Lawn Tennis tournament between Swiss Roger Federer and American Andy Roddick was the fifth most watched TV event of the year, generating an audience of 89 million people who looked in on at least some of the action, and 29 million who watched the whole match on their screens. Along with the other three Grand Slam events in the USA, Australia, and France, this has established tennis as one of the top attractions in world sport.

The Slams are complemented by an expanded schedule of events around the calendar so that – as with the professional golf tour – the jobbing international competitor of whom few have heard might make a healthy income. Unlike their golfing counterparts, women tennis players have established earning parity with men.

Each November since 1970, the ATP (Association of Tennis Professionals) men's tour has ended with the (Barclays) ATP World Tour Finals. In 2009, the world's top eight players competed at London's O2 arena for a share of the $5 million prize money. The ATP heralds its end-of-season event

as a "head-to-head in one-on-one gladiatorial battles in their purest form".

Tennis also retains its popularity as a participation sport, at recreational levels. Over 874,000 adults in England reported playing more than once a month in 2005, placing tennis as the ninth most played sport in the country. But there is no necessary relationship between such recreational and often informal play, and the production of champions; at Wimbledon 2010 there was, for the first time ever, no Englishman competing – the top-ranking British player, Andy Murray, being a Scot.

Over a third of a million boys and girls played competitively in US high schools in 2009–10, although international competitions and professional titles were less dominated by US men than at any time in the modern era. Tennis writers and analysts began to ask how Serbia, a country of 10 million, with such a traumatic recent history, could produce the same number of top ten players as the USA.

Most successful men's Grand Slam winner ever, with 16 titles, Roger Federer displays both the elegant style that characterized his play at its peak, and the profile of the Nike swoosh in the top tier of the game.

Serving notice: Maria Sharapova, top earner in the women's game in 2009, looks up and aims high.

### The tennis models

From Suzanne Lenglen (1899–1938) to Anna Kournikova and Maria Sharapova, competitive tennis has provided a stage not just for female athletic excellence, but a means of profiling sexual attractiveness. Sharapova, with only three Grand Slam titles to her name, out-earned the more competitively successful Williams sisters in the 2008/09 season.

Women tennis players have also broadened the boundaries of cultural tolerance. Billie-Jean King and Czech star Martina Navratilova came out as lesbians, and made inestimable contributions to the public understanding of sexuality.

**TOP 8**

#### Top earners from winnings and endorsements *2008/09*

| | |
|---|---|
| Roger Federer | $36m |
| Maria Sharapova | $23m |
| Rafael Nadal | $20m |
| Serena Williams | $18m |
| Andy Roddick | $16m |
| Venus Williams | $15m |
| Andy Murray | $12m |
| Novak Djokovic | $11m |

# International tennis

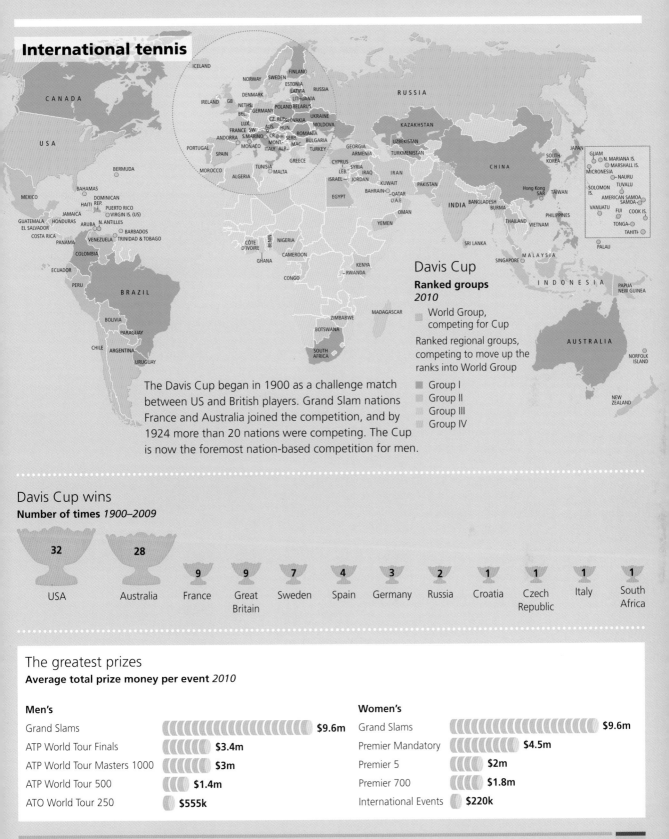

## Davis Cup
### Ranked groups
*2010*

- World Group, competing for Cup

Ranked regional groups, competing to move up the ranks into World Group

- Group I
- Group II
- Group III
- Group IV

The Davis Cup began in 1900 as a challenge match between US and British players. Grand Slam nations France and Australia joined the competition, and by 1924 more than 20 nations were competing. The Cup is now the foremost nation-based competition for men.

## Davis Cup wins
**Number of times** *1900–2009*

| USA | Australia | France | Great Britain | Sweden | Spain | Germany | Russia | Croatia | Czech Republic | Italy | South Africa |
|---|---|---|---|---|---|---|---|---|---|---|---|
| 32 | 28 | 9 | 9 | 7 | 4 | 3 | 2 | 1 | 1 | 1 | 1 |

## The greatest prizes
**Average total prize money per event** *2010*

**Men's**

| | |
|---|---|
| Grand Slams | $9.6m |
| ATP World Tour Finals | $3.4m |
| ATP World Tour Masters 1000 | $3m |
| ATP World Tour 500 | $1.4m |
| ATO World Tour 250 | $555k |

**Women's**

| | |
|---|---|
| Grand Slams | $9.6m |
| Premier Mandatory | $4.5m |
| Premier 5 | $2m |
| Premier 700 | $1.8m |
| International Events | $220k |

# TRACK AND FIELD

## Citis, altius, fortius

### The sub-four-minute mile

Englishman Roger Bannister was the first to break the four-minute barrier, running 3.59.4 in May 1954. The Australian John Landy broke the record within days. Landy went on to become Governor of Victoria, while Bannister pursued a successful career in medicine and public service. Together, they represented one of the last moments of the amateur athlete, as the Soviet system and creeping acceptance of professionalism produced more full-timers, and raised the aspirations of runners. Morocco's Hicham El Guerrouj ran the world's fastest-ever mile in Rome in 1999 at 3.43.13.

Modern track and field athletics embodies the sporting skills featured in the ancient Greek Olympics, but today's top practitioners are also full-time professionals in an entertainment business.

For most of the 20th century, international and Olympic athletes had to be amateur, although college-based athletes in the USA were, in effect, sponsored performers, and from the 1952 Olympics the Soviet model of talent-spotting produced full-time athletes with bogus positions in state employment or the military. The USSR and other East European countries also supported women athletes, particularly in explosive, strength-based throwing events. Many countries turned a blind-eye to financial support that found its way to so-called amateurs. But by the 1980s, such was the hypocrisy surrounding what was dubbed "shamateur" status, with trust-funds allowing athletes to take money from sponsors as long as it was declared as training support not income, that the International Olympic Committee gradually loosened its rules, and by the early 1990s abandoned its insistence that all Olympians (the one exception being boxing) should be amateur. Marking this transformation, the International Amateur Athletics Federation (IAAF) became the International Association of Athletics Federations in 2000.

Sponsors have poured in, television has lapped up the expanded athletics programme, and those who realize the Olympic slogan – *Citius, Altius, Fortius* (Swifter, Higher, Stronger) – accrue substantial personal wealth. The IAAF annual competitive circuit of one-day meets, the Samsung Diamond League, was inaugurated in 2010. From mid-May to late August, athletes in 32 disciplines contest a World Number One position with a cash prize and, more significantly, expanded and unlimited branding and marketing possibilities. As high-earning full-timers, modern athletes must prepare for more events than their genuinely amateur predecessors. Their training schedules are tougher, they must peak more often, and they must balance physical performance with commitments to their corporate paymasters.

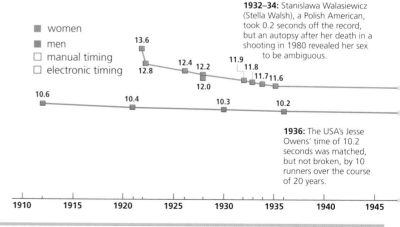

With the top 10 jumps of all time to her name, Russia's Monaco-resident Yelean Isinbayeva has been dubbed the Princess of the Pole Vault. She won gold at Beijing 2008 and went on to receive the women's athlete of the year award (and $159,000) for the third time. She is supported by Li Ning (a leading Chinese sports brand), Colgate-Palmolive, Spanish jewellery giant Carrera y Carrera, and UCS, leading USA sports equipment company.

## 100 metres
### World records, *1912–2009*

Despite improvements to sportswear, track surfaces and training, men have only shaved just over a second off the record. Women sprinters made great strides early on as they were given more opportunities to train.

The introduction of electronic timing enabled timings to a hundredth of a second. For a while, this method was used in tandem with older methods, but since 1977, the IAAF has required automated timing for a record to be recognized.

■ women
■ men
□ manual timing
□ electronic timing

**1932–34:** Stanislawa Walasiewicz (Stella Walsh), a Polish American, took 0.2 seconds off the record, but an autopsy after her death in a shooting in 1980 revealed her sex to be ambiguous.

**1936:** The USA's Jesse Owens' time of 10.2 seconds was matched, but not broken, by 10 runners over the course of 20 years.

Women: 13.6, 12.8, 12.4, 12.2, 12.0, 11.9, 11.8, 11.7, 11.6

Men: 10.6, 10.4, 10.3, 10.2

1910  1915  1920  1925  1930  1935  1940  1945

# World Athletics Championships

Beyond the historic Cold War rivalry, several developing countries are notable for their gold medal success. Two Caribbean countries, Cuba and Jamaica, have provided the superstars of the sprints, and two African countries, Ethiopia and Kenya, are the masters of long-distance. Incentives have been offered to African runners to change nationality. Bahrain made it into the top 10 for the 2009 Championship, with gold in the 1,500 m for Ethiopian-born Maryam Yusuf Jamal, and Kenyan-born Yusuf Saad Kamel.

| | Track events | | | | | Field events | |
|---|---|---|---|---|---|---|---|
| Sprints | Middle-distance | Long-distance | Hurdles | Relays | | Jumps | Throws |
| 100 m | 800 m | 5,000 m | 100 m (women) | 4×100 m | | Long jump | Shot put |
| 200 m | 1,500 m | 10,000 m | 110 m (men) | 4×400 m | | Triple jump | Discus |
| 400 m | 3,000 m | | 400 m | | | High jump | Hammer |
| | | Marathon (road) | 3,000 m steeplechase | | | Pole vault | Javelin |

For combined events see Multi-sports.

## TOP 10

### World Championships gold medals, *1983–2009*

USA 120
Russia 37
Kenya 31
Germany 28
Soviet Union 22
Cuba 18
GDR 18
Ethiopia 18
Great Britain 16
Jamaica 14

| Berlin 2009 | Gold |
|---|---|
| USA | 10 |
| Jamaica | 7 |
| Kenya | 4 |
| Russia | 4 |
| Bahrain | 2 |
| South Africa | 2 |
| Australia | 2 |
| Poland | 2 |
| GB | 2 |
| Ethiopia | 2 |
| Germany | 2 |

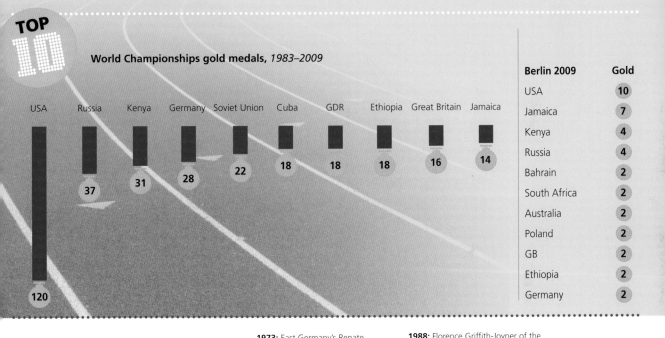

**1973:** East Germany's Renate Stecher was the first woman to run under 11 seconds, but in 1977 it was revealed that this was achieved while taking the anabolic steroid oral-turinabol.

**1988:** Florence Griffith-Joyner of the USA set a stunning record, then retired on the eve of the introduction of compulsory random drug-testing.

**1968:** Jim Hines (USA) set the first sub-10-second record, refining it to 9.95 in high-altitude Mexico City.

**1988–94:** The USA's Carl Lewis and Leroy Burrell contested the record, reducing it by 0.08 seconds in the process.

**2006–09:** Jamaicans Asafa Powell and Usain Bolt contested the record, reducing it by 0.19 seconds.

# VOLLEYBALL & BEACH VOLLEYBALL

## Sand, sun and sky

### Old folks at play

Volleyball was devised in 1895 by William Morgan, of the YMCA, Holyoke, Massachusetts. He was looking for a sport less frenetic than basketball, suited to the older adults attending his classes.

The game spread beyond the YMCA, shed its tranquil origins and expanded worldwide. It is now a vigorous young person's sport, especially popular among young women, with nine times as many girls as boys playing it in US high schools

Women enjoying a game in the early days of the sport.

**404,000**
girls play volleyball in the USA

Volleyball is a vigorous six-a-side team game, played in a gym. The equipment needed is simple and cheap, and the sport has a wide international appeal. The Fédération Internationale de Volleyball (FIVB) was established in 1947, and world championships for men and women were inaugurated in 1949 and 1952 respectively.

Volleyball became an Olympic event for both sexes at the 1964 Tokyo Olympics, where the host nation provided the gold medal winning team in the women's event, and the bronze medallists in the men's. Hirofumi Daimatsu, coach to the Japanese women, drew 10 of the 12 members of his squad from a spinning mill near Osaka, where he was a departmental manager. He enforced a brutal regime, the players training and playing for a minimum of six hours a day, every day throughout the year, and the Japanese team was never remotely challenged.

Beach volleyball has eclipsed its parent discipline. It became an Olympic sport for both men and women in 1996, when it was the third hottest ticket in town. The sport originated on the beaches of Santa Monica, California in the 1920s, and competitions for trophies were held after World War II, with the first Manhattan Beach Open (Southern California) held in 1960. Brazil and the USA have dominated the men's events at the Olympics, although an Australian women's pair won the gold at Sydney in 2000. On the professional tour in 2008, Brazil provided five of the top 15 women's teams, and four of the top 15 men's pairings.

Professional beach volleyball has boomed, and although the number of events on the Tour has declined substantially in recent years, the total prize money on offer seems to be holding up comparatively well. Unlike most other sports, women's earnings match those of the men.

> Briefs should be a close fit and be cut on an upward angle towards the top of the leg. The side width must be maximum 7cm; tops must fit closely to the body.
>
> FIVB regulations for women volleyballers, Athens 2004

## Sex appeal

Bondi Beach, Sydney 2000 Olympics beach volleyball venue, drew many spectators new to the sport. "Sand, Sun and Sky – get involved" was the running head of the FIVB in the run-up to the Beijing 2008 Olympics. The fourth "S" was of course implicit. Beach volleyball's success testifies to the voyeuristic side of sport spectating. US Olympian Holly McPeak told *Sports Illustrated*: "If people want to come and check us out because they're scoping our bodies, I don't have a problem with that, because I guarantee they'll go home talking about our athleticism... The sex appeal is unavoidable, but it's not the basis of the sport."

# Volleyball

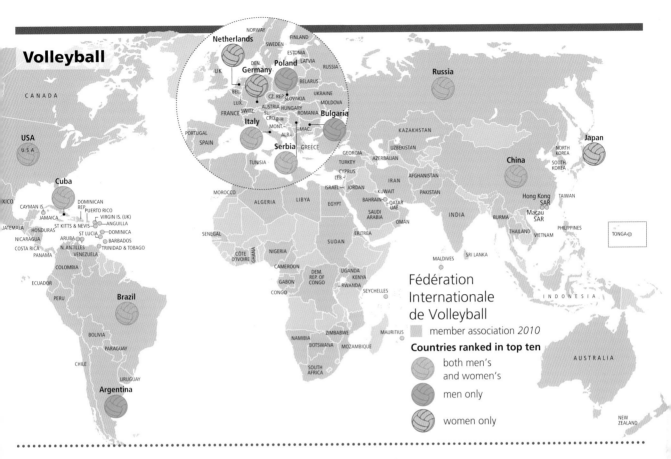

Fédération
Internationale
de Volleyball

member association *2010*

**Countries ranked in top ten**

both men's
and women's

men only

women only

## Olympic medals

After the barnstorming performance of the Japanese women's volleyball team at Tokyo 1964, the USSR secured the gold medal in the two subsequent Olympics, with Japan only reclaiming it in 1978. Outstanding women's teams emerged from China and Cuba, the latter winning gold three times in succession from 1992 to 2000. Men's champions have included Brazil, the Netherlands, the USA and Yugoslavia, as well as the former USSR.

**Gold medals for both men and women** *1964–2008*

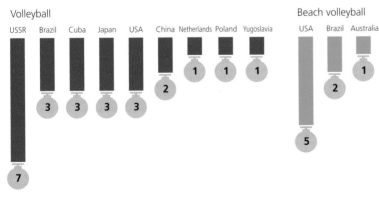

Volleyball: USSR 7, Brazil 3, Cuba 3, Japan 3, USA 3, China 2, Netherlands 1, Poland 1, Yugoslavia 1

Beach volleyball: USA 5, Brazil 2, Australia 1

## Beach volleyball

**Number of events and prize money on Swatch FIVB World Tour** *2005–10*

**Men**

| Year | Number of events | | Total prize money |
|---|---|---|---|
| 2005 | 30 | | $3.8m |
| 2006 | 20 | | $3.3m |
| 2007 | 22 | | $4.2m |
| 2008 | 27 | | $4.4m |
| 2009 | 14 | | $3.4m |
| 2010 | 14 | | $3.3m |

**Women**

| Year | Number of events | | Total prize money |
|---|---|---|---|
| 2005 | 26 | | $3.9m |
| 2006 | 20 | | $3.4m |
| 2007 | 23 | | $4.2m |
| 2008 | 26 | | $4.2m |
| 2009 | 16 | | $3.8m |
| 2010 | 15 | | $3.5m |

15 number of events    total prize money

# WRESTLING

## Holds, grabs and falls

### To the death

Ancient Greek boys were trained not only in grammar and mathematics, but in wrestling. Although wrestling was considered more a skill than a martial art, when it came to the big competitions it was a serious business.

Arrachion of Phigaleia was three-time Olympic champion, although he knew little of his third triumph in 564 BC. Dying in a stranglehold, he nevertheless managed to dislocate the ankle of his opponent, who then submitted to a victorious corpse.

19th-century engraving of Ancient Greek wrestlers.

All-in wrestling, as featured in the ancient Olympics, lived up to its name – *pankration*, literally "all-powerful". It involved punching, choking, kicking, and assault on the genitals, though not biting or gouging. Comparisons have been made between this and "total" or "ultimate fighting", and a companion format, cage-fighting, popularized in Japan and the USA, in particular, since the 1990s (although attacks on genitals are outlawed). John McCain, 2008 Republican presidential candidate, has called this ultimate variant "human cockfighting…a commentary on the sickness at the heart of American life".

*Pankration*, as a form of mild mixed martial arts, remains one of the disciplines overseen by the Fédération Internationale des Luttes Associées, wrestling's world governing body, founded in 1921. The others are: Greco-Roman, with no holds below the hips, or use of legs; Freestyle, in which leg holds predominate; Female, an adaptation of the men's freestyle model; Beach, acknowledged in 2004 as a festive variant; Grappling, another mixed martial arts hybrid; Belt Wrestling, in which fighters hold on to each other's belts whilst trying to throw the opponent; and Traditional Wrestling, embracing surviving folk forms.

In the Olympics, men's Freestyle appeared in the 1904 St. Louis Games. Greco-Roman was invented in France in the 19th century, in tribute to the sporting cultures of Greece and Rome, and entered the Olympic programme at the 1924 Paris Games. Women's wrestling, based on the freestyle form, was included in the Olympics for the first time at the 2004 Athens Games.

### Men in tights

Wrestling's popularity as a televized spectacle has gone in waves. In the 1960s and 1970s in the UK it was family viewing on Independent Television's Saturday afternoon *World of Sport*, and Martin Ruane (aka Giant Haystacks) was told by Frank Sinatra that British wrestlers were world-leading entertainers. But in 1988 the network axed wrestling from its schedules, chasing a more affluent and upmarket viewer.

The World Wrestling Federation (WWF), established in the early 1950s, combined staged pantomime with sado-masochistic physical performances that attracted huge numbers of mainly male viewers and fans in the USA in the mid-1980s. It created large-than-life stars such as Hulk Hogan. A "Summerslam" event staged at Wembley, London, in 1992, drew a capacity crowd of 81,000. In 2009, the 25th Anniversary of its showcase event, WrestleMania, drew more than 72,000 fans.

The Federation changed its name to World Wrestling Entertainment (WWE) after losing a court case to the World Wildlife Fund over the rights to the acronym, but has retained a buoyant and loyal fan base around the world. In addition to those attending its events, in 2009 it reached viewers in 145 countries through 7,500 hours of television.

## 267,000
boys took part in competitive wrestling in US schools in 2009

## 2.3m
Number attending WWE events worldwide in 2009

# Sumo

In Japan, the superstars of wrestling are the Sumo men. Sumo is an explosively short physical contest, as the fighter seeks to throw the opponent off balance, but dignity, expressed in the ritual surrounding the bouts, is a core Sumo value. This has recently been somewhat tarnished by revelations of connections between stars and the Japanese mafia. Nevertheless, in its amateur form Sumo has spread worldwide, with 80 national associations, plus Hawaii, affiliated to the International Sumo Federation, which has been lobbying for the sport to be included in the Olympics.

## International Sumo Federation

Countries with associations 2010

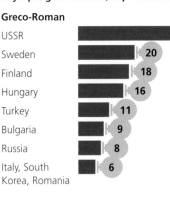

One of the rituals of Sumo – the ring-entering ceremony.

## Olympic wrestling

Some countries excel in one or other style of wrestling – but some, such as Finland, Russia, Sweden and Turkey are highly successful in both.

Wrestling has been marred by drug scandals, with the most recent offenders coming from Bulgaria and Turkey.

Asian women, particularly Japanese, dominate at the Olympics and at the Women's World Championships, held since 1987 – and also in 2008, when so few top-ranked women could compete at the Beijing Olympics.

### Olympic gold medals, top countries, all weights 1904–2008

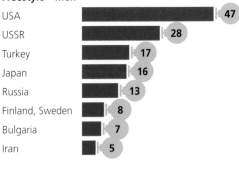

**Greco-Roman**

| | |
|---|---|
| USSR | 34 |
| Sweden | 20 |
| Finland | 18 |
| Hungary | 16 |
| Turkey | 11 |
| Bulgaria | 9 |
| Russia | 8 |
| Italy, South Korea, Romania | 6 |

**Freestyle – Men**

| | |
|---|---|
| USA | 47 |
| USSR | 28 |
| Turkey | 17 |
| Japan | 16 |
| Russia | 13 |
| Finland, Sweden | 8 |
| Bulgaria | 7 |
| Iran | 5 |

**Freestyle – Women**

| | |
|---|---|
| Japan | 4 |
| China | 2 |
| Canada, Ukraine | 1 |

# 3

# THE ECONOMICS OF SPORTS

Sports are organized by legions of volunteers at the local level, where clubs and teams play for fun and leisure as well as local pride. But at the high-performance level, sporting mega-events at which top players compete are organized by national and international associations, or federations. SportAccord, a rebranding in 2009 of the General Association of International Sports Federations (GAISF), shares its name with an annual convention of powerbrokers of world sports. In 2010, it listed 87 international federations and 17 associated members – bodies that organize international games and/or events, or operate as a sports-related international association. Outside SportAccord, but supported by it, is the International Olympic Committee (IOC) – the overarching body for the world's prime multi-sports event.

International federations were initially INGOs (International Non-Government Organizations), but as the commercial value of sports increased, many were transformed into BINGOs, business-oriented versions of the INGO. Unpaid volunteers, for whom running federations was a form of public service, were replaced by individuals who saw in certain sports and events – soccer, athletics, the Olympics – opportunities for expansion, commercial exploitation of sports as products, and, in some cases, personal profit as well as self-aggrandizement. In a pivotal period of change between 1974 and 1981, the IOC in Lausanne, FIFA in Zurich, and the IAAF in Monaco transformed the economic basis of modern sports, auctioning their sports and events to new partners in the media and the corporate world.

## Where the power lies

**Location of headquarters of international sporting federations**
*2010*

Number of federations:
- 25
- 8
- 1 – 5

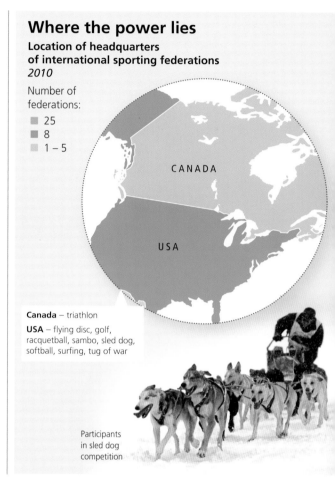

CANADA

USA

**Canada** – triathlon

**USA** – flying disc, golf, racquetball, sambo, sled dog, softball, surfing, tug of war

Participants in sled dog competition

## The growth of the federations

⊘ FIFA events  ⊘ IAAF events  ⊘ IOC events  ⊘ establishment of other INGOs

France was a major influence upon the internationalization of sports administration. The French roots of the Olympics made French the first language of international sports administration, and the desire to gain recognition by the IOC and entry to the Olympic programme stimulated many of the initiatives in the administration and control of international sports.

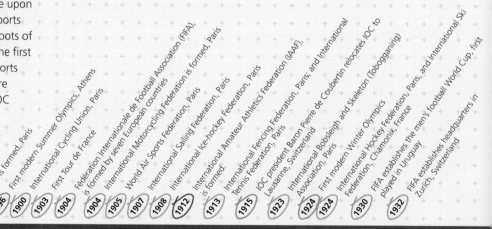

- **1894** IOC is formed, Paris
- **1896** First modern Summer Olympics, Athens
- **1900** International Cycling Union, Paris
- **1903** First Tour de France
- **1904** Fédération Internationale de Football Association (FIFA), is formed by seven European countries
- **1904** International Motorcycling Federation is formed, Paris
- **1905** World Air Sports Federation, Paris
- **1907** International Sailing Federation, Paris
- **1908** International Ice-hockey Federation, Paris
- **1912** International Amateur Athletics Federation (IAAF), Paris; and International Tennis Federation, Paris is formed.
- **1913** International Fencing Federation, Paris
- **1915** IOC president Baron Pierre de Coubertin relocates IOC to Lausanne, Switzerland
- **1923** International Bobsleigh and Skeleton Association, Paris
- **1924** First modern Winter Olympics Federation, Chamonix, France
- **1924** International Hockey Federation, Paris, and International Ski Federation (Tobogganing)
- **1930** FIFA establishes the men's football World Cup, first played in Uruguay
- **1932** FIFA establishes headquarters in Zurich, Switzerland

NORWAY
FINLAND
UK
IRELAND
NETH.
BELGIUM GERMANY
CZECH. REP.
FRANCE SWITZ. AUSTRIA HUNGARY
SPAIN MONACO ITALY
BULGARIA
GREECE

U.A.E. – cricket

CHINA

SOUTH KOREA
JAPAN

**South Korea** – soft tennis, taekwondo

**China** – dragon boat, wushu

**Japan** – aikido, go, kendo, sumo

U.A.E.

THAILAND

MALAYSIA

SINGAPORE

**Thailand** – muaythai

**Singapore** – bowling, sepak takraw

**Malaysia** – badminton

**Switzerland** – air sports, aquatics, archery, baseball, basketball, boxing, canoe, cycling, equestrianism, fencing, football/ soccer, gymnastics, handball, hockey, ice hockey, mini golf , motorcycling, mountaineering, rowing, skating, skiing, table tennis, volleyball, water skiing, wrestling

**Italy** – bobsleigh, boules sport, fistball, kickboxing, roller sports, sport climbing, sport fishing, subaquatics

**Austria** – biathlon

**Belgium** – billiard sports, lifesaving

**Bulgaria** – ju-jitsu

**Czech Republic** – casting

**Finland** – floorball, orienteering

**France** – American football, bridge, polo

**Germany** – luge, powerlifting, shooting

**Greece** – chess

**Hungary** – judo, weight lifting

**Ireland** – rugby union

**Monaco** – athletics, modern pentathlon, powerboating

**Netherlands** – draughts, korfball

**Norway** – darts

**Spain** – basque pelota, bodybuilding, dancesport, karate

**UK** – curling, netball, sailing, squash, tennis

Global sports need regulating, and international federations grew out of, or were formed by clusters of, national associations. They were the product of a globalizing world in which teams could travel, and people had the time and the money to watch sports. Many were relocated to or established in Switzerland, ensuring proximity to the IOC, and also benefitting from the country's generous financial and legal systems and procedures.

## International Olympic Committee

The IOC was rocked by corruption in the 1990s, with IOC members accepting bribes from candidate cities in the bidding process to host events. Dr Jacques Rogge won the presidency in 2000, on the resignation of the 20-year incumbent Samaranch (a former political careerist, seen here kneeling in uniform before the fascist Franco). Rogge has brought about reforms, but the credibility of world sport remains threatened by corruption and doping. Critics of the IOC call for the United Nations to develop a global sports policy.

## Lack of accountability

In an assessment of their transparency, the participation and engagement of their stakeholders, their general performance, and responses to complaints, neither FIFA (in 2007) nor the IOC (in 2008) scored at all well.

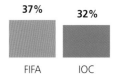

37%      32%

FIFA      IOC

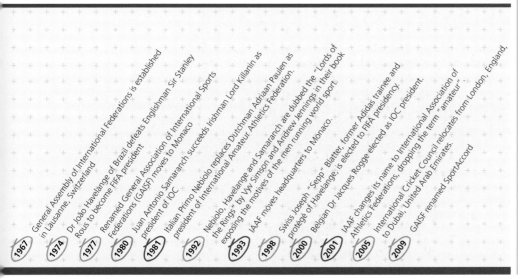

1967 General Assembly of International Federations is established in Lausanne, Switzerland

1974 Dr João Havelange of Brazil defeats Englishman Sir Stanley Rous to become FIFA president

1977 Renamed General Association of International Sports Federations (GAISF) moves to Monaco

1980 Juan Antonio Samaranch president of IOC

1981 Italian Primo Nebiolo succeeds Irishman Lord Killanin as president of International Amateur Athletics Federation.

1992 Nebiolo, Havelange and Samaranch are dubbed the "Lords of the Rings" by Vyv Simson and Andrew Jennings in their book exposing the motives of the men running world sport.

1993 IAAF moves headquarters to Monaco.

1998 Swiss Joseph "Sepp" Blatter, former Adidas trainee and protégé of Havelange, is elected to FIFA presidency.

2000 Belgian Dr Jacques Rogge elected as IOC president.

2001 IAAF changes its name to International Association of Athletics Federations, dropping the term "amateur".

2005 International Cricket Council relocates from London, England, to Dubai, United Arab Emirates.

2009 GAISF renamed SportAccord

# MEDIA

In 1996, News International's Rupert Murdoch called sports a "battering ram" for the expansion of his global pay television network, noting: "Sport absolutely overpowers film and everything else in the entertainment genre". In 2010, ESPN president George Bodenheimer reaffirmed the centrality of sports and big sporting moments to the changing global media landscape: "You can read about it in the business section, in the entertainment section, in the social section. It's all pervasive. It's no longer just the sport; it's a major part of the culture of the world."

Although often demeaned as the "toy department" of the journalistic superstore, sports journalism was important to the expansion of print media in the 19th century, at local, regional, and national levels, promoting, advertising, and sponsoring as well as reporting. In the early 1880s, four sporting dailies competed in the UK for a growing market, and weekly publications targeted both general and specialist readerships. The new sporting public was also targeted by the established dailies, which, by 1900, offered regular and increasing sports pages, and by the Sunday papers, which brought Saturday's actions into the homes of the fans.

Specialist sports publications have had sustained success in Italy and France. The Italian *Corriere dello Sport* and *La Gazzetta dello Sport* have survived into the web age; in France, *L'Equipe* continues to have a huge profile in sports promotion as well as coverage. In the USA, *Sports Illustrated* sells 3 million copies a week, with 23 million adult readers (including 5 million women). The print success in the UK in the 1990s was the sports sections of the quality press. But the print media have come under siege from the extending reach of broadcast and new media.

Social scientists point to the globalization, digitization, and marketization of sports-media culture, a dismantling of a paternalistic media system and its replacement with a more commercially driven and demand-led system. The chase for profitable new or old niche markets of fans/viewers, and for unprecedentedly large worldwide audiences for the highest-profile events, has created a lucrative global sports-media industry. ESPN showed a minority of English Premier League soccer games in season 2010–11, but it got into the pockets and handbags of iPhone and Android owners, relaying goals and scores within minutes to those willing to pay a modest subscription.

## Top media events

### Global TV viewing figures for selected events
*2009*

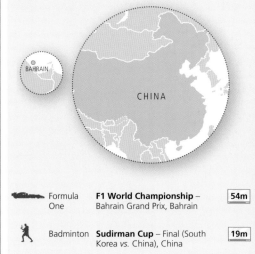

| | | |
|---|---|---|
| Formula One | **F1 World Championship** – Bahrain Grand Prix, Bahrain | 54m |
| Badminton | **Sudirman Cup** – Final (South Korea *vs.* China), China | 19m |

Huge global audiences are created by the televizing of live sports events, although the number watching may be affected by the team or player involved, and the time-zone in which the event takes place. Superstar performances, such as Michael Phelps swimming in Rome, Usain Bolt running in Berlin, and Roger Federer playing at Wimbledon, generate huge interest. This level of audience keeps the broadcasters queuing for rights, and the advertisers buying up primetime exposure.

## The rising price of Olympic coverage
**Revenue from sale of broadcasting rights**

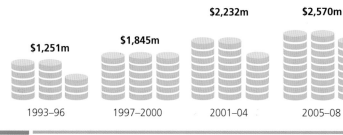

| | | | |
|---|---|---|---|
| $1,251m | $1,845m | $2,232m | $2,570m |
| 1993–96 | 1997–2000 | 2001–04 | 2005–08 |

## Where events were watched
*2009*

- highest proportion of population viewing
- host country

UEFA Champions League Final

| | | |
|---|---|---|
| Soccer | **UEFA Champions League** – Final (Barcelona *vs.* Manchester United) Italy | 109m |
| Athletics | **IAAF World Athletics Championships** – Men's 100 Metres Final, Germany | 33m |
| Tennis | **Wimbledon Lawn Tennis Championships** – Men's Singles Final, (Roger Federer *vs.* Andy Roddick), UK | 29m |
| Motor Cycling | **MotoGP World Championship** – Italy | 19m |
| Cycling | **Tour de France (Stage 20)** – Provence, France | 18m |
| Ice Hockey | **IIHF World Championship** – Final (Russia *vs.* Canada), Switzerland | 17m |
| Handball | **Men's World Handball Championships** – Final (France *vs.* Croatia), Croatia | 17m |
| Cricket | **ICC World Twenty20** – Final (Sri Lanka *vs.* Pakistan), UK | 13m |
| Skiing | **FIS World Alpine Skiing Championships** – Men's Slalom, Val D'Isère, France | 13m |
| Swimming | **World Aquatics Championships** – Men's 100 Metres Butterfly Final, Italy | 12m |
| Cricket | **Indian Premier League** – Final (Deccan Chargers *vs.* Royal Challengers Bangalore), played in South Africa for security reasons | 11m |

The presence of Michael Phelps at the World Aquatic Championships boosted its viewing figures.

| | | |
|---|---|---|
| American Football | **NFL Super Bowl XLIII** (Pittsburgh Steelers *vs.* Arizona Cardinals), USA | 106m |
| Baseball | **World Baseball Classic** – Final (Japan *vs.* South Korea), USA | 27m |
| Baseball | **MLB World Series** – Game 6 (Philadelphia Phillies *vs.* New York Yankees), USA | 26m |
| Basketball | **NBA finals** – Game 5 (Los Angeles Lakers *vs.* Orlando Magic), USA | 26m |
| Golf | **US Masters** – Final Day, Augusta, USA | 21m |
| NASCAR | **Daytona 500**, USA | 16m |
| Ice Hockey | **Stanley Cup Final** – Game 7 (Pittsburgh Penguins *vs.* Detroit Red Wings), USA | 12m |

**$908m**

**Amount agreed by consortium in 2008 for TV rights to Indian Premier League**

NFL Super Bowl XLIII

F1 World Championship

IAAF World Athletics Championships

Wimbledon Lawn Tennis Championships

# SPONSORSHIP

Sponsorship and global TV coverage have transformed the modern sporting event, turning international competitions into branding opportunities for corporate sponsors. The association of sports stars with a particular product is not new, and in the early history of modern sports many individuals had endorsement deals for clothes or personal products such as hair cream. But as the media expanded its global reach during the second half of the 20th century, marketing through sporting events became an even more lucrative industry.

Coca-Cola was a pioneering exponent of this form of marketing, ripe for recruitment into the expanding football market. When Brazilian Dr João Havelange won the presidency of La Fédération Internationale de Football Association (FIFA) in 1974, his organization had virtually no budget for the implementation of his manifesto. Aided by Adidas boss of the time, Horst Dassler, FIFA contracted Coca-Cola (a veteran of 1928 Olympics and 1950 World Cup advertising) in a worldwide deal that transformed the economics of sports mega-events.

A golden triangle of sports, television, and sponsor was established, emphasizing exclusivity and a partnership role for the sponsor. The UEFA Champions League in European football moved to a select list of just six partners at the end of the 21st century's first decade: Dutch drinks giant Heineken, German financial services Unicredit, US car manufacturer Ford, US-based credit company MasterCard, and – a double here for leading Japanese conglomerate – both Sony and Playstation. The FIFA World Cup also had six such partners, including Sony. The International Olympic Committee, during the global economic recession of 2008–10, looked more volatile in its sponsor partnerships: three North American-based companies – Johnson & Johnson (health care and pharmaceuticals), John Hancock/Manulife (financial services), and Kodak (film/electronics) – ended their association with the IOC in that period.

Nevertheless, enough companies with the capacity to buy in to the exclusive partnership role continue to pay huge sums for association with the biggest profile events: more than two weeks, across three weekends, for the Summer Olympics; a full month of extended exposure at the men's FIFA World Cup, or in the cycling classic the Tour de France. The profile of a new brand or product can be dramatically enhanced by effective association, as Formula 1's Red Bull motor-racing team can confirm. As

There is nothing subtle about the advertising at the Tour de France.

## Olympic sponsorship

TOP (The Olympic Programme) sponsorship has, along with broadcasting revenue, funded the Olympic Games since the 1980s. In return for an average $72 million each, the partner sponsors in TOP VII (2005–08) got "exclusive global marketing rights and opportunities within a designated product or service category", as the IOC put it. This included partnerships with the IOC, and with national Olympic committees and teams, as well as organizing committees of the Summer and Winter Games.

> The Olympic Games are one of the most effective marketing platforms in the world, reaching billions of people in over 200 countries and territories throughout the world.
> IOC website, sponsorship section

**Amount paid by partner sponsors to The Olympic Programme** *1993–2008*

| | |
|---|---|
| 1993–96 | $279m |
| 1997–2000 | $579m |
| 2001–04 | $663m |
| 2005–08 | $866m |

# The golden triangle

The flow of money and other benefits between the points of the triangle has enriched organizations and individuals, boosted media markets and established global brands.

**TV**

raised profile

increased viewing figures

money

money

**SPONSORS**

marketing rights • logos on official literature
tickets • kudos associated with high-quality event

**SPORTS EVENTS ORGANIZATIONS, ATHLETES AND PLAYERS**

## An un-free market

People buying FIFA World Cup tickets buy more than the right to watch a live football game; they also surrender the opportunity to exercise consumer choice. FIFA partners and sponsors are granted not just wide exposure but exclusive marketing rights.

Visa's status as a FIFA partner for the World Cup 2010 ensured that it was the "preferred" payment system for many services, and the only accepted way of paying for items purchased inside the stadiums. Fans were not permitted to bring drink or food into the stadiums, where sponsors Budweiser and Coca-Cola had the monopoly on expensively priced beer and soft-drink sales.

Heavy-handed protection of its partners' and sponsors' interests by FIFA officials included the expulsion from Johannesburg's Soccer City of 36 Dutch and South African women sporting orange mini-dresses adorned with tiny hemline labels reading "Bavaria beer". The women were ejected from the Holland–Denmark game, threatened with arrest and jail sentences, and a FIFA spokesperson confirmed that "ambush marketing" was a criminal offence in South Africa, and prohibited by "the stadium code of conduct and ticketing terms and conditions".

## Value of sponsorship

South Korean company Hyundai has no doubts about the value of sport sponsorship, reporting "impressive results" for its investment in the 2006 World Cup. Its name and brand were transmitted to a cumulative TV audience estimated at 34 billion, and it had the highest recognition of all sponsors by fans at the FIFA Fan Fest. At South Africa 2010 this was reaffirmed by the fleets of Hyundai coaches, limousines and vehicles that dominated the sites and venues of the World Cup.

**Increased brand awareness of Hyundai following its investment in 2006 Football World Cup** *2006*

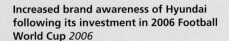
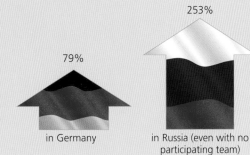

79%

in Germany

253%

in Russia (even with no participating team)

"Football sponsorship is ... perhaps one of the most favorable tools in increasing the company's image to become a top tier automotive brand.

Corporate marketing division

# CONSUMING SPORTS

The sports product is bought and experienced in a variety of ways by modern media audiences and fans. The immediate experience of being there – the spectator focused intensely upon the event – was traditionally linked to reading about the action and the build-up to the next game – a rhythm of fandom akin to the episodes of a soap opera. Radio and television transformed this by bringing the live action to the fan, a more distant experience in which people are engaging with the event but with no direct influence upon it. Today, with global transmission, and non-stop coverage on TV and internet, millions around the world can identify 24/7 with their chosen sports.

Following sports can create strong subcultures that give positive identities to members, at varying levels of commitment and intensity. But there is also a dark side. Sports-spectating can be voyeuristic. And it can bring out the worst in male fans. A woman in Buffalo, New York, recalled how her partner reacted after a defeat for his home team: "…the first beating happened after the first trip to the Super Bowl. He lost a large sum and beat me up bad." The "cultural drinking fountain" of televized sports can spell fear.

The new media age has provided fans with expanded opportunities to consume sports. They can fantasize about their expertise and influence; insert themselves into the play; and get close up to their favourite sports star in the electronic arts of the computer game – a new, virtual sports world.

The biggest football clubs in Europe draw fans – and consumers – from around the world. Premier League players' names roll off the tongues of children in remote villages, creating a bizarre shared language between locals and travellers.

## Sports subcultures

Sports encourage strong and enduring fan subcultures, in which following the game of your choice is an authentic lifestyle decision, matched by the commitment of time and resources. For some, their chosen sport is a primary source of identity; others relate to the subculture only from the margins.

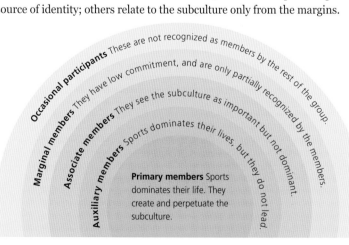

**Occasional participants** These are not recognized as members by the rest of the group.

**Marginal members** They have low commitment, and are only partially recognized by the members.

**Associate members** They see the subculture as important but not dominant.

**Auxiliary members** Sports dominates their lives, but they do not lead.

**Primary members** Sports dominates their life. They create and perpetuate the subculture.

## Fan types

**Traditional supporters** – those with a long-standing commitment to, and personal investment in, one club or team.
**Followers** – those who form links with other fans with an interest in different aspects of the game.
**Consumer fans** – those who follow a particular club, show brand-loyalty and consume club merchandise even though they may see a game only on television or the internet.

Fan, flâneur, or consumer? South Africans dressed in their national colours for a game between New Zealand and Slovakia at the 2010 Football World Cup.

**Flâneurs** – the modern urban stroller, with market-dominated relationships to the club or clubs, constantly searching for a new look in a couture aesthetic rather than a grounded commitment to any single club or legacy.

## Cheerleading

Cheerleading was organized in US universities in the late 19th century, when all-male groups urged on college football teams. In 1948 a US National Cheerleaders' Association was founded, and competitive cheerleading soon claimed to be a competitive sport in its own right.

Cheerleading is a stage for the reaffirmation of sexual stereotypes, as crowds of mainly males watch the young females performing.

# Virtual Sports

## Fantasy Football

Fantasy football leagues bring the fan into the imagined world of the manager or coach. First formulated in the USA as early as 1962, the form took off in regional newspapers in the late 1980s, and boomed in newspapers – national and regional – in the 1990s. The web and the internet have widened participation, and male fans in particular choose to play in their own time and space, whilst feeling part of a wider virtual subculture of networked participants. Sports management games such as *Championship Manager* bring out the passion of the fan.

> " You do get very emotionally involved in the game, and feel like you are managing a real team, and you want to interact with your players more ... tell them to pull their socks up ... their performance was rubbish or praise them. "
>
> 29-year-old Dean, a PR consultant

## Computer Games

Leading games company Electronic Arts (EA) produces games based on real-world sports leagues, venues, events, and players' reproductions in lifelike graphics. Sports fans flock to buy them, thereby putting money in the pockets not just of EA, but of the teams from whom EA buys the franchise. For the American National Football League, sports games were rivalling replica shirts as the main source of merchandizing income as early as 2002. EA's 2010 profits were boosted by sales of *2010 FIFA World Cup South Africa*, released six months before the event, and promising fans the opportunity to experience the World Cup "in spectacular detail" – including the thrill of that moment when they score a goal for their country.

**$97m**
The amount spent on sports-based computer games in North America in 2009

**8**
of the 20 best-selling video games in North America in 2009 were sports-based

## Wii

Wii allows fans to mimic real games. A hand-held pointing device – the Wii Remote wireless controller – detects movement in three directions, and the "player" of Wii Sports can compete with onscreen opponents at his/her selected sport, from baseball to tennis, boxing to golf. Participants can not only play matches against real or virtual opponents, but can also monitor their own "fitness" levels.

As of December 2009, over 509 million copies of Wii games had been sold. Apart from Wii Sports, which comes bundled with the console, the biggest seller is Wii Play, which includes duck-shoots and table tennis, and has sold 27 million copies.

**71m**
The number of Wii consoles sold 2006 – mid-2010

The Wii generation is reported to suffer from psychological and physical maladies ranging from repetitive stress injury to addiction and sleep disorder.

# MERCHANDISING

Sports sell. For every social reformer for whom sports are a means of character building, there is an entrepreneur who knows that fortunes can be made by trading on the image of the sportsman or sportswoman. Equipment and kit make millions, and the sports goods industry lives off the dynamic of merchandising. It is as if there is a magical relationship between the image and skill of a top player and the performance potential of the ordinary individual: buy the same racket as Rafael Nadel and what can stop you?

Albert Spalding manufactured for, as well as administered, US baseball in its expansionist phase. The ball manufacturer Gilbert, whose goods were used by the boys of Rugby School in the early 19th century, was still doing business at the end of the following century, immortalized in Clint Eastwood's focus on the classic brand in the movie *Invictus*.

Apparel on the tennis court could make or break company profiles, and women's fashions in the 1920s were challenged by players capturing a spirit of individualism and modernity, but also presaging the consumerism of the new international era. Fred Perry, English tennis star of the 1930s, might have been snubbed by the Wimbledon establishment, but the Fred Perry brand was a pioneer in the casual clothing revolution.

The merchandising of events, teams and players is a lucrative business.

**The number of Adidas Jabulani footballs sold during 2010**

Micro-markets catering for specialist sports are hugely profitable, especially when cheap labour is harnessed to production for rich markets. But the biggest demand is for "trite" sports goods – the "leisure" football, the t-shirt with endless uses, the sports shoe for any surface – for which there are macro-markets. Fans buying tickets for the 2010 football World Cup were urged to register with a "FIFA club". Within days of Spain's victory, they received unsolicited emails offering "Spain Adidas Champions T-shirts". Adidas did €1.5 billion of business as a result of its sponsorship of the 2010 World Cup – 25 percent more than during the 2006 World Cup. Every World Cup, it creates a newly named football. Each tournament, sales soar.

## Popular pressure – Honduras

The profits of providers such as Adidas and Nike continue to be underpinned by workers paid negligible wages by ruthless employers.

In January 2009, 1,800 workers at two Nike subcontractors – Hugger and Vision Tex – lost their jobs, and received none of the severance pay due under Honduran employment law. United Students Against Sweatshops mobilized public opinion. The University of Wisconsin, Madison terminated its licensing deal with Nike, and Cornell threatened to do the same if Nike did not resolve the dispute.

Nike agreed, in July 2010, to make $1.54 million available as a workers' relief fund. "This may be a watershed moment", said Scott Nova, executive director of the Worker's Rights Consortium, comprising 186 US universities that monitor factories making college-logo apparel.

## Three Steps to Heaven

The Nike swoosh is marketed brilliantly. First, sign up your sports star for celebrity grooming. Second, destroy the opposition by taking over or inaugurating sports events. Third, as Naomi Klein puts it, "brand like mad". Nike revolutionized corporate branding with its innovative Michael Jordan ads, sport's first rock 'n' roll videos.

Branding reaches everywhere. The smallest objects, marked by the simplest of logos, can make huge profits.

**replica football jerseys sold by Adidas in first half of 2010, double the 2006 figure**

## Labour pains

As children look for soft and makeshift balls with which to play barefoot on the rough streets of African villages and townships, and in the favelas on the edge of Rio de Janeiro, the big shoemakers and apparel manufacturers continue to carve up the world's markets. Sports goods producers balance their ethics and consciences against profits as they commission manufacturing processes from ruthless subsidiaries with no qualms about the conditions and remuneration of workers in the labour markets of the less developed world.

### Stitched up in India

In the Meerut and Jalandhar districts of India, children and families have been producing footballs for less than 5 rupees, which are then sold for more than 100 rupees. Sharp needles and knives used to stitch the balls have left the children with wounds that often go untreated, and can turn septic. Working in poor light, children's eyesight deteriorates. Although reports emerged of this exploitation in the mid-1990s, home-based production has continued, beyond the reach of regulation. Many children (especially girls) have been deprived of the opportunity to go to school, although the situation has been improved in recent years by the efforts of NGOs.

**School attendance of stitchers aged 6–17 years surveyed in Meerut** *2008*

- ■ attend school and work
- ■ only work

| | Girls | Boys |
|---|---|---|
| attend school and work | 57% | 43% |
| only work | 19% | 9% |

> ❝ I have been stitching footballs for as long as I can remember. My hands are constantly in pain. It feels like they are burning. ❞
>
> Geeta, aged between 10 and 12 years old

### Pakistan

In Sialkot, in north-east Pakistan, 2,000 factories have employed 300,000 workers making goods for Western markets, including footballs for Adidas. The city has thrived for the entrepreneurs, its $1.3 billion in exports even generating its own international airport. Employers have denied that they have employed child labour, and continued to produce footballs at a seventh the cost of Western counterparts.

### West Java, Indonesia

Hamdani worked for six years for an Adidas supplier in West Java. He and 32 workmates were dismissed after striking for better wages. For five years he has been unemployed, despite pledges from Adidas that he would be helped in getting employment elsewhere.

Hamdani asks the world's consumers not to be "influenced by the sports shoe advertisements that are all about luxury, wealth, strength.... Instead, try to look behind the scenes at the workers who make those shoes and see the human face of production."

### Vietnam

Consultants Ernst & Young visited one of Nike's subcontractor factories in Bien Hoa City in 1997, where 9,200 workers, many of them young women, produced 400,000 pairs of athletic shoes each month. Workers were found to be exposed to the carcinogen toulane, which could harm the liver, kidneys, and the central nervous system. More than three-quarters of employees had respiratory problems. The Korean owner of the subcontractor paid the workers the equivalent of $10 for a 65-hour week. This was just one of 150 factories working for Nike in Asia and employing 450,000 workers.

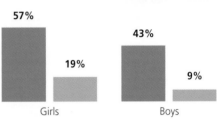

PAKISTAN

Sialkot

Jalandhar

Meerut

INDIA

VIETNAM

Bien Hoa City

INDONESIA

West Java

# GAMBLING

In 1992, US federal legislation, the Professional and Amateur Sports Protection Act, outlawed betting on sports. Senator Bill Bradley argued that sports betting converts "sports from wholesome athletic entertainment into a vehicle for gambling" and raises "people's suspicions about point-shaving and game-fixing." In 2003, Nevada was the only state in which sports betting was legal, though by early 2010 Delaware, Oregon, and Montana had over-ridden federal law and permitted parlay betting (on two or more sporting events), so releasing the "magic bullet" of tax revenues from gambling income. Online gambling is technically illegal in most of the USA, although millions participate on "off-shore" sites.

In Europe, gambling plays a major role in sports. It is an established leisure pursuit, and part of the social reality of the sports experience. Gambling is also a potential source of sports finance, as demonstrated by the way in which funds from the UK lottery have been redistributed to sporting projects and individuals throughout the country.

There is concern, however, about the impact of gambling on sports. Match-fixing threatens the basic integrity of the sporting contest. Football referees in Germany and Poland have been suspended and prosecuted, and China's football fans turn to televized coverage of foreign clubs and leagues, rejecting manipulated results of their own competition. In the UK, a 2010 government panel urged sports authorities to treat the "issue of integrity ... in relation to betting ... with the same importance as they treat other serious issues affecting their sport, e.g. doping." An unfortunate illustration of the power of gambling to corrupt occurred later in the year, when several Pakistani cricketers were accused of bowling no balls or of manipulating scoring rates – aspects of the game on which "spot-bets" could be laid – in a Test Match against England.

The social side of betting is important. The dynamic of the wager and the meaning of the bet are about more than economics. Placing a bet or raising the stakes are forms of social display. Most punters lose, but a win can spark spontaneous, common jubilation, the triumph celebrated collectively.

People gamble in different ways. Some have the occasional bet, or "flutter"; for others, addictive wagering can be ruinous. For the professional, a rational approach is a potential investment. In 2007, almost half of the US population, and more than two-thirds of people in the UK, bet on something. Hotbeds of gambling around the world also include Australia, South Africa, and the Indian subcontinent.

## Sports betting

### Most globally successful licensed gambling operators, 2008

| | |
|---|---|
| Gala Coral | €1,000bn |
| Ladbrokes | €900bn |
| William Hill | €700bn |
| Betfair | €180bn |
| Paddy Power | €170bn |
| Unibet | €90bn |
| bwin | €24bn |
| bet-at-home | €24bn |

### Gross winnings from global sports betting 2004–08, 2009–12 (projected)

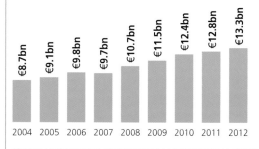

| 2004 | 2005 | 2006 | 2007 | 2008 | 2009 | 2010 | 2011 | 2012 |
|---|---|---|---|---|---|---|---|---|
| €8.7bn | €9.1bn | €9.8bn | €9.7bn | €10.7bn | €11.5bn | €12.4bn | €12.8bn | €13.3bn |

### Global online sports betting 2004–08, 2009–12 (projected)

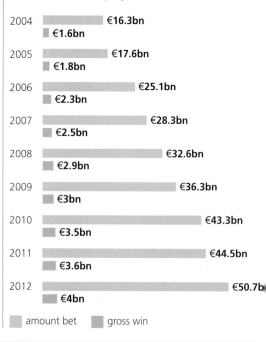

| 2004 | €16.3bn | €1.6bn |
|---|---|---|
| 2005 | €17.6bn | €1.8bn |
| 2006 | €25.1bn | €2.3bn |
| 2007 | €28.3bn | €2.5bn |
| 2008 | €32.6bn | €2.9bn |
| 2009 | €36.3bn | €3bn |
| 2010 | €43.3bn | €3.5bn |
| 2011 | €44.5bn | €3.6bn |
| 2012 | €50.7bn | €4bn |

■ amount bet  ■ gross win

### Global gambling market, 2009

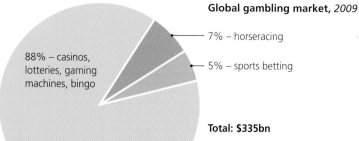

88% – casinos, lotteries, gaming machines, bingo

7% – horseracing

5% – sports betting

Total: $335bn

# Power of prohibition

## Sponsorship gains

Football-shirt sponsorship in Europe's Big 5 leagues (England, France, Germany, Italy, Spain) plus the USA totalled €512 million in 2008, of which almost 15 percent came from gambling companies – even with around half of that market prohibited to private gambling operators. Austria-based online betting company bwin is a major player in the sponsorship game. Where bwin stays in the game in Italy and Spain, the rich get richer. This is not the case in the more highly regulated France and Germany, where deals with bwin and Gamebookers for their logos to appear on shirts have had to be cancelled following court rulings.

**Value of advertising bwin on team shirts**

to AC Milan

**€75m** over four seasons from 2006/7

to Real Madrid

**€45m** over three years from 2007/8

**Status of advertising by gambling companies at sporting events in Europe,** *2009*

- ■ prohibited
- ■ permitted
- ░ no data

 **35%** of English Premiership teams were sponsored by gambling operators in 2009/10 season, which was broadcast to TV audiences in 200 countries

## UK National Lottery funding

Lottery funding directed to sports is used to support grassroots projects, thereby widening sporting opportunities for all. But it is also used to boost elite performance, and has been crucial in raising the success of the UK's athletes on the world stage. It has paid for equipment, facilities, coaches, physiotherapy, and enabled them to focus full-time on their training. It is ironic that money from the pockets of some of the country's most disadvantaged people, themselves pursuing a dream of wealth and fame, effectively creates the time and environment to enable others to realize their ambitions.

 **€4.5bn** The amount of UK National Lottery funding distributed in support of nearly 50,000 sporting projects 1995–2009

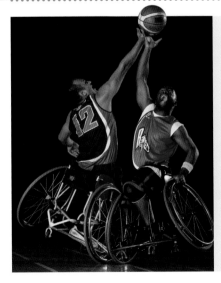

Wheelchair basketball, one of the many sports supported by Sport England, which distributes funds from the UK National Lottery.

# SPORTS TOURISM

For someone active in a particular sport, the expanding global holiday industry, with its emphasis on outdoor adventures and focused individual activity, presents many opportunities. Sports tourism covers a multitude of possible activities, destinations and sites, from white-water rafting to skiing and snowboarding; from golf courses to tennis training camps and self-organized cycling breaks; from the Olympics and football World Cup to city-based marathons.

Estimates have put the interest in (though not necessarily the take-up of) sports activity holidays at between 10 and 20 percent of the holidaying population of affluent nations. This is a lucrative potential market, and both commercial operators and the public sector have looked to sports for forms of economic development or regional regeneration. Mountain ranges from Bulgaria to the Rockies, from Scandinavia to the Pyrenees, have been transformed into playgrounds of the rich. Climbers, skiers, walkers and cyclists provide work throughout the year for what were previously rural-based communities. Outdoor sports enthusiasts have been targeted by regions keen to complement traditional industries such as winemaking. Landscapes have been adapted, even transformed, as in the case of Vallée and Lac du Salagou (L'Hérault, France), a haven for sailors, windsurfers, mountain-bikers, hang-gliders, and walkers, created in 1968 and attracting tourists to an economically declining region.

Sports tourists come in different levels of intensity and commitment, from the casual to the connoisseur. Specialist providers chase the latter, and the growth of some niche markets is fuelled by consumers seeking increasingly challenging experiences in their chosen activity – to enhance their skills, as well as simply enjoy themselves. The skilled consumers on the ski slopes, the golf course or the tennis court are valued returning customers.

Much sports tourism is by its nature seasonal. Snowdon, the highest mountain in Wales, attracts over 340,000 walkers from April to September, but is effectively closed for the winter. The most ambitious developers, though, defy seasons and the rhythms of nature. Dubai, in the United Arab Emirates, markets itself as the "Sports Capital of the Middle East", where the season never ends.

## Pros and cons of sport tourism

Potential positives include:
- new uses for land, employment
- strengthening of national heritage, identity, community spirit
- international profiling, as visitors get to know foreign people and their culture
- development and improvement of the built infrastructure and the natural environment

Potential negatives:
- erosion of traditional communities, endangering the balance of a local economy
- contribution to the loss of cultural identity and heritage
- tensions between hosts and visitors
- environmental threats

The noise and erosion caused by automotive vehicles in natural environments can adversely impact the experience of other users.

**60m**
number of visits made to US ski slopes in 2009/10 An increase of 5% on 2008–09

**Water sports**
Beautiful beaches, and the desire to enjoy water sports, brings tourists flocking to the Caribbean, but the employment benefits for local people tend to be limited, and most of the profits are retained by the business investors.

## Types of sports tourism
**Extent to which sports are part of the experience**

| Supplementary | Sports participation | Sports training | Sports events | Luxury sports |
|---|---|---|---|---|
| The visitor may play a sport spontaneously or casually while on holiday, but the choice of destination is not defined by the sport. | Holidays aimed at fans and amateur players, focusing on sporting activities, and including visits to famous sports facilities and museums. | An opportunity for high-performance athletes to improve their skills out of their normal environment, including training sessions in high-quality facilities. | Organized holidays to specific events, ranging from small-scale, specialist events to international meets and mega-events. | Socially exclusive activity in top-of-the-range hotels, such as elite ski resorts, country-house golf, salmon-fishing, or corporate hospitality at the Monaco Grand Prix. |

# Striking a delicate balance

**Barcelona Summer Olympics**
The 1992 Olympics appear to have boosted the Catalan city's profile in the international tourist market.

Donations from visitors have enabled further work to be carried out on Gaudi's unfinished Sagrada Familia.

**Proportion of tourists from outside Europe**

| 1990 | 2000 |
|------|------|
| 17%  | 29%  |

**Artificial snow**
More than 5,000 snow cannons on the Alpine pistes use huge amounts of water diverted from Europe's major rivers to enhance the experience of the paying public.

**Climbing Mt. Everest**
The world's highest mountain has been used as a garbage dump by the hundreds of climbers who test themselves each year on its slopes. Several missions have been launched to clean its slopes, but the problem will only be solved by all mountaineers behaving responsibly.

**Mallorcan cyclists**
Serious amateurs and competitive professionals populate the roads and the accommodation of the Mediterranean island in winter and early spring in an example of successful niche-marketing of the needs of the specialist sports tourist.

**Sensitive skiing**
All-pedestrian developments such as Avoriaz in the French Alps are more sensitive to the environment than most ski resorts.

**Climbing Mt. Kilimanjaro**
Erosion of soil, burnt or chopped vegetation, and disappearing wildlife are the price to pay for this human adventure, though eco-tourism initiatives provide dependable local employment.

**Number of climbers a year**

| 1950s | 1990s  | 2010s  |
|-------|--------|--------|
| 1,000 | 11,000 | 35,000 |

**Eco-tourism**
Active vacations in remote locations, such as the Amazon or Patagonia, need to be carefully managed in order to ensure that the local environment and economy benefit. Accommodation built using traditional materials and methods is just one aspect of this.

**Golf courses**
North Africa and the Gulf States are attracting golfing tourists in a relentlessly expanding international market. Environmentalists point to golf's contribution to the destruction of delicate eco-systems, and the over-use of limited water, but golf continues to grow.

**Coral reefs**
While divers provide a valuable source of income for local economies, corals and bottom-dwelling organisms are often disturbed, and sometimes physically damaged, at regularly dived sites.

**America's Cup**
New Zealand prepared for its defence of the America's Cup in 1999 by redeveloping an underused and polluted water-basin in the capital city Auckland at a cost of $NZ60m. Creating this "America's Cup Village" and staging the race had some impact on the marine eco-system, but was considered worthwhile for the international profile of the event and the boost to the local economy of millions of dollars.

# 4

## COUNTRY PROFILES

# COUNTRY PROFILES

These country snapshots give some indication of the place of sports in their national contexts, and in relation to international sporting encounters and competition. The benefits of the boom in the global profile of the biggest sports remain unevenly distributed, as many of the case studies covered in the previous section demonstrate. But, while the international dimensions of sports frame their modern form in the media, the regional dimensions of competitions also allow smaller or less well-off countries to compete at an appropriate level. Country profiles are valuable ways of showing these variations, and of considering the political, economic, and cultural influences that have shaped the sporting life and achievements of a nation.

In doing this, we have not attempted to cover every country. Football – both watching and playing – is the most popular sport in the world, and many argue that basketball runs it a close second. So, comprehensive coverage would involve telling the same story over and over again. And countries with similar political and social profiles can have much in common in terms of sport, so to relate the post-Soviet history of every new or restored East European nation, or to cover every Caribbean country, would run the risk of repetition. We have therefore made representative selections, and in the case of the Caribbean, covered the (British) West Indies in a single entry, and the striking distinctiveness of Cuba in a separate entry. Generally, the selection takes a view of the world as it is organized by sport's governing bodies, with what are often called continental confederations: Africa, the Americas, Asia, Europe, and Oceania. In all, the 77 countries covered here convey a useful picture of the global trends and national idiosyncrasies of sports culture in the smallest, poorest societies, as well as in the leading economies of the world.

The profiles are also informed by personal observation and acquired local knowledge. We authors have, between us, visited more than 50 of the countries, discussing the sports of individual countries with sports administrators and sports academics, and sometimes sampling the sports as participants and onlookers. This is not to claim that we can only write about what we observe and do; any such claim would be close to denying the possibility of history and comparative studies. But it is to say that being in the crowd, or talking to the shapers of the sporting life of a country, can provide hugely valuable insights into the cultural value of a sport, or sporting institution. Sitting in the Skydome high above the playing area of Stanford University's American football stadium, watching the college football squad in training, and then seeing the comparatively minor scale of the Stanford soccer first team as it plays its early evening match in front of just a few hundred enthusiasts, is a vivid reminder of the institutional and economic power of the grid-iron game.

There is then an inevitable element of the personal in these profiles. There are no reliable data for country-by-country participation, so many of the entries are shaped by what has caught the eye of the author. Other writers might pick out a different feature, another sporting practice. But the personal can be objective, not merely subjective. And the profiles concentrate upon what the atlas sets out to demonstrate – the who, where, what, and why of our sporting lives. In particular, they reaffirm the importance of understanding the interrelated dimensions – historical, political, economic – that have made sport such a significant cultural force in the world.

**Alan Tomlinson and Lincoln Allison**

• • • • • • • • • • • • • • • • • • • • • • • • • • • • • • • • • • • • • • • • • • • •

## ⬎ Afghanistan

Isolation, violent conflict and traditionalism have all played a part in restricting the Afghan impact on global sport. The most longstanding sporting tradition in the country is generically known as *buzkashi*, and consists of men on horseback using a variety of methods of seizing animal heads and carcasses and getting them to a goal: loosely, we might say that if polo is hockey on horseback, *buzkashi* is rugby.

The Taliban government in Afghanistan between 1996 and 2001 was one of the last in the world to prove actively hostile to most forms of modern sport. Women were excluded from sport, *bukhashi* was banned, and the playing of association football was restricted in a number of ways, including an interdiction on wearing modern football clothing. However, out of this period of repression there did emerge a sporting success story. Afghan cricket has grown in stature largely because of the increase of population movement between the country and Pakistan. The national team has won a number of tournaments, including a victory in the 2010 Asian Cricket Council Trophy, a competition that excludes the four test-match playing countries in Asia.

## ↘ Argentina

Known for its football expertise, and winner of two football World Cups, Argentina also excels in polo, has produced world-class tennis champions and motor-racing drivers and, at Beijing 2008, gold-medal-winning field hockey teams. The Argentinean elite learned football well from the British, and replaced them as Olympic champions in 1924. A year before that, in an example of the nationalization of the sports culture of a colonizing elite, a British Polo Association of the River Plate was replaced by the Asociación de Polo de Argentina. The country has been the uninterrupted world polo champion since 1949.

The contrast between polo, with its expensive upkeep of horses and limited number of players, and football, which is accessible to the poorest of shanty-town kids, conveys the extremes of privilege and poverty that shape sporting opportunity even in a less economically developed nation. Other sporting legacies of British residents include men's and women's cricket, rugby union, and golf. The Argentinean national rugby side finished third in the 2007 Rugby World Cup, and Angel Cabrera won both the US Open in 2007, and the US Masters in 2009.

Within its region, Argentina is a highly competitive sporting nation, fourth after the USA, Canada, and Cuba in the all-time rankings of the Pan American Games. In the Olympics, it has won most of its gold medals in boxing, though mainly between 1928 and 1948. In the 1950s, the country's president Juan Perón, declared *pato* – a cross between polo and basketball, once played with a live duck rather than a ball – the country's national sport, but the more orthodox form of polo sustained its profile within the culture of the nation's elite.

## ↘ Australia

For a country with a population of around 22 million, Australia has an impressive record in international competition, including at the Summer Olympics, at which it has competed since 1896. When hosting its second Summer Games, at Sydney in 2000, it finished fourth in the medal table, behind the superpowers of the USA, Russia, and China, and above the combined strength of the re-united post-Cold War Germany. At Athens 2004, it replicated this success, though at Beijing 2008 it slipped to sixth, behind the resurgent Great Britain, and Germany. Australia also excels in

an alternative Olympic medal table compiled, unsurprisingly, by the Australian Bureau of Statistics, in which gold medals are related to the country's population. On that reckoning, it was third behind the Bahamas and Norway, with the USA and China a distant 34th and 53rd respectively. Australia's traditional strengths in Olympic disciplines include track and field, and, especially, swimming. The latter has produced legendary performers, such as Dawn Fraser in the 1960s, and Ian Thorpe in the early years of the new century.

Much of Australia's success from the 1980s onwards has been attributed to the foundation in 1981 of the Australian Institute of Sport (AIS), the country's own version of Soviet-style central planning for sports performance and competitive excellence. A lowly 32nd in the medal table at Montreal 1976, with no gold medals, the government-backed AIS harnessed coaching and scientific support to targeted sports (including non-Olympic ones that had competitive international profiles), and has been hailed as a world-leading model for the transformation of an underachieving competitive sports system. The country's most popular sports also include several non-Olympic ones, at which Australia also excels internationally: netball, cricket, rugby union, rugby league, and rugby sevens (though this will feature in future Games). Australian Rules football is the country's most nationally distinctive sport.

## ↘ Austria

The Austro-Hungarian Empire generated a court and a military establishment that supported particular sporting practices such as riding and shooting, and a remaining legacy of this is the famous Spanish Riding School sustained by the Austrian army. In the more democratic Austria of the 1920s, Vienna was a centre of cultural life in which sports were embraced as an element of that culture. Winter sports flourished, and Austria has remained famous for its world-beating Alpine skiers. The Mitropa Cup for club football sides was, in part, an Austrian initiative. In the 1930s, the Austrian national football team was nicknamed the Wunderteam, and threatened to outclass all national opponents with a swift passing game, but the German occupation of Austria in 1938 led to the dissolution of the side and the integration of its most skilful players into the German team for the World Cup. Pre-World War II, Austria won four Olympic gold medals in weight-lifting. Post-war, it has produced more outstanding Alpine and Nordic skiers, motor-racing champion Nikki Lauda, and, choosing bodybuilding over football in his youth, Arnold Schwarzenegger, 38th governor of California a third of a century on from becoming Mr Universe in 1968.

## ⬇ Bahrain

An island country in the Persian Gulf, Bahrain has coasts and shores perfect for scuba diving and snorkelling. Rich beyond the imagination of most territories or nations in the world, it has little substantive sporting pedigree. Its indigenous sporting culture comprises camel racing, and horse racing is a popular spectator event. But, with such levels of finance at its disposal, the country has sought to achieve Olympic and international success by giving citizenship to already established athletes. The country sent 15 athletes to the Beijing 2008 Games, in shooting, swimming, and track and field athletics. Rashid Ramzi, a Moroccan runner who gained Bahraini citizenship in 2002, won the 1,500 metres, but was stripped of the gold medal after testing positive for blood-boosting doping. Ethiopia and Kenya have provided world-class (nationalized) Bahrainian marathon runners.

## ⬇ Bangladesh

Bengal was considered one of the least sporting regions in British India, and lagged behind the rest of South Asia in its development of cricket. However, since East Pakistan, as it was then called, became an independent nation in 1971, its cricket has begun to catch up with that of the rest of the subcontinent. Bangladesh acquired test match status in 2000, and has gradually become more competitive since then. The other popular sports in the country are hockey, football, *kabbadi* and rugby.

## ⬇ Belgium

Sports both embody and transcend the linguistic and administrative divisions of Belgian society, which is divided into Flemish-speaking Flanders, and French-speaking Wallonia. In the capital, Brussels, German is spoken by a third official community. Sports have expressed the interests of these different communities, in, for instance, the Flemish

movement in the late 19th century and the early years of the 20th, when gymnastics and cycling were significant elements in the articulation of Flemish cultural identity. Sports also embody national integration, through bodies such as the country's single Olympic committee and the national football side.

The annual Tour of Flanders bicycle race draws more than a million spectators to the roadside, for many of whom it is a celebration of Flemish identity. But the sport also produces national heroes. Cyclist Eddy Merckx won the Tour de France five times from 1969 to 1974, and in 2000 was voted Belgium's greatest sports figure of the century. Belgium has also provided two presidents of the International Olympic Committee: Henri de Baillet-Latour (from 1925 to his death in 1942), and Dr Jacques Rogge (from 2001 to 2012/3).

## ⬇ Brazil

The world knows Brazil as the home of football, the "beautiful game". It has won the men's World Cup five times, and provides top European leagues with a continual flow of talented players. Brazil has also produced great athletes, long-distance runners for instance, and has prioritized sports in its general cultural and economic development. The men's World Cup takes place in Rio de Janeiro in 2014, the Summer Olympics two years later. Only Mexico (1968 and 1970) and Germany (1974 and 1976) have previously achieved this hosting coup. Brazil likes to portray sports as a big outdoor party, associating them with the hedonism of carnival. Connecting Copacabana Beach with the medal podium, its women have excelled in beach volleyball at the world championships and the Olympics.

Brazil has had a serious influence upon world football administration in the person of Dr João Havelange, president of FIFA from 1974 to 1998, a period in which the men's World Cup expanded, the women's World Cup was introduced, and other competitions broadened the international base of the game.

A particular Brazilian strength is in motor racing. Three Brazilian drivers have won the world Formula 1 title, from 1972 to 1991: Emerson Fittipaldi, Nelson Piquet, and Ayrton Senna. When Senna, son of a wealthy businessman and rancher, was killed in a crash in 1994, three-mile queues formed to file past his coffin in São Paulo. In Formula 1's 2010 line-up, Brazil had four drivers. In tennis, Maria Bueno represented grace and style as well as competitive strength in the tournaments of the late 1950s and the 1960s.

## ↘ Bulgaria

An established Balkan nation-state before being absorbed into the Soviet empire, Bulgaria brought with it a well-established men's football culture, influenced by enthusiasts who had established the sport in neighbouring Turkey. Bulgaria peaked at international level at the 1994 World Cup Finals in the USA, taking fourth place. During the Soviet period and before robust and systematic drug-testing began, Bulgaria was one of the top Olympic nations in medal counts of Summer Games, fearsomely effective in wrestling and weight-lifting. Its men volleyballers have been internationally competitive. In the post-Soviet period, the country has looked to expand its skiing industry and has trained high-quality biathlon competitors on its slopes.

## ↘ Cameroon

Cameroon has been one of the strongest of the emergent African football nations. At the 1990 World Cup in Italy, it shocked eventual finalists Argentina with a first-round victory, and all but matched England in a tight encounter in the quarter-finals. At the Sydney Olympics in 2000, it defeated Argentina to take the men's football gold medal. Typical of the problems faced by most African nations, though, it has not developed its full potential, with many star players earning a living in Europe, and little sustained or consistent infrastructural development of the domestic game.

## ↘ Canada

With a colonial legacy from the British Empire, Canada has cricket and rugby traditions, but its sports are really shaped by its own geo-political history, and its proximity to, and rivalry with, its neighbour the USA. Ice-hockey is a Canadian invention, and the National Hockey League straddles Canada and the USA. Canadian Football, though, is distinct from American Football. Canada boasts the world's largest rodeo, the Calgary Stampede, which attracts more than 1.2 million visitors. With a population of just 33 million, in an area constituting the second-largest country in the world in terms of land mass, Canada has also hosted two Winter Olympic games, at Calgary in 1988 and Vancouver in 2010. Sports also provide a focus for political identification, the ice hockey team the Montreal Canadiens expressing the French-Canadian identity of that province.

## ↘ Chile

Chile is 2,700 miles long, and its remarkable variety of terrain gives scope for every kind of outdoor activity including some of the world's best surfing and mountaineering. However, the country does not have an impressive record in competitive sports, having won, for example, only 13 Olympic medals in its history. Football is by far the most popular sport, with tennis in second place – the country's only two Olympic golds being for tennis at Athens in 2004. In 1962, Chile hosted the Football World Cup, and achieved its best result, third place. The national side has qualified for the final stages of the competition on seven other occasions.

## ↘ China

Many historians and contemporary commentators have stressed that the culture of China has been more hostile to sports and physical achievement than any other. The roots of this paradox go deep into Chinese history and involve rival concepts of masculinity: *wu*, incorporating military virtues and akin to Western ideas of chivalry, and *wen*, a more fastidious, scholarly ideal influenced especially by the thought of Confucius. An established historical account suggests that in Imperial China, the absolute importance of intellectual achievement for social mobility and status, encouraged by the *keju* or civil service exam, helped devalue any aspirations to physical achievement. Thus, anything we might call sports have been socially peripheral in China, though "dragon boat" racing and martial arts were the principal survivors, and table tennis (*ping pong*) was one of the few Western games to gain a popular following in 20th-century China.

Thus, for a long time the Chinese impact on international sports was minimal, particularly for a country with the largest population in the world. The People's Republic made a rather nominal appearance at the Summer Olympics in 1952, but thereafter was not represented at any games until 1980, or at a Summer Olympics until 1984. Representation was bedevilled by a diplomatic dispute with the regime in Taiwan, which also claimed to be the "Republic of China", but also by a lack of interest on the part of the ruling Communist Party.

However, Chinese leaders since the death of Mao Zedong in 1976 have prioritized sports, seeing the winning of medals, and the successful hosting of events as an effective riposte to a perceived lack of respect on the part of Western countries in particular. To this end, they have imitated Soviet practice in selecting children for early sporting training, and they have also, to a greater extent than the Soviet Union, targeted sports that are not commercial and professional sports in the West, and where there are many Olympic medals available. An overwhelming majority of Chinese gold medals in the Olympics have come in five sports: swimming, diving, weightlifting, gymnastics, and shooting. The culmination of this policy came in 2008, when China hosted the Summer Olympics, and came top of the official medal table. Even so, Chinese sports remains a very "top down" phenomenon, with very low numbers of participants and organizations, and very poor access to facilities for ordinary people.

## ↘ Côte Ivoire (Ivory Coast)

Football dominates the sporting landscape of this former French colony. As it produces footballers of a world-class level, the anomalies of global inequalities are exposed through the activism and intervention of those who have prospered in the money markets of the world game. Didier Drogba, Chelsea star of the English Premier league, has spent years, and millions of pounds fighting disease and poverty in his home nation. He funnels money from sponsorship deals with Pepsi, Nike, and Orange France into projects in the homeland that he left at the age of five. Drogba has also organized events raising millions of pounds for his foundation's cause, and in 2010, building was about to start on a £3 million hospital in Abidjan, the city of his birth.

## ↘ Croatia

Croatia had a brief existence as a Nazi puppet state between 1940 and 1944, but only became a fully independent country in 1991, when it seceded from Yugoslavia. Since then, its impact on global sports has been remarkable, particularly in football and tennis. Playing in a distinctive red and white chequered uniform, the national football team qualified for the final stages of the European Football Championship in 1996, and in the 1998 World Cup was placed third, behind France and Brazil. In tennis, arguably, the success has been even more remarkable, as the country has continuously produced high-ranking players. Goran Ivanesevic won the Wimbledon championships in 2001, and the national team won the Davis Cup in 2005. Put alongside other successes in, for instance, basketball and Alpine sports, these achievements make this small country (of fewer than 4.5 million people) one of the great per capita successes of world sports.

## ↘ Cuba

Fidel Castro, born 1926, led the 1959–60 Cuban revolution, and guided the country towards the support of the Soviet Union, in so doing moving Cuba more fully towards a communist state. This political development in turn shaped the country's sports culture. Sports were immensely important to Castro and his revolutionary philosophy, for they could enhance health, and so be part of the production of the new citizen in the new society; they could also give the country a worldwide profile in international sporting competition, particularly on the Olympian baseball diamond against the USA. Castro himself had enjoyed organized sports as a schoolboy at a Jesuit institution, and excelled in baseball, so his reform strategy was in part a form of personal evangelism. This could produce contradictions: Castro may have enjoyed golf, but it was seen as a bourgeois sport, so not supported by the post-revolutionary state. Castro's Cuba established the National Institute of Sport, Physical Education and Recreation (INDER) in 1961, for planning and implementing sports provision for the masses and for high-performance athletes. The school curriculum prioritized physical education, after mathematics and science, and talented athletes were selected to enter national training schools in a particular sport.

Post-revolutionary Cuba had inherited strong traditions, in particular in boxing and baseball. The latter was so well-established within wider Cuban society that it was not considered necessary to include it in the school curriculum. Along with athletics, and some women's sports such as volleyball, boxing and baseball became the flagship sports of Cuba's highly developed sporting system. Talent identification and full-time practitioners produced remarkable achievements on the international stage for the small Caribbean island. At the widely boycotted Moscow Olympics of 1980, Cuba finished fifth in the medal table, above Italy, Great Britain, Sweden, and Australia. Aided by Soviet expertise in coaching and competing, Cuba has also exported its coaching and organizational prowess in turn, to the Republic of Ireland for instance. Its all-time greats on the track and in the ring include "White Lightning" Alberto Juantarena, double Olympic champion in 400 and 800 metres at Montreal 1976, and boxer Teófilo Stevenson, who won three Olympic gold medals in heavyweight boxing (1972, 1976, 1980).

## ⬊ Czech Republic

The two most popular sports in the Czech Republic are football and ice hockey. Ice hockey mobilized national feeling in matches with the USSR after the Soviet invasion of the country in 1968. Top Czech players have played in the National Hockey League in North America. Czechoslovakia, which was dissolved in 1993, also produced a remarkable number of outstanding tennis players, from 1954 Wimbledon winner Jaroslav Drobny to Ivan Lendl and Martina Navratilova. All these champions left the country, and took up citizenship elsewhere, Drobny in the UK after winning his Wimbledon title as an Egyptian following his defection from communist Czechoslovakia. The others became US citizens.

## ⬊ Denmark

Whilst often categorized as one of a Scandinavian cluster of nations sharing common values, in sports Denmark has, for obvious climatological reasons, a lower profile in winter sports than those of its more northerly Scandinavian neighbours. It has produced outstanding performers in cycling but, most distinctively, numbers badminton amongst its most popular sports. Its men and women badminton players have won several Olympic gold medals. Sailing, shooting, and rowing are also disciplines in which Danes have excelled in international competition. In football, its national side won the men's European Nations title in 1992, many of its players having been recalled from holiday to replace the Yugoslavia side that had qualified for the tournament but was disqualified due to the wars that had

broken out within the country. This became a byword for laid-back triumph, though Denmark has never since matched that achievement. Denmark's women handball players held Olympic, world, and European titles simultaneously in 1997.

## ⬊ Egypt

The record of Egypt in sports is in general unimpressive: the majority of the country's two dozen Olympic medals have been achieved in either weightlifting or wrestling. By far the most popular sport is football, and Egypt's record in the biannual Africa Cup of Nations is impressive: six victories, including three in succession (2006–10). Otherwise, the most successful sport is squash, in which Egypt has produced a number of winners in international tournaments.

## ⬊ El Salvador

With not a single medal to its name at the Olympics, El Salvador – the smallest, but also most densely populated of Central America's countries – is one of the weakest of competitive sporting nations in the Americas. It attracts surfers to its Pacific coastline, but has little in the way of established sports culture beyond the national passion for football, which gave it some notoriety in the so-called Football War with neighbour Honduras, in 1969 (see entry for Honduras).

## ⬊ Ethiopia

At the Beijing 2008 Olympics, Ethiopia was the fifth-ranked athletics nation, confirming its remarkable pedigree in the production of middle-distance and long-distance runners. At the 2010 New York marathon, when Haile Gebrselassie pulled up with knee trouble after 16 miles, bringing his 20-year career to an end, his retirement marked one of the most distinguished and sustained profiles in modern athletics. Abebe Bikila, his Ethiopian predecessor, had been an inspiring example when taking Africa's first Olympics athletics gold, running barefoot in Rome in 1960. Derartu Tulu was Africa's first black woman to win gold, in the 10,000 metres in Barcelona in 1992. The quality of Ethiopian runners, and their counterparts in other African countries such as Morocco and Kenya, has reshaped the horizons of competitive distance running. Their achievements dwarf those of Ethiopians in any other sport.

## Fiji

Many traditional Fijian games, including forms of wrestling and javelin throwing, died in the 19th century when the country became part of the British Empire, though the form of canoeing known as outrigger paddling still thrives. Although football and golf are popular among the Indian population, ethnic Fijians have taken particularly strongly to forms of rugby. Rugby union is the predominant sport, and Fiji reached the World Cup quarter-finals in 1987 and 2007, but it has twice been world champion at the smaller-scale seven-a-side version. There is also a national rugby league competition, and a number of Fijian players have gone on to play professionally in Australia.

## Finland

Winter sports are less dominant in Finland than in neighbouring Sweden and Norway. The national sporting pastime is *pasäpallo* (also known as *pasis*), which is broadly a local form of baseball. A wide variety of sports are practised in Finland, but outside its own borders the country is mainly known for success in two generic fields of sports: track and field athletics and motor sports, leading Anglophone journalists to refer to a succession of "Flying Finns". The first of these on the track was Hannes Kolehmainen, who won three gold medals at the Stockholm Olympic Games in 1912; great Swedish middle-distance runners of later generations include Paavo Nurmi and Lasse Viren. Nurmi introduced new levels of endurance training to athletics, and was in this sense a modernizing influence. Lasse Viren has a more controversial legacy, in the form of his intense preparations for peaking at the Olympics, and his indifferent performances in competitions between those events. In motor sports, Finland, the densely forested "land of a thousand lakes" (actually, there are tens of thousands) has dominated rally driving, and some Finnish drivers have gone on to be successful drivers on the track: Keke Rosberg, Mika Häkkinen and Kimi Räikönen have all been Formula 1 World Champion drivers.

One curiosity of Finnish athletics has been consistent success in the javelin event, with over 20 Olympic medals.

## France

Modern sports came to France mainly from England in the years following the country's comprehensive defeat in the Franco-Prussian war of 1870. Political elites saw sports as the source of a necessary process of national reinvigoration, and indigenous sports such as *jeu de paume* were displaced by the Anglicized form of lawn tennis. Although many sports established themselves in France, cycling and rugby were disproportionately popular. The Tour de France cycle race, founded in 1903, became a great national institution, watched, in short sections, by more than half the nation, and used in schools to instil pride in the geography and culture of the country.

After World War II, France saw sports as a means of building a third way between the sporting ideologies of the Cold War superpowers. President De Gaulle instituted policies for the cultivation of sports in youth, and state policies prioritized physical education programmes in the school curriculum and sports initiatives in the community.

Frenchmen also had important roles in the globalization of modern sports, originating the two greatest institutions of global sports. The driving force behind the formation of the modern Olympic movement, Baron Pierre De Coubertin, was a French aristocrat, and the Fédération Internationale de Football Association (FIFA), was founded in Paris in 1904. Its first president, Robert Guérin, was French, as was the third, Jules Rimet, who in 1930 established the World Cup that originally bore his name and has become the world's most watched sporting competition. In 1998, France not only hosted the competition but also won it. The 1924 Paris Olympics were also a catalyst for the foundation of numerous international sporting federations, stimulated by the aspiration to receive Olympic recognition.

In the 2000s, France's men's handball side became the first ever country to hold at the same time the Olympic (Beijing 2008), World (2009), and continental (European, 2010) titles.

## Georgia

The Republic of Georgia was incorporated into the Soviet Union in 1921, and its sporting development then followed the Soviet pattern, with a near-eradication of traditional sports including varieties of wrestling and equestrianism, and the fostering of Olympic sports after World War II. Georgian football became outstandingly successful. Dinamo Tbilisi knocked Liverpool out of the European Cup in 1979, and in 1981 won the European Cup Winners' Cup. On occasions in the early 1980s the majority of the Soviet representative side was Georgian.

Following the collapse of the Soviet Union, a badly declining Georgian economy was matched in the near-collapse of Georgian football, crowds plummeting from 80,000 to 200 for a purely Georgian league. The newly formed national team had little success.

Rugby, however, is another story. In Georgian it is called *lelo*, and treated as the English modernization of an ancient Georgian game. The country has reached final stages of World Cups, and many players have gone abroad, especially to France, to earn a living. Rugby, in short, has provided a successful paradigm for Georgians in how a new state can take its place in global sports.

## ⬎ Germany

German sports draw on ideas of competition and physical development that have deep roots in the national culture. Under the German Empire (1870–1914) there was, initially, some resistance to the importation into the country of English ideas of organized games, and attempts were made to restrict the country to traditional national activities such as German gymnastics (*Turnen*). But these were largely unsuccessful, and Germany emerged as one of the great powers of modern sports, though its sporting history was complicated by its political history. Between 1945 and 1991 the country was divided into Communist East Germany and non-Communist West Germany, whose diplomatic disputes had complex effects on German sporting representation (see Glossary, p.133).

Germany has provided globally leading figures in a wide variety of sports: Boris Becker and Steffi Graf in tennis, Franz Beckenbauer and Gerd Muller in football, Michael Schumacher in motor racing, and Bernhard Langer in golf are just a few examples. If the medals of both Germanies are aggregated, then the country lies third in the overall Olympic medals table, behind the USA and the Soviet Union/Russia. But an important factor in this success, in the German Democratic Republic, was the systematic development of drug or doping programmes in preparation for competition.

The national football team of the Federal Republic, West Germany, has been world champion three times, in 1954,

1974 and 1990, on each occasion beating more fancied opposition. This elite success is based upon a vigorous grassroots system of sporting competition: approximately one-third of Germans are members of sports clubs and, although one must have reservations about international statistical comparisons and the possibility of multiple counting of memberships, this is arguably the highest in the world.

## Great Britain *see* UK

## ⬎ Greece

The place of Greece in world sports will always be primarily associated with the country's role as creator of the ancient Olympic Games, to which the modern games pay homage. Athens hosted the first modern games in 1896, and hosted them again in 2004. In the late 1970s and early 1980s, the campaign by some Greek politicians to establish a permanent site for the modern games at Olympia, where the ancient games had been held, almost succeeded, but the success of the "free enterprise games" in Los Angeles in 1984 revived the interest of many cities in hosting the games, and killed interest in the Greek project.

Otherwise, football is the most popular sport in Greece, and the national team achieved a remarkable feat by winning the 2004 European Football Championship, defeating several more fancied opponents. Greek teams and individuals have also had disproportionate success at basketball, water polo and athletics. At the 2004 Athens Olympics, though, the 200-metre gold medallist from Sydney 2000, Kostas Kenteris, who was scheduled to light the Olympic flame in the stadium for the Opening Ceremony, was disgraced when faking a motor-cycle accident with training partner Katerina Thanou (100-metre silver medallist in Sydney), to avoid drug testing. The grubby and sordid story of their evasion soils the idealistic rhetoric of the Olympic event and movement.

## ⬎ Honduras

With its proximity to the USA, Honduras has adopted baseball and American Football, but football/soccer is the country's major sport, and its men's national side qualified from the North, Central America, and Caribbean group for the World Cup Finals in South Africa 2010, along with the two superpowers of that group, the USA and Mexico. This was its second appearance in a Finals, after its debut in Spain in 1982. In its six games at those two Finals, Honduras has yet to register a victory. After rioting and violence at World Cup qualifying games between Honduras and El Salvador, in June 1969, El Salvador launched military attacks on its neighbour in what became known as the Football War, though disputes had simmered for years over immigration issues, and the conflict was in no real sense generated by the football games.

## ⬊ Hungary

Hungary, at the zenith of the Austro-Hungarian Empire, shared with Austria some highly developed and military-related sporting practices. Some of these were the basis of early Hungarian achievements on the international sporting stage. In the Summer Olympics, Hungarian men and women have excelled in fencing, shooting, swimming, wrestling, and gymnastics. In any overall medal table for the Summer Olympics, up to Beijing 2008, Hungary holds a top-ten position, but at Beijing itself was only 20th in the table.

Hungary's fabled national football side – nicknamed the Magic Magyars – of the 1950s was destined to be one of the great Beautiful Losers of world sports history. The players were essentially full-time state socialist employees. Hungary humbled England twice in 1953, inflicting the host's first Wembley defeat (6–3) to a non-British side, and inflicting on England its worst ever defeat (7–1) in the return fixture in Budapest later in the year. But in the 1954 World Cup final, West Germany turned the tables after an 8–3 thrashing by Hungary in an earlier round, winning 3–2 in what Germany remembered as The Miracle of Berne. In the post-Soviet era, Hungary's sporting infrastructure has deteriorated, if not collapsed.

## ⬊ India

India is a country of enormous cultural diversity where more than a hundred languages are spoken. Some of the cultures within the country have traditions of physical prowess that have adapted well to modern sports, whereas some have not. The Sikhs of the Punjab, for example, have adapted their

warrior *khalsa* leagues into sporting organizations, playing Western games alongside traditional ones such as *kabbadi*, and the princes of Rajasthan were relatively easily assimilated into the ethos of sportsmanship promulgated by the British "public schools" and their Indian imitators. But the Brahmin cast, with its traditional disdain for physicality and muscularity, and the intellectually oriented culture of Bengal proved more difficult territory for the spread of organized games.

Many sports are played in India, and there are several whose origins are wholly or partially Indian. The country has been particularly successful at field hockey, winning eight Olympic titles. However, India can be classified as one of the countries that has internalized a foreign sport as its own dominant activity: cricket is to India as rugby union is to New Zealand and football is to Brazil. As Ashis Nandy has put it, cricket is an Indian game accidentally discovered in England. The national team has become one of the world's leading teams, beating all of the world's other leading nations in test series over the years, and winning the third World Cup in 1983 in the one-day version of the game. The Indian batsman Sachin Tendulkar, in the first decade of the 21st century, became both the country and the sport's best-known personality. Correspondingly, the Board of Control for Cricket in India (BCCI) has become the leading player financially and politically in world cricket, and the Indian Premier League (IPL) has dominated the 20-over form of the game by offering the highest wages in cricket. As these developments have taken place, the centre of administrative power in world cricket has switched from London to Dubai, United Arab Emirates.

## ⬊ Indonesia

Indonesia has no great sporting heritage. Football is the most popular sport, but badminton is the most successful: all of Indonesia's Olympic champions have been badminton players, both men and women, and the only other sport in which the country has won more than a single medal is weightlifting.

## ⬊ Iran

Freestyle wrestling and football are the most popular and established sports in Iran. In 2009, four members of the national football side were suspended after wearing green wristbands in a match to symbolize their support for the opposition party in the country's national elections.

Women's sporting potential is curtailed by the Islamic culture's restrictions on contact between men and women. To provide male trainers for sportswomen would be, in the words of a top Iranian Olympic official, a "subjugation to Western customs and practices", so women athletes are only supported if women trainers and coaches can be found.

## ⬂ Iraq

Blighted by war and its aftermath, Iraq astonished the world by taking the Asian Football Confederation's Asian championship in 2007. Other sports, such as wrestling and basketball, are popular in Iraq, but football gives the country its strongest sports-based profile. "No one thinks that sports are just for men," Nadia Yasser, captain of Iraq's national women's soccer team, observed in 2002. Women have played basketball, golf and participated in wrestling, and sports have been seen as a medium for challenging the more traditional Islamic view of the gender order.

## ⬂ Ireland

Sports have been an essential ingredient in the cultural and political mix that has made the modern independent Republic of Ireland. It was identified early as a catalyst for the mobilization of a nationalist consciousness and a Gaelic culture. The GAA (Gaelic Athletic Association) was founded in 1884, and banned British games, promoting Gaelic alternatives, although in parts of the country, and especially rural areas, cricket continued to be the popular choice of young men. After partition, and the creation of the Irish Free State in 1922, Ireland could compete in international sports as an independent nation. But its Gaelic sports had little competition available, a consequence of the nationalist project that established them. International sports were therefore played in the previously repressed sports of cricket, rugby, and football in particular.

An Olympic Council of Ireland was formed in 1922, and a team representing the whole island of Ireland travelled to the Paris Olympics of 1924. Athletes from Northern Ireland have represented Ireland at the Olympics, in those sports organized throughout the two countries on an all-Ireland basis. This capacity of sports to transcend – indeed reshape – political divisions and boundaries has been notable. Ireland's rugby union team continued to represent the whole of the island after independence and partition. This internationalism of sporting competition has also underpinned the growing popularity of football in the Republic, though the nationalist sports of hurling (women's version camogie), and Gaelic Football continue to have a strong hold on regional sporting passions and identities.

## ⬂ Israel

Israeli sports pre-date the state of Israel in that hundreds of Maccabis across Europe and beyond encouraged Jewish youth to take up sporting activities. The Rabbi Moses Mainonides (1135–1204) had preached the importance of a healthy body as well as a healthy mind. On the foundation of the state of Israel in 1948, sports were recognized as of national significance but not of top priority. Defence and security, education and health, welfare and prosperity were the key drivers of state policy. Nevertheless, a young Marc Spitz could challenge stereotypes of the non-sporty Jew at the 1965 Maccabiah (the international Jewish Olympics), where he took six gold medals. Outstanding athletes have been given non-combatant roles during their spells of national service.

Israel was expelled from Asian sports federations after the Arab–Israeli conflict of 1973, but this strategy backfired, as Israel's national sports teams were accepted into European federations in football, athletics, swimming, and basketball, giving them a higher level of regular competition. Other popular sports are volleyball and a range of water sports. The potential of Israeli sports and their athletes remains constrained, though, by the imperatives of national security and the low priority of sports on the state's agenda. Also, sponsors have been reluctant to be associated with a national image that is seen to evoke aggression and hostility as much as inter-cultural understanding.

## ⬂ Italy

Italy is mainly known in world sports as the second most successful national football team after Brazil, with four World Cup victories. The Italian language is one of the few that does not describe football with a word derived from the English. It is called *il calcio* (kick), as was the medieval Florentine game played between Epiphany and Lent; this game was revived in the 20th century, though it is now played mainly in the summer and is referred to as *il calcio antico*. Several Italian football clubs have had major successes in European football competition; these are mainly concentrated in the industrial north of the country, and include Internazionale Milano, AC Milan, and Juventus (in Torino).

Motor sports have always been prominent in Italy: the Ferrari team is the only one that has competed throughout the history of Formula 1 racing, and it has been the most successful in the sport; it also has the largest following. In rugby union, Italy competes (along with France) against nations from the British Isles in the European elite Six Nations tournament.

Mussolini saw in all levels of sports a powerful tool for the inculcation of fascist thinking. At the International University Games of 1933, a pamphlet lauded the achievements of the fascist state in placing "the health and physical improvement of the Italian race" at the forefront of the fascist regime's policies, and praised the "successful efforts made to give a sporting education to young men which will strengthen their muscles today and mould their character in the future". Mussolini's Italy won the Football World Cup on home territory in 1934, in France in 1938, and was placed second behind the USA at the 1932 Los Angeles Olympics, and fourth in the rankings at Berlin 1936. Mussolini also championed the victories of boxer Primo Carnera when he briefly held the world heavyweight boxing title in the 1930s.

Italy has always been prominent in Olympic sports. Rome hosted the 1960 games, and Italians have consistently won medals throughout the history of the games, most of them in fencing, skiing, cycling, boxing, and track and field athletics. The majority of successful Italian competitors in the Winter Games have come from the Alto Adige province, also known as the Sud Tyrol, where the majority of the population speak German as a first language.

It has often been remarked that Italians are less nationalistic or patriotic than most Europeans when it comes to sports (as in other matters), seeing their primary allegiance as being to club, city, or region rather than to country.

## ↘ Japan

Modern Japanese culture is often said to be a blend of Japanese tradition and Western modernity, and Japanese sports fall neatly into this pattern. Until 1945, Japan could be described as a martial society, and its equivalent of sports were a wide variety of martial arts. Some of these, such as *judo, jujitsu, aikido, karate,* and *sumo* were forms of unarmed combat, whereas *kendo* used staffs and *kyudo* bows and arrows. In all cases, as with European sports in the Classical period, the activities had religious and ethical meanings.

But it is also the case that Japan began to take to western conceptions of sports as early as the 1870s. Baseball, cricket, rugby, and golf were all adopted as elite activities and spread downwards into Japanese society, mainly through the education system. In contemporary Japan, baseball is the most popular sport, followed by football, with *sumo*, the traditional heavyweight wrestling, in third place, and golf fourth.

For a country of its size Japan has not proved to be particularly successful at the global level of sports. However, given the large population, their enthusiasm for sports of all kinds, their level of wealth and their orderly patterns of behaviour, it has been regarded as the ideal venue to hold major global events. Japan hosted the Olympic games in 1964, the Toyota (or Intercontinental) Cup match between the football champions of Europe and South America from 1980 to 2004, the football World Cup (with South Korea) in 2002, and in 2019 will host the Rugby World Cup.

## ↘ Kazakhstan

In the largest landlocked country in the world, with a mere 15 million people, Kazakhstan has been outstanding in ice hockey, a legacy of its Soviet past, and its government has supported talent development in cycling. Independent of the USSR since 1991, it has since then had a proud record in regional competition, its athletes winning 316 medals at the Summer Asian Games from 1994 to 2006 (92 gold, 95 silver and 129 bronze), and taking fourth place, after Japan, China, and South Korea in the Asian Winter Games up to 2007.

## ⬎ Kenya

Along with Morocco and Ethiopia, Kenya has produced some of the most remarkable long-distance and middle-distance runners. Kip Keino's Olympic gold medals in Mexico (1968) and Munich (1972) confirmed the emergence of African runners as a new world elite. At 13th position in the 2008 Beijing Olympics medal table, Kenya was Africa's top-placed nation. Cricket, football, and rugby union are also organized at competitive levels, as befits the legacy of the country's status under British Colonial rule. But the country's men and women runners dominate the sporting image and achievements of the country.

## ⬎ Madagascar

Sports in this island nation off the south-east coast of Africa are primarily recreational, or take the form of facilities for tourists. As well as football, established school-based sports in Madagascar are boxing, track and field athletics, judo, women's basketball, and women's tennis.

## ⬎ Malaysia

Like much else in Malaysia, sports have tended to be divided along ethnic lines, with the Chinese community dominating athletics and table tennis, those of Indian origin cricket and hockey, and the Malays football and traditional sports such as *sepak raga*, a three-a-side sport played in a space like a badminton court. Football in Malaysia has never quite recovered from very serious problems with betting and corruption that peaked in relation to the 1994/95 season. Nevertheless, the Malaysian capital Kuala Lumpur retains the headquarters of the Asian Football Confederation.

The sport that most unites Malaysia is badminton, also the one at which all Malaysia's Olympic medals have been won.

## ⬎ Mexico

Games were played in pre-Columbian Mexico, including the notable Mesoamerican ball game (or games), but these traditions were broken by conquest and we do not even know the rules that governed them. Modern Mexican sports are the result of a mixture of influences from Spain and North America. Bullfighting is popular, as is *charreria*, a rodeo-like collection of events based on cowboy skills. Most of the principal sports of the USA are played and followed in Mexico, the most popular being baseball. Boxing is arguably the most successful Mexican sport, and the total number of world champions the country has produced is second only to the USA. The country has not been a prodigious winner of Olympic medals; diving and boxing have been the most successful sports in this respect. Nor has the national team been massively successful at its most popular sport, football, its greatest achievements being to be twice runners-up in the Copa America, and twice quarter-finalists in the World Cup. Mexico has twice hosted the World Cup – in 1970 and 1986 – and once, in 1968, the Olympics.

## ⬎ Morocco

Most of Morocco's Olympic medals have been in track and field athletics, particularly in middle-distance running. Football is the most popular sport, and the country has regularly produced professional players who have played in top European leagues; the greatest success of the national side was in winning the Africa Cup of Nations in 1976. Although Alpine events take place in the Atlas Mountains, the country has competed only intermittently at the Winter Olympics and without success.

## ⬎ Netherlands

Given that the Netherlands is a low-lying, Northern European country, it is perhaps not surprising that skating is a traditional sport. Unfortunately, because of climate change, the old-established long-distance outdoor forms of skating have declined in the 21st century. But Dutch traditions have transferred to the indoor skating rink, where Dutch competitors have accrued a total of more than 80 speed skating medals at the Winter Olympics. Perhaps surprisingly, these skills have not transferred to ice hockey; the national side has never been ranked among the elite nations in this sport. It is, though, a world-class competitor in field hockey.

The Netherlands has had both high rates of participation in sports and considerable international competitive success. More than a quarter of the population are members of a sports club. Football is the most popular sport, and the national team has been runners-up in the World Cup on three occasions. The most successful team sport has been (field) hockey: the women's national team has won six world championships, and the men's three. Swimming and cycling are the two sports at which Dutch competitors have won most medals at the Summer Olympics, and tennis and golf are also popular individual sports. Cricket, baseball, volleyball, basketball, and handball are all minority sports at which Dutch teams have competed at a high level.

Of all the Dutch sports competitors who have appeared on the world stage, two can be said to stand out historically: Fanny Blankers-Koen, who won four gold medals at the 1948 Olympics, and footballer Johan Cruyff, who played for Ajax Amsterdam, Barcelona, and the Netherlands national team in the 1970s, and who is widely considered to be one of the greatest footballers of all time.

## ⬊ New Zealand

For a small country, New Zealand has consistently produced sportsmen of global significance in a wide variety of sports. These include the mountaineer Edmund Hillary, the cricketer Richard Hadlee, the runner Peter Snell, Ivan Mauger in speedway, Michael Campbell in golf, and the yachting crew that, in 2000, made New Zealand only the fourth country to win the America's Cup. Rugby union, though, dominates New Zealand sports, producing a source of national unity symbolized in the *haka*, the Māori war dance and poetic chant performed by New Zealand rugby teams before matches. In no other colonial country do the colonialists regard a "native" war dance as a key component of their culture. The other principal symbol of New Zealand rugby is the "All Black" strip or uniform worn by the national teams. Yet, at the international level, New Zealand has underachieved, winning the world title only once, when hosting a relatively low-key inaugural affair in 1987.

## ⬊ Nigeria

For the most populous country in Africa, Nigeria has a low level of success in international sports. At the Olympics, its only two gold medals were won at Atlanta 1996, in the women's long jump, and the men's football competition. It has been more successful in regional competitions, and at the Commonwealth Games. A National Sports Council, set up in 1962, augmented by a National Sports Commission in 1971, aimed to promote physical fitness and the general well-being of the nation, and to raise the standards of sports performance in the country. Its successes have been limited, though, and the layers of administration, and the endemic nature of financial and administrative corruption, have worked against any effective implementation of such policies.

## ⬊ Norway

Norway has considerable state investment in sports, and the government claims that more than 40 percent of the adult population are active in sports. Although the country has produced many players at the global elite level in such sports as football, handball, and ice hockey, there is no doubt that the real national sports are the Nordic events in winter sports, especially cross-country skiing and biathlon. Norwegians believe that these sports are an essential part of their culture, relating them to their landscape and their traditions. They are mass participation sports, but Norwegians also have high expectations of their national competitors at the elite level. In 2010, the country came fourth in the medals table at the Winter Olympics in Vancouver.

## ⬊ Pakistan

As part of British India, what is now Pakistan absorbed British sports practices in much the same way as the rest of India. The landowning upper classes readily absorbed the ethos of "sportsmanship" and the English "public school" system, playing hockey and cricket, and transferring their equestrian skills to polo. Cricket has proved to be by far the most popular and important sport in Pakistan; the country first played a test match as an independent nation in 1952. In shorter versions of the game, Pakistan were world champions at the 50-over game in 1992, and at the 20-over game in 2009.

Unfortunately, Pakistani sports – and cricket in particular – have suffered severely from the political instability of Pakistani society. In the 21st century the situation has been so bad that the national team has had to play its "home" games in the United Arab Emirates and the UK. Because Pakistan is poorer than most other major cricket-playing societies, and their players are denied access to the lucrative Indian Premier League for political reasons, they have become prey to gangsters running illegal gambling rings, and corruption and match-fixing have become endemic.

## ↘ Papua New Guinea

Like much else in the country, sports in Papua New Guinea have been a consequence originally of British, and latterly of Australian, influence. Cricket was the first game to take root, but rugby league is now considered to be the unofficial national sport. Australian Rules football and rugby union are also played, but league is dominant. The country has the unfortunate distinction of never having won an Olympic medal of any kind, and of having been ranked bottom of all FIFA members in football. On the other hand, it is, along with Australia, New Zealand and England, one of the global "Big Four" in rugby league.

## ↘ Philippines

Boxing, basketball, billiards, football, and volleyball are the main sports in the Philippines, but boxing gives the country its highest international profile, with Manny Pacquiao recognized by many experts as the best pound-for-pound fighter in the world in 2010. In May 2010, he was elected to Congress as he moved into a future political career away from the ring. At the other end of the spectrum to world-title boxing fights, the Traditional Games and Sports Act of 2010 stated a commitment to the revival and protection of traditional sports: "It is hereby declared the policy of the State to foster patriotism, nationalism and sportsmanship by giving priority to a sports program that shall revive, promote and enhance the country's traditional games and sports."

## ↘ Poland

Polish competitors have excelled at a wider variety of sports than those of most former Communist countries, including speedway and other forms of motor racing, and men's volleyball. The country's most successful sports at the Olympic Games have been boxing, and track and field athletics. Football is the most popular sport, and the national team has twice finished third in the World Cup, in 1974 and 1982. Poland will host the 2012 European Football Championship jointly with the Ukraine. For a northern European country that contains the high Tatra Mountains, Poland has made surprisingly little impact on winter sports.

## ↘ Portugal

The country has produced numerous world-class long-distance and cross-country runners. Its four Olympic gold medals include the men's marathon at the Los Angeles 1984 Games, and the women's marathon at Seoul four years later. The dominant sport in the country is football, and the Real Madrid player Ronaldo is a celebrity figure across the world.

## ↘ Qatar

A minnow in performance terms, with just two bronze medals to its name at the Olympics (boxing and running), Qatar has nevertheless established itself as a power base of sorts in global football politics. When Japan failed to qualify for the World Cup Finals of 1992, conceding a goal to Iraq at the very end of a critical game, what became known as The Tragedy of Doha haunted Japanese ambitions for years thereafter, and also profiled Qatar as a centre and venue for international events. It provides one of the most influential sports administrators in world football, Mohamed Bin Hamman, who tried and failed to relocate the headquarters of the Asian Football Confederation to his home country. But Bin Hamman remained a powerful figure on the Executive Committee of football's world governing body, FIFA, and in 2010 Qatar was successful in its bid to host the 2022 World Cup.

## ↘ Romania

Boosted by the adoption of a Soviet model of sports development, and state support for high-performance athletes, Romania was a high-profile and successful nation in the Olympics of the Cold War period. It was particularly prominent in gymnastics; in 1976, at the age of 14, Nadia Comaneci was the first gymnast in Olympic history to be given a maximum 10/10 score, for her routine on the uneven bars.

Although within the orbit of Soviet domination, Romania also showed some independence in the world of sports politics, ignoring the USSR's tit-for-tat boycott of the 1984 Los Angeles Olympics, and finishing second in the medal table, behind the USA. In the 1960s and 1970s, men and women's national teams won the Handball World Cup.

Romania has produced strong football teams, from club sides in the Mitropa Cup in the 1930s through to national sides in more recent World Cup Finals. It was one of just four European nations to compete at the first World Cup tournament, in Uruguay in 1930. The country has competed at every Rugby World Cup tournament. It produced one of the most charismatic stars of the newly professionalized tennis era in Ilie Nâstase, world number one in 1973–74, and the first professional athlete to sign an endorsement deal with emergent shoe giant Nike. But since the collapse in 1989 of the communist state, Romanian sports have declined. At the Beijing 2008 Olympics, the country was 17th in the medal table, its four gold medals all won by women, in judo, rowing, gymnastics and the marathon.

## ↘ Russia

Russian sports draw on traditions of acrobatics and circus-style physical prowess that have always been part of the country's culture, and were expressed in the early Soviet period in the *spartakiad*, multi-sports events bringing young people together from all over the Soviet Union, and named after Spartacus, the rebel slave of ancient Rome. But Soviet sports were given a different – wider and more aspirational – direction by the decision of the USSR in the late 1940s to compete in the Olympic Games as a prestige project. As with other well-defined objectives, such as the "space race", the Soviet command economy was able to achieve spectacular success; the USSR dominated every Olympic Games from its entry in 1952 until 1988, the last occasion on which it competed as such.

Post-Soviet Russian sports have subsequently declined, but not by as much as in some of the ex-Soviet republics. Russia has remained strong in a wide variety of Olympic sports, although weak in some of the more commercial Western sports that were not part of the Olympics, such as golf and motor racing. The most popular sports in Russia are football, ice hockey and basketball. *Bandy* is a popular local variant on ice hockey, played on natural ice and over much greater

areas than the international version. One sport in which post-Soviet Russia has proved particularly successful is tennis; the country has produced numerous champions, particularly in the women's game, several of them passing through Nick Bollettieri's Florida academy, a joint venture with International Management Group. In 2009, 13 Russian women were in the world's top 100, more than from any other nation.

Russia has also been very successful under the leadership of Vladimir Putin and Roman Abramovich in winning the right to host major international events: the 2014 Winter Olympics for the city of Sochi, and the 2018 Men's World Cup.

## ↘ Rwanda

As in the vast majority of African countries, football is the most popular sport, although rugby – including for women – is also fairly well-established. But the most notable indigenous sport, and focus of revivalist initiatives as a means of restoration of national pride and identity in a society ravaged by the massacres of 1994, is Rwandan high jump, which astonished European explorers and colonizers in the early 20th century. Regardless of such a pedigree of apparently natural talent, Rwanda awaits its first Olympic medal.

## ↘ Saudi Arabia

Saudi Arabia has a thriving football competition with modern facilities funded by oil revenues. The national team has reached the final stages of the World Cup on four occasions and has won the Asian Championship three times. There has been little Saudi success in the Olympics with only two medals in total. The *Wahabi* form of Islam, which is Saudi Arabia's official religion, makes women's sports almost impossible.

Camel racing, a traditional sport patronized by the royal family, has continued to thrive in modern conditions as in several other countries in the Arabian peninsula.

## ↘ Serbia

Serbia emerged from the dissolution of communist Yugoslavia in the 1990s, and from the split with Montenegro in 2006. Basketball and football are Serbia's most prominent sports, a legacy it inherits from Yugoslavia, which was twice runner-up in the European Football Championship (1960 and 1968). The Socialist Federal Republic of Yugoslavia's men's basketball team won Olympic gold at the 1980 Moscow Games, whilst also holding the 1978 World Championship title, and won five European championships. Marshal Tito, president of the League of Communists of Yugoslavia, recognized the value of successful sports teams for the fostering of a sense of national Yugoslavian identity. This legacy has sustained Serbian men and women's volleyball in the world's top ten.

It is in tennis, though, that Serbia has shone in the 21st century, producing world-class competitors and Grand Slam event winners Novak Djokovic and Ana Ivanovic. Monica Seles, born in Novi Sad, Yugoslavia (now Serbia) but an ethnic Hungarian, won eight Grand Slam titles whilst a Yugoslavian citizen, before taking US citizenship in 1994/5. The rise to stardom of her successors has become the stuff of myth, success stories based on relentless practice in defiance of the bombs that were falling on Belgrade, and in make-do facilities such as a converted swimming pool.

## ⬊ Singapore

Surrounded by the ocean, Singapore provides obvious opportunities for water-sports, including scuba-diving. At international level, it has produced outstanding women table-tennis players. Football is the country's top spectator sport, and a professional football league, the S-League, was established in 1996, modelled on Japan's J-League. This has met with modest success, seen as one of the top ten professional leagues in Asia. As a mini Asian Tiger, an independent state from 1965, Singapore's government has looked to use sports to boost the visitor and tourist economy, and the country hosted Formula 1's first-ever night-time race in 2008.

## ⬊ Slovakia

One of the two nations formed in 1993 following the dissolution of Czechoslovakia, Slovakia shares the same sporting pedigree and legacies as the Czech Republic. Its men's football team qualified for the World Cup Finals in South Africa in 2010, performing creditably in getting to the last 16, defeating defending champions Italy 3–2 in the process.

## ⬊ South Africa

The Republic of South Africa has an exceptional sporting history: no other country has put its organization of sporting activity on the global diplomatic agenda in the way that South Africa did in the 20th century, and in no other country have sporting institutions played such a large part in internal politics. The Nationalist party's victory in the elections of 1948 led to the introduction and implementation of the policy of apartheid, or separateness. Racial discrimination was implemented in every aspect of society, including sports, with South African representative teams in the major sports of rugby union and cricket drawn only from the minority white population. In the years that followed, individuals, governments and sporting institutions increasingly joined the bandwagon of support for a boycott of South African sports in opposition to a system contradicting fundamental sporting principles not just political principles.

In 1961, South Africa withdrew from the Commonwealth, and in 1964 the Republic was expelled from the Olympic movement. By the 1970s, the country was largely isolated from international sports, in Afrikaaner-dominated rugby, in cricket, and also football, the main sport of the African population. In 1977, Commonwealth countries – including sporting rivals in Australia, New Zealand, and the UK – agreed to implement a complete boycott of all sporting connections with South Africa. South Africa's response was to allow some wider representation in, for instance, rugby, though this could not counter the argument that there could be "no normal sport in an abnormal society".

In 1988, ANC representatives, surprisingly, committed themselves to supporting South Africa's re-entry into international sports before the institution of universal suffrage. Thus, the rugby authorities played their part in the acceptance by their compatriots of regime change, which began the following year. Post-apartheid South Africa has rejoined all the major international sporting organizations. Sports have remained immensely important in the country's politics and culture and have often been presented as a unique forum for a sense of national unity and reconciliation. The white population reciprocated Nelson Mandela's gesture of wearing a Springbok jersey at the country's Rugby World Cup triumph in its support for *Bafana Bafana* (the national football team) in its victory in the 1996 Africa Cup of Nations and in its hosting of the World Cup in 2010. All has not been sweetness and light, however, as there has been bitter controversy about quotas and targets for African players –

promoted as an antidote to a structural racism privileging white players.

## South Korea (Republic of Korea)

In the wake of the Korean War (1950–53), during which South Korea was supported by the United Nations in a military conflict against North Korea (the Democratic People's Republic of Korea), sports have been an important tool of national restoration and national pride. Japan ruled the Korean peninsula from 1910 to the end of World War II, and included Korean athletes in its teams at the 1936 Berlin Olympics. Re-establishing a Korean identity through sports included staging the 1988 Summer Olympic Games in Seoul, and gaining co-hosting status with Japan in the staging of the 2002 football World Cup. Without doubt, staging the Olympic Games marked Seoul as a modern city and the country as a serious player in economic and political terms. Its corporations also saw the value of association with sports. Hyundai has been a long-term sponsor of the men's football World Cup, while Samsung first sponsored the Olympics from 1997, and is signed up as a top sponsor through to 2016.

Taekwondo is a Korean individual combat sport that was developed, from the 1950s onwards, into an Olympic sport, and introduced at the 2000 Sydney Games. Koreans have since won nine gold medals in this event. Korean men and women have become competitively strong in golf, and Yang Yong-eun in 2009 became the first Asian-born golfer to triumph in one of the four major annual tournaments in the golfing calendar.

## Sri Lanka

Although the official national sport of Sri Lanka (previously Ceylon) is volleyball, and rugby is also popular, Sri Lanka is typical of South Asia insofar as cricket is by far the dominant sport. The national team won the (50-over) Cricket World Cup in 1996 and has remained competitive with the world's elite ever since, especially in shorter forms of the game. This level of success is out of all proportion to any other Sri Lankan sporting achievements.

## Spain

Spain has established itself as a powerhouse of world sports in the 21st century. The national football team won the European Championship in 2008 and the World Cup in 2010, and the country's two most prominent clubs, Barcelona and Real Madrid, have established themselves as permanent members of the global elite. Spain has also produced many other megastars of modern sports, including Rafael Nadal in tennis, Fernando Alonso in motor racing, and champion cyclists such as triple Tour de France winner Alberto Contador (though suspended in late 2010 for testing positive for drugs on a rest day during that year's Tour). The country is also the main locus of European golf outside the UK.

Much of Spanish success is based on the idea of the multi-sports club, usually with municipal backing. Real Madrid, for example, puts out teams and competitors in a wide variety of sports and is the world's largest sports club defined by financial turnover.

Spanish prominence in global sports is a relatively recent phenomenon. For the first three quarters of the 20th century the country was marginalized by backwardness and civil war and the dictatorship of Francisco Franco. The marginalization was sporting, as well as political and the country was largely identified with bull-fighting and hunting. The 1992 Barcelona Olympic Games was a watershed in the development of a modernized national sports system.

## Sweden

With a population which has never reached 10 million, Sweden's astonishing success in world sports gives the country a serious claim to the title of the world's greatest sporting nation. Swedes have won championships at an astonishing variety of sports and games. In handball, the men's team has been world champions four times, and in ice hockey eight times. In football, the national team was runner-up to Brazil in the 1958 World Cup, and the Malmö club were runners up in the 1979 European Cup. In tennis, Bjorn Bjorg, Mats Wilander, and Stefan Edberg have all been multiple winners of Grand Slam tournaments. Sweden has produced a world heavyweight boxing champion in Ingemar Johansson, and arguably the world's greatest woman golfer in Annika Sorenstam. Swedish speedway has been a world leader, and *bandy*, a form of hockey played on large outdoor surfaces, is also played at a high level. Swedes have won more than 600 Olympic medals, the most common categories being in winter sports, track and field athletics (notably in the modern pentathlon), equestrianism, wrestling and shooting. The pale blue and gold colours of Sweden are to be feared and respected in most of the world's major sports.

Such disproportionate success requires explanation, and has been much studied by less successful nations. It is firmly based on mass participation; more than 20 percent of Swedes are members of sports clubs, and many more are involved informally in varieties of winter sports and orienteering. The Swedish government, for long periods under the Social Democratic party, has invested massively in sports facilities and sports science. There is undoubtedly a culture of physical prowess in Sweden; organized traditional games, winter sports and gymnastics were thriving in the 19th century long before international organized games came to the country. Swedes have also been influential in sports administration. At the Stockholm Olympics of 1912, Sigfrid Edström was a key figure in the formation of the International Amateur Athletics Federation, and held the presidency from 1912–46, when he became the fourth president of the International Olympic Committee. Or perhaps the explanation is very simple: the tennis player Mats Wilander, asked by an English interviewer why Swedes were so successful in sports, replied: "Have you been to Sweden? There is nothing else to do."

## ↘ Switzerland

Switzerland is not just the land of cuckoo clocks (as Harry Lime in *The Third Man* put it), punctual trains and Alpine-inspired chocolate bars. It is the home of many of the world's governing bodies of sports. The International Olympic Committee relocated to Lausanne, Switzerland from Paris in 1915, and since then many world governing bodies of sports have followed suit, lured in part by the attraction of generous tax laws and the financial discretion for which the Swiss are so well known; and in part by the Swiss claim of neutrality that is associated with other Swiss-based global organizations such as the United Nations (including the World Health Organization) and the Red Cross.

Individual sports at which the Swiss themselves have excelled in Olympic competition include winter sports (Alpine skiing), and, by dint of the national service that all citizens must undertake, military disciplines such as shooting and riding. Many sports activities are organized in clubs, and gymnastics clubs have been the most organized participant activity in Swiss sports, with gymnasts also garnering numerous gold medals. The country's professional football teams have been quite strong, usually expecting to qualify from the Europe region for the men's World Cup Finals.

## ↘ Taiwan

Formerly Formosa, Taiwan's sports have been shaped by its position at the centre of 20th-century Cold War politics. It continues to lay claim to the title of the Republic of China, established on mainland China in 1912, but is known as Chinese Taipei at the Olympic Games, as a concession to the People's Republic of China (established in 1949), which itself continues to claim the island of Formosa. Sports in Taiwan have therefore been bound up with both the persisting nationalist project represented by the country's opposition to Chinese communism, and its support from the USA. Introduced during Japanese rule, baseball is the most popular spectator sport, and basketball its most played sport. In international competition, it has been more likely to take individual honours (a taekwondo gold at Athens 2004, and two taekwondo and two weight-lifting bronze medals at the 2008 Beijing Olympics), and has produced top-class contenders in tennis and golf. But its men's baseball teams have been competitive at the lower tiers of the non-professional game, in the Intercontinental Baseball tournament, actually hosted by Taiwan in 2006.

## ↘ Thailand

European visitors to Siam (as it was then called) in the 19th century often remarked on the extreme skill shown by some inhabitants in playing with wicker objects, mostly balls, but also more complex shapes. This was the national pastime – shared, in different forms, with neighbouring countries – of *sepak takraw*. It has evolved into a number of organized games and the version based on volleyball has been part of the Asian Games since 1991. Along with kickboxing, it can be considered to be a "national sport".

Thai sport has always been relatively advanced. The country has hosted the Asian Games four times – more than any other – since their inception in 1951 and lies sixth in the Games' overall medal table. This is largely an expression of the national pride of a country which is unique in South Asia in never having been part of a European empire. The Bangkok elite have never wavered in their aspiration to international sporting success, irrespective of whether there has been an elected or a military government in power. When Somluck Kamsing won the country's first Olympic gold medal, in the featherweight division of the boxing competition in Atlanta in 1996, he was rewarded by the King and the government with property and honorary academic qualifications as well as a sum of money estimated at $1.5 million.

## ⬎ Tunisia

As a former French colony, independent since 1956, Tunisia has tended to follow French patterns of sporting activity. Rugby, handball, basketball, and volleyball are all played, as is *pétanque*, but football is the dominant sport. The national team (*Les Aigles de Carthage*) has qualified on four occasions for the final stages of the World Cup and, though it has never progressed to the knockout stages, it does have the distinction of having been the first African team to win a match at the group stage of the competition; this was a 3–1 victory over Mexico in 1978. In 2004, Tunisia won the Africa Cup of Nations when hosting the tournament, beating Morocco 2–1 in the final.

## ⬎ Turkey

The most distinctive sport in Turkey is what outsiders call "Turkish wrestling", which involves competitors being covered in olive oil. This sport has very ancient origins, and the annual tournament held in Edirne in European Turkey has been in continuous existence since approximately 1361. It claims to be the oldest sporting tournament in the world. Turkish wrestling has skills transferable to more international forms, and the overwhelming majority of Turkish medals at the Olympic Games have been in forms of wrestling, with most of the rest being in other types of combat and weightlifting.

Otherwise, Turkey is known for the extreme passion of its football fans at both club and national level. The most successful achievement of the national side was in coming third at the 2002 World Cup.

## ⬎ UK

The United Kingdom of Great Britain and Northern Ireland – some narrow it down to England – is credited with the invention of some of the most widely played sports in the world, including golf, athletics, football, cricket, rugby union, rugby league, tennis, badminton, and boxing. In the elite (fee-paying) public schools such as Rugby School, boys were encouraged to organize their own team sports, a practice continued in the ancient universities of Oxford and Cambridge to which many of those boys progressed. Horse-racing and golf had acquired governing bodies as early as the late 18th century. And it was to Rugby School, as well as the ancient universities and the USA's top colleges, that France's Baron Pierre de Coubertin travelled when looking for the inspiration to establish the modern Olympic Games.

Football in England was established in its professional league form in 1888–89, though amateur teams had contested the Football Association (FA) knockout trophy since 1871. England's professional national side has won only one international trophy, the Jules Rimet World Cup in 1966, playing all its matches at Wembley, London, giving it more recovery time between matches than any of its rivals.

Football and cricket have long dominated the sports pages in the UK press, though when a potential British champion emerges – in motor racing, tennis, or boxing for instance – the balance of coverage varies. Within the UK itself, the Celtic countries of Scotland, Wales, and Northern Ireland promote their own cultural and national identities through sports and particular sports events. These include the Highland and Caledonian Games in Scotland, a particular passion for rugby union in Wales, and Gaelic Football and hurling in (Northern) Ireland.

The UK is the only nation state able to field four separate, independent, national football teams in world football competition, a curious, widely resented and little understood historical anomaly. The UK (Great Britain, as recognized by the International Olympic Committee) has not fielded a football team at an Olympic Games for many years, knowing that if it did send a "unified team", other countries and nations around the world would dispute its right to have four full members of FIFA. Entering GB men's and women's teams at the London 2012 Olympics is therefore a risky commitment, given the ambitions and ruthlessness of many powerful players in the world of international football politics.

At the level of participation in regular organized team games, sports have been shaped by social class and status, but are in decline. In England's largest-ever survey of sports activity, in 2005/6, pilates overtook rugby union and track and field athletics, and entered the country's Top 20 list of participation sports. Yet, sports watching – particularly on television and via newer technologies – has never been higher.

........................................................

## ⬎ United Arab Emirates (UAE)

Of the UAE's seven emirates, oil-rich Abu Dhabi and Dubai are the most prominent. Dubai and Abu Dhabi have sought the labels of sports capital of the world, attracting high-profile events such as end-of-season tennis championships, golf circuit tournaments, and Formula 1 motor racing (in 2010, the last and deciding race on the circuit was in Abu Dhabi). The emirates have seen sports as a way of boosting the tourist industry, and also promoting the image of the country. Football has also been promoted by the state with some, but scarcely sustained, success. The sports agenda for UAE citizens, though, is heavily male-dominated. Women football players have organized, but face continuing difficulties and disapproval.

........................................................

## ⬎ Uruguay

Next to its neighbour Argentina across the River Plate, Uruguay has a small and undistinguished sporting tradition and pedigree. But its place in sports history is assured by its achievements in international football competitions. Double Olympic champion in the 1920s, the country helped FIFA president Jules Rimet launch the men's football World Cup in 1930. South America had its own (sub)continental federation, and Uruguay was looking for a hallmark event through which to celebrate the centenary of its constitution. The Centenario Stadium in Montevideo was constructed for this purpose, and Uruguay progressed inexorably to the title, defeating its giant rival Argentina in the final. At South Africa 2010, the men's football team lost narrowly in the semi-final. Basketball and rugby union are the country's other most popular sports.

## ⬎ USA

The Big Four – American football, basketball, baseball, and ice hockey – dominate the landscape of team sports in the United States of America. A combination of college athletics – operated in the big team games on a hugely commercial basis – with the interests of the professional leagues is a distinctive feature of the US sports system. College and university teams provide recruits to the professional ranks of American football and basketball, through the "draft" system. Indeed, universities cultivate a system of student-athletes across a wide range of sports. Golfer Tiger Woods and tennis player John McEnroe, who attended Stanford University, California, for instance, are examples of elite athletes and potential future champions who combined academic study – not always completed – with close-to-full-time athletic commitment. This system has also enabled the USA to excel at the Olympic Games and other international competitions, with college-sponsored athletes producing peak performances tailored to the cycle of the event.

A peculiarity of US sports culture is the relatively low profile of football, or soccer, at least in comparison to the Big Four. The USA has a fairly strong pedigree in international football competition, playing in early World Cup Finals and defeating England 1–0 in a stage match at the 1950 finals, and progressing to the later stages of Finals in 2002 and 2010. But the sport is still seen as marginal in the USA, despite increasing popularity among Hispanics, and a globally competitive profile for the national women's team. US companies, though, see the global prominence of football as an irresistible marketing opportunity, and their endorsement of top European and world competitions has undoubtedly raised the profile of the sport in the USA. The same could be said for certain Olympic sports that hardly feature in the everyday perceptions of sports fans.

Sports offer meritocratic possibilities for social mobility in the USA, as in almost any other society. But the country's wide range of established sports – from skiing to sailing, boxing to NASCAR stock-car racing, as well as the established professional team sports – does not simply confirm the myth of classlessness. Privileged people succeed in sports, and Olympians emerged early from the corridors of the New York Athletic Club and the elite universities of the east and west coasts. Even in the land of opportunity, with the ideology of the rise from log cabin to White House, it helps to know the right people in the right places.

## ⬃ Vanuatu

A small island nation in the South Pacific, Vanuatu participates in international sports through its membership of the Oceania federations, in football and rugby. Some football development has been secured for the island through FIFA's Goal project, and the national side boasts a memorable 4–2 win over giant fellow federation members New Zealand in the Oceania Nations Cup in 2004. But it is in world football politics, rather than on the field of play, that a tiny country like Vanuata can have some influence. Johnny Lulu, long-term secretary of its national football association, has the same voting rights at a FIFA congress (which elects the president) as his counterpart from Brazil, Italy, or Germany.

## ⬃ West Indies

The "British West Indies" are a loosely defined group of up to 18 states and territories in and around the Caribbean. They have defied attempts to federate them from the 17th century through to the 20th, but are linked by the English language and close relations with the UK. The West Indies are geographically dispersed and culturally disparate, and it is often said that there are only two West Indian institutions per se: the University of the West Indies and the "national" cricket team. Although individual islands compete separately in cricket, as in other sports such as football, the West Indies has always competed as a whole in test match cricket and in international one-day competitions. The overwhelming majority of West Indian cricketers have come from six countries: Trinidad and Tobago, Guyana, Barbados, the Leeward Islands, the Windward Islands, and Jamaica. For about 30 years, from the 1960s to the 1990s, the West Indies was the dominant power in world cricket, beating all other countries in test matches, and winning the first two World Cups in 1975 and 1979.

The decline of West Indian cricket since the 1990s has often been put down to Americanization, including the influence of American media, migration and sports scholarships, mainly in basketball and athletics, to colleges in the USA. Football has also gained a hold in some countries, and Jamaica (France, 1998) and Trinidad & Tobago (Germany, 2006) showed the quality of Caribbean football, qualifying for the men's World Cup Finals from the regional confederation. Those two countries have also provided the world's most outstanding sprinters of the 21st century.

## ⬃ Zimbabwe

With the exception of South Africa, Zimbabwe (originally Southern Rhodesia, then just Rhodesia) was the British colony in Africa with the largest white population. It has been the white population that has led the way in sports. For example, of Zimbabwe's eight Olympic gold medals one was won by the overwhelmingly white women's (field) hockey team in Moscow in 1980, and the other seven by swimmer Kirsty Coventry in 2004 and 2008. Zimbabwean rugby has also been dominated by the white minority, who were never as much as 10 percent of the population.

The most important and controversial sport in Zimbabwe has been cricket. The national team achieved test match status in 1992 based on an unsegregated, but predominantly white, body of players. Their greatest achievements were a test series victory over Pakistan, and fifth place in the 1999 World Cup. Zimbabwean cricket has declined markedly in the 21st century as players of all races have gone into exile because of President Robert Mugabe's repressive policies, and international teams have refused to travel to Zimbabwe. In many sports, including cricket and rugby, the dominant word in Zimbabwean sports has been "exodus", as players raised in the country have chosen to leave and play elsewhere.

# GLOSSARY OF COUNTRY NAMES

The following team names used in the maps, graphics and text require further explanation. The full names of two organizations sometimes referred to only by their initials are also given.

**China**  People's Republic of China

**Taiwan**  An island state not recognized by the United Nations, and referred to by the International Olympic Committee and other sporting organizations as **Chinese Taipei** out of deference to the People's Republic of China, which claims the island as part of its territory.

**Czechoslovakia**  The state that existed from 1918–92, after which it divided into the Czech Republic and Slovakia.

**GDR**  The German Democratic Republic, the socialist state established in northeast Germany in 1949, under the influence of the Soviet Union. It was reunified with the Federal Republic of Germany in 1990. On three occasions during that period, a combined German team competed at the Olympics as the **United Team of Germany**. The GDR participated as a separate state in the Olympics from 1968 to 1988.

**England**  An area of the **UK** represented in a number of international tournaments, notably those involving football, rugby, and at the Commonwealth Games.

**FIFA**  Fédération Internationale de Football Association.

**Germany**  In the medal tables in the atlas the total for Germany includes medals accumulated by the German team prior to the division of the country in 1949, to the teams in which West Germany (FDR) participated from 1949–90, and to the team that has represented a reunified Germany since 1990. *See also* **United Team of Germany**.

**Great Britain (GB)**  The name used by the International Olympic Committee and other organizations for the United Kingdom of Great Britain and Northern Ireland.

**IOC**  International Olympic Committee

**Ireland**  The Irish Republic (Eire). For rugby and hockey, players from Eire join with those from Northern Ireland (part of the UK) to form a combined Ireland team.

**Northern Ireland**  Six counties in the north of the island of Ireland that are part of the UK, and are represented in a number of international tournaments, notably football, and at the Commonwealth Games. For international rugby and hockey, players from Northern Ireland join with those from the Irish Republic to form a combined Ireland team.

**Scotland**  An area within the UK (partly self-governing), represented in a number of international tournaments, notably those involving football, rugby, and at the Commonwealth Games.

**Soviet Union**  Union of Soviet Socialist Republics (USSR), formed in 1922, and dissolved in 1991 into Russia and 14 independent states. *See also* **Unified Team.**

**UK**  Short form for United Kingdom of Great Britain and Northern Ireland.

**United Team of Germany**  A team comprising competitors from both West Germany (FDR) and East Germany (GDR), which competed at the Summer and Winter Olympics in 1956, 1960, and 1964.

**Unified Team**  A team comprising the states of the former **Soviet Union** (excepting Estonia, Latvia, and Lithuania), which competed at the 1992 Olympics.

**USSR**  Union of Soviet Socialist Republics, also known as **Soviet Union**.

**Wales**  An area within the UK (partly self-governing), represented in a number of international tournaments, notably those involving football, rugby, and at the Commonwealth Games.

# SOURCES

**9–12 INTRODUCTION**
A Tomlinson. 2005. Magnificent trivia: Olympic
spectacle, opening ceremonies, and some paradoxes
of globalization. In *Sport and leisure cultures*.
Minneapolis: University of Minnesota Press.
**Who plays?**
J Huizinga. 1949. *Homo ludens: A study of the play
element in modern culture*. London: Routledge.
J Hargreaves. 1994. *Sporting females: Critical issues
in the history and sociology of women's sports*.
London: Routledge.
MA Hall. 1996. *Feminism and sporting bodies: Essays
in theory and practice*. Champaign, IL: Human
Kinetics Press.
**What is sport?**
K Roberts. 2004. *The leisure industries*. Basingstoke:
Palgrave Macmillan.
A Guttmann. 2004. *Sports: The first five millennia*.
Amherst: University of Massachusetts Press.
Sport England. 2006. *Active people survey*. London:
Sport England.
P Bourdieu. 1984. *Distinction: A social critique of the
judgement of taste*. London: Routledge & Kegan Paul.
A Tomlinson (ed). 2007. *The Sport Studies Reader*
(section 1). London: Routledge.
R Giulianotti (ed). 2004. *Sport and modern social theorists*.
Basingstoke: Palgrave Macmillan.
**Where?**
J Bale. 1989. *Sports geography*. London: E & FN Spon.
S Cushion, J Lewis (eds). 2010. *The rise of 24-hour news
television: Global perspectives*. Oxford: Peter Lang.
**Why?**
S Terkel. 1975. Eric Nesterenko. In *The sporting life*, book
seven of *Working*. Harmondsworth: Penguin.
L Allison. 2001. *Amateurism in sport: An analysis and a
defence*. London: Frank Cass.
G Whannel. 2002. *Media sport stars: Masculinities and
moralities*. London: Routledge.
J Maguire. 1999. *Global sport: Identities, societies,
civilizations*. Cambridge: Polity Press.
Juvenal. 1992. *The satires*. Oxford: Oxford University Press.
HU Gumbrecht. 2006. *In praise of athletic beauty*.
Cambridge: Belknap/Harvard University Press.
**Why sports matter**
E Dunning. 1999. *Why sport matters: Sociological studies
of sport, violence, and civilization*. London: Routledge.
V de Grazia. 2005. *Irresistible empire: America's advance
through 20th-century Europe*. Cambridge: Harvard
University Press.
T Miller et al. 2001. *Globalization and sport: Playing the
world*. London: Sage.
RD Putnam. 2001. *Bowling alone. The collapse and revival
of American community*. New York: Touchstone/Simon
& Schuster.
C Lasch. 1979. *The culture of narcissism: American life in
an age of diminishing expectations*. New York: WW
Norton & Company.

**14–15 NATIONAL SPORTS**
EP Archetti. 1999. *Masculinities: Football, polo and the
tango in Argentina*. Oxford: Berg.
A Guttmann. 2004. *Sports: The first five millennia*.
Amherst: University of Massachusetts Press.
A Tomlinson. 2010. *A dictionary of sports studies*. Oxford:
Oxford University Press.
J Walton. Sports and the Basques: Constructed and
contested identities 1876–1936. *Journal of Historical
Sociology*. Forthcoming 2011.
J Bale. 2002. *Imagined Olympians: Body culture and
colonial representation in Rwanda*. Minneapolis:
University of Minnesota.
D Wallechinsky, J Loucky. 2008. *The complete book of the
Olympics*. London: Aurum Press.
Jump Up! Rwanda. www.jumpuprwanda.org

**18–19 THE OLYMPIC GAMES**
A Guttmann. 2002. *The Olympics: A history of the
modern Games, Second Edition*. Urbana and Chicago:
University of Illinois Press.
D Miller. 2008. *The official history of the Olympic Games

and the IOC: Athens to Beijing, 1894-2008*. Edinburgh:
Mainstream Publishing.
**Cold War games; Summer Olympics; Winter Olympics**
Olympic Medals. www.olympic.it [Acc. 2010 June 23]
**Usain Bolt** J Kollewe. Champion sprinter Usain Bolt helps
Puma trainers fly out of shops. 2009 Aug 24.
www.guardian.co.uk
**4.7bn TV audience...** Beijing Olympics draw largest ever
global TV audience. 2008 Sept 5.
http://blog.nielsen.com

**20–21 THE FOOTBALL WORLD CUP**
FIFA publications, including 2009 Financial Report and
FIFA.com website on ticketing.
**FIFA points ranking** FIFA/Coca-Cola World Ranking.
www.fifa.com [Acc. 2010 Aug]
**World Cup Winners 1930-2010; Location of World
Cup finals** Past FIFA World Cups. www.fifa.com
**FIFA Rights revenue** 2009 FIFA Financial Report.

**22–23 THE COMMONWEALTH GAMES**
Commonwealth Games Federation. www.thecgf.com
**Sub-Saharan Africa competes** Commonwealth
Games Results. www.thecgf.com [Acc. 2010 Sept];
Commonwealth Games medals table.
http://news.bbc.co.uk [Acc. 2010 Oct 22]
**Participating countries 2010** Delhi 2010.
www.thecgf.com
**2bn people in Commonwealth** The Commonwealth
Conversation.
www.thecommonwealthconversation.org
**Growing games** Story and growth of the Games.
www.thecgf.com

**24-25 DRUGS IN SPORT**
G Hunter. China cleans up its game. www.rdasia.com
[Acc. 2010 Aug 3]
J-L Chappelet, B Kübler-Mabbott. 2008. *The International
Olympic Committee and the Olympic system: The
governance of world sport*. London: Routledge.
D Wallechinsky, J Loucky. 2008. *The complete book of the
Olympics*. London: Aurum.
S Holt. Stars dimmed by Balco's shadow. 2004 Dec 6.
http://news.bbc.co.uk
T Knight. Beijing Olympics: Spectre of doping blights the
Games. 2008 Aug 1. www.telegraph.co.uk
**Positive support** www.wada-ama.org [Acc. 2010 July 23]
**Prohibited enhancements 2010** WADA. *The 2010
Prohibited List international standard, effective from
1 Jan 2010*. 2009 Sept 19. www.wada-ama.org
**Out in the open** Wallechinsky, Loucky op. cit.;
Holt op. cit.
**Bulgaria medals** www.olympic.org [Acc. 2010 Aug 18]

**26–27 TACKLING DISABILITY**
International Wheelchair & Amputee Sports Federation.
www.iwasf.com
PD Howe. 2011. Children of a lesser god: Paralympics
and high-performance sport. In J Sugden, A Tomlinson
(eds). *Watching the Olympics: Politics, power and
representation*. London: Routledge.
A Tomlinson. 2010. *A dictionary of sports studies*. Oxford:
Oxford University Press.
D. Whitteridge. Guttmann, Sir Ludwig (1899–1980).
www.oxforddnb.com
**International Paralympic Committee** National
Paralympic Committees. www.paralympic.org
[Acc. 2010 July 25]; Past Games. www.paralympic.org
**Criteria for disability** Parasport. www.parasport.org.uk
**Blade Runner** K Eason. Amputee sprinter Oscar Pistorius
allowed to compete in Beijing. 2008 May 17.
www.timesonline.co.uk

**28-29 GAY GAMES**
J Hargreaves. 1994. *Sporting females: Critical issues
in the history and sociology of women's sports*.
London: Routledge.
**"The City of Cleveland..."; $80m value to Cleveland
2014** Gay Games: Cleveland to host in 2010. 2009
Sept 29. www.huffingtonpost.com

**Too late for some** F Deford. 1977. *Big Bill Tilden: The
triumphs and the tragedy*. New York: Simon
& Schuster.
Brian Deer on Justin Fashanu. The Mail on Sunday.
1998 July 12. http://briandeer.com
**Matthew Mitcham** Matthew Mitcham shows: Everyone
can participate. www.gaygames.com
**Cologne 2010; Number of participants; Gender
breakdown; Sports with highest number of
participants** Participants Information.
www.games-cologne.de [Acc. 2010 Aug 20]

**30–31 DEVELOPMENT AND PEACE**
F Coalter. 2009. Sport in development. Accountability
or development? In R Levermore, A Beacon (eds).
*Sport and international development*. Basingstoke:
Palgrave Macmillan.
RS Gruneau. 2010. Sport, development and the challenge
of slums. Unpublished mss, forthcoming 2011.
J Sugden. 2010. Critical left-realism and sport
interventions in divided societies. *International Review
for the Sociology of Sport* 45/3. pp258-72.
Peace and Sport. www.peace-sport.org [Acc. 2010 Oct 7]
**Puma programmes**
Who We Are. http://vision.puma.com
PUMA vision sustainability report 2007/2008.
Herzogenaurach, Germany: PUMA AG Rudolf Dassler
Sport. http://images.puma.com
**Football4Peace** Football 4 Peace International.
www.football4peace.eu [Acc. 2010 Oct 22]
**Right to Play** Right to Play. www.righttoplay.com
**UNESCO programmes** Sports for peace and
development. www.unesco.org
**$147m FIFA to Africa...** FIFA. 2010. *A legacy for Africa*.
Zurich: FIFA Communications & Public Affairs Division.

**34–35 AMERICAN FOOTBALL**
J Sayre. He flies on the wing. 1955 Dec 26.
http://sportsillustrated.cnn.com
American Sports Data, Inc. 2008. *The superstudy of sports
participation® Volume II: Recreational sports 2007*.
Cortland Manor, NY: American Sports Data, Inc.
M Ozanian, K Badenhausen, D Bigman. The business of
football, 2009. 2009 Sept 2. www.forbes.com
Sports industry overview. Plunkett Research Ltd. 2009.
www.plunkettresearch.com [Acc. 2010 May 8]
ViewerTrack – The most watched TV sporting events
of 2009. 2010. Tinceline: futures sport +
entertainment. www.futuressport.com
Why did Super Bowl 2010 become the most watched TV
program ever? 2010 May 20. http://blogs.wsj.com
US Census. Table 1209. Adult attendance at sports events
by frequency: 2008.
**The gridiron camp** A Tomlinson. 2010. *A dictionary of
sports studies*. Oxford: Oxford University Press.
**Stacking**
R Smith. 1988. *Strikes, lockouts and Super Bowl: Inside
American football*. London: Heinemann Kingswood.
J Coakley. *Sports in society: Issues and controversies*,
10th Edition. Maidenhead: McGraw-Hill, 2009.
Super Bowl history. www.nfl.com
History: African-Americans in pro football.
www.profootballhof.com
N Halling. *American Football: Young, gifted and black
quarterbacks beat racism to lead NFL revolution*.
2004 Oct 27. www.independent.co.uk
**Footballers larger than life...** Weights taken from
NFL listings of players, analysis by Marcus Hunt.
www.nfl.com [Acc. 2010 May 11]
**The American Game** National Federation of State High
School Associations, Participation statistics: sports
statistics. www.nfhs.org [Acc. 2010 Apr 16]; US
Census. Table 16. Resident population by age and
state: 2008.
**Top 5 NFL Teams** NFL team valuations. 2009 Sept 2.
www.forbes.com
**Top NFL players** J Freedman. *The 50 highest-earning
American athletes*. 2009.
http://sportsillustrated.cnn.com
**19% increase...**American Sports Data, Inc. op. cit.

**Foreign fields** B Oliver. *Sport gears up for global revolution*. 2007 Oct 28. www.guardian.co.uk

### 36–37 BASEBALL
American Sports Data, Inc. 2008. See under AMERICAN FOOTBALL.
TF Carter. 2008. *The quality of home runs: The passion, politics, and language of Cuban baseball*. Durham and London: Duke University Press.
National Federation of State High School Associations. Participation statistics: sports statistics. www.nfhs.org [Acc. 2010 Apr 16]
World Baseball Classic. http://web.worldbaseballclassic.com
S Roberts, D Epstein. *Sources tell SI Alex Rodriguez tested positive for steroids in 2003*. 2009 Feb 7. http://sportsillustrated.cnn.com
GJ Mitchell. Report to the commissioner of baseball of an independent investigation into the illegal use of steroids and other performance enhancing substances by players in major league baseball. 2007 Dec 13. http://mlb.mlb.com
**A reflection of the nation**
N Dawidoff (ed). 2004. *Baseball: a literary anthology*. New York: The Library of America and Penguin Putnam Inc.
JA Michener. 1975. *Sports in America*. New York: Fawcett Press/Random House.
**12% of US adults...**US Census. Table 1209. Adult attendance at sports events by frequency: 2008.
**Babe Ruth** Stats, achievements. www.baberuth.com [Acc. 2010 Nov 12]
**Breaking through the color bar**
MLB Decline 1975-2010. [Acc. 2010 Nov 12] http://africanamericanbaseballleague.com
R Adams. *Jackie Robinson day*. 2010 Apr 21. www.guardian.co.uk
N Lanctot. 2004. *Negro league baseball: The rise and ruin of a black institution*. Philadelphia: University of Pennsylvania Press.
**The American game**
National Federation of State High School Associations op. cit.
US Census. Table 16. Resident Population by Age and State: 2008
**Top 5 Major League Teams** K Badenhausen, M Ozanian, C Settimi. The business of baseball. 2010 Apr 7. www.forbes.com
**Top Major League Players** J Freedman. *The 50 highest-earning American athletes, 2009*. http://sportsillustrated.cnn.com [Acc. 2010 Apr 17]
**27m TV viewers...** ViewerTrack – The most watched TV sporting events of 2009. 2010. London: Initiative, futures sport + entertainment. www.futuressport.com
**World Baseball Classic event** World Baseball Classic. http://web.worldbaseballclassic.com

### 38–39 BASKETBALL
American Sports Data, Inc. 2008. See under AMERICAN FOOTBALL.
K Badenhausen, M Ozanian, C Settimi. The business of basketball. 2009 Dec 9. www.forbes.com
N George. 1992. *Elevating the game: Black men and basketball*. New York: Harper Collins.
Sports industry overview. Plunkett Research Ltd. 2009. www.plunkettresearch.com [Acc. 2010 May 8]
2007-08 Player Survey: Mr. Average. 2007 Nov 21. www.nba.com
Players. www.nba.com
Season opens with record-tying 83 international players. 2009 Dec 9. www.nba.com
I Berkow. *Looking over Jordan: David Halberstam examines the life and times of the world's greatest athlete*. 1999 Jan 31. www.nytimes.com
M Novak. 1976. *The joy of sports: Endzones, bases, baskets, balls, and the consecration of the American spirit*. New York: Basic Books.
**Inventing the game** A Tomlinson. 2010. *A dictionary of sports studies*. Oxford: Oxford University Press.
**32m enjoy...** American Sports Data, Inc. op. cit.
**Olympic rivalries** D Wallechinsky, J Loucky. 2008. *The complete book of the Olympics*. London: Aurum Press. www.olympic.org [Acc. 2010 Apr 19]
**The American Game**
National Federation of State High School Associations, Participation statistics: sports statistics. www.nfhs.org [Acc. 2010 Apr 16]
US Census. Table 16. Resident population by age and state: 2008.
**Top 5 NBA Teams** Badenhausen, Ozanian, Settimi op. cit.
**Top NBA Players** J Freedman. *The 50 highest-earning American athletes, 2009*. http://sportsillustrated.cnn.com [Acc. 2010 Apr 17]
**The European Game** Euroleague Basketball. www.euroleague.net [Acc. 2010 Nov 12]

### 40–41 BOXING – AMATEUR
EJ Gorn. 1986. *The manly art: Bare-knuckle prize fighting in America*. Cornell University Press: Ithaca and London.
T Hughes. 1958. *Tom Brown's school-days* (1857). Macmillan & Co Ltd: London.
J Sugden. 1996. *Boxing: An international analysis*. Manchester: Manchester University Press.
**The Queensberry Rules; Boxing – the language of everyday life**
J Davis. Douglas, John Sholto, ninth marquess of Queensberry (1844–1900). www.oxforddnb.com
MA Bryant. Chambers, John Graham (1843–1883). www.oxforddnb.com
S Shipley. 1989. Boxing. In T Mason (ed). *Sport in Britain: A social history*. Cambridge: Cambridge University Press.
A Tomlinson. 2010. *A dictionary of sports studies*. Oxford: Oxford University Press.
**The politics of boxing** J Riordan. 1981. *Sport under Communism: The USSR, Czechoslovakia, the GDR, China, Cuba*. 2nd edition revised. London: Hurst.
**Olympic boxers** D Wallechinsky, J Loucky. 2008. *The complete book of the Olympics 2008 edition*. London: Aurum Press.
**Olympic medals** www.olympic.org [Acc. 2010 Mar 14]

### 42–43 BOXING – PROFESSIONAL
K Jones. 2001. A key moral issue: Should boxing be banned? *Sport in Society* 4/1. pp63-72.
P Radford. 2001. *The celebrated Captain Barclay: Sport, gambling and adventure in Regency times*. London: Headline Book Publishing.
S Shipley. 1989. see BOXING – AMATEUR.
**Bare-knuckle fighting**
GC Boase. Cribb, Tom (1781–1848), rev. Julian Lock. www.oxforddnb.com
EJ Gorn. 1986. see BOXING – AMATEUR
R Nevill. 1910. *Sporting days and sporting ways*. London.
G Le G Norgate. Winter, Thomas [Tom Spring] (1795–1851), rev. Julian Lock. www.oxforddnb.com
Radford op. cit.
**The rise of the heavyweight black boxer**
B Considine. 1988. The Louis-Schmeling fight, 22 June 1938. In J Carey (ed). *The Faber book of reportage*. London: Faber & Faber.
C Lemert. 2003. *Muhammad Ali: Trickster in the culture of irony*. Cambridge: Polity Press.
M Marqusee. 1999. *Redemption song: Muhammad Ali and the spirit of the sixties*. London: Verso.
**World organizations**
IFB/USB History. www.ibf-usba-boxing.com
World Boxing Association. www.wbaonline.com
World Boxing Council. http://wbcboxing.com
World Boxing Organisation. www.wbo-int.com
**The value of boxing**
Big bout is sure to break records. 1921 June 26. http://query.nytimes.com
J Doyle. Dempsey vs. Carpentier, July 1921. 2008 Sept 8. www.pophistorydig.com
S Povich. 1927. Tunney vs. Dempsey. 1927 Sept 22. www.washingtonpost.com
D Margolick. 2005. *Beyond glory: Joe Louis vs. Max Schmeling, and a world on the brink*. New York: Alfred A. Knopf.

Mayweather-De La Hoya fight sets pay-per-view records. 2007 May 9. www.cbc.ca
Battle for supremacy in Manila. 1975 Oct 13. www.time.com
M Hirsley. The Dempsey-Tunney fight. www.chicagotribune.com
Lennox Lewis versus Mike Tyson (2002 June 8). www.torrentdownloads.net

### 44–45 CRICKET
J Kaufman, O Patterson. Cross-national cultural diffusion: The global spread of cricket. 2005 Feb. *American Sociological Review*. vol. 70. p82-110.
P Wilby. *The Empire strikes back*. 2009 July 2. www.newstatesman.com
S Szymanski. The rise of the Indian Premier League. Seminar presentation, Judge Business School, Cambridge. 2010 Feb 22.
**A sporting legend** GMD Howat. Grace, William Gilbert [WG] (1848–1915). www.oxforddnb.com
**The bodyline controversy**
R Holt. 1989. *Sport and the British: A modern history*. Oxford: Oxford University Press.
D Hamilton. 2009. *Harold Larwood*. London: Quercus Publishing PLC.
GMD Howat. Jardine, Douglas Robert (1900–1958). www.oxforddnb.com
P Wynne-Thomas. Larwood, Harold (1904–1995). www.oxforddnb.com
**Sachin Tendulkar caption**
Sachin Tendulkar vs Ricky Ponting : Most career century & runs: Test + ODI. www.itsonlycricket.com
BBC Sport. Australia vs. India 2nd Test. 2009 Oct 21. www.bbc.co.uk
**International Cricket Council** ICC Member Countries. http://icc-cricket.yahoo.net [Acc. 2010 May 30]
**32m television audience** ViewerTrack. The most watched TV sporting events of 2009. 2010. London: Initiative, futures sport + entertainment. www.futuressport.com
**ICC Cricket World Cup winners**
Past Events. http://icc-cricket.yahoo.net
ICC Womens World Cup 2009 – Event history. http://iccwomensworldcup.yahoo.

### 46–47 CUE SPORTS
G Burn. 1986. *Pocket money: Bad-boys, business-heads and boom-time snooker*. London: Heinemann.
N Polsky. 1967. *Hustlers, beats and others*. Chicago: Anchor Books.
D Trelford. 1986. *Snookered*. London: Faber and Faber.
*Sport by sport factsheet*. 2006 Dec 6. London: Sport England.
*Sport market place directory*. 2008. Millerton, NY: Grey House Publishing.
World Confederation of Billiard Sports. www.billiardworld.org
**A man's world** Polsky op. cit.; Mosconi Cup. www.matchroompool.com
**Structure of the WCBS** World Confederation of Billiard Sports. www.billiardworld.org
**Top 5 Pool earners** AZBilliards.com. www.azbilliards.com
**Allison Fisher** Allison Fisher. www.allisonfisher.com
**Professional snooker** Burn op. cit.; Trelford op. cit.
**Top 5 Snooker Earners** Rankings. www.worldsnooker.com [Acc. 2010 May 20]

### 48–49 CYCLING
L Armstrong. 2001. *It's not about the bike: My journey back to life*. London. Yellow Jersey Press.
Union Cycliste Internationale. www.uci.ch
**Champion material** A Tomlinson. 2010. *A dictionary of sports studies*. Oxford: Oxford University Press.
**Lance Armstrong caption** Lance Armstrong sparks mass ride through Paisley. 2009 Aug 18. www.guardian.co.uk
**Tour de France**
CS Thompson. 2008. *The Tour de France: A cultural history*. Berkeley: University of California Press.
Union Cycliste Internationale op. cit.

# SOURCES

**Speed, endurance and artistry** Union Cycliste Internationale op. cit.
**Olympic medals** www.olympic.org [Acc. 2010 July 9]
**20 millions bikes sold...** COLIBI – COLIPED report. European bicycle market - industry and market profile 2009 edition. www.colibi.com

## 50–51 FOOTBALL – INTERNATIONAL
AH Fabian, G Green (eds). 1960. *Association Football volume one*. London: The Caxton Publishing Company Limited.
D Goldblatt. 2006. *The ball is round. A global history of soccer*. New York: Riverhead/Penguin.
P Lanfranchi et al. 2004. *100 years of football: The FIFA centennial book*. London: Weidenfeld & Nicholson.
Pele, with O Duarte, A Belos. 2006. *Pele: The autobiography*. London: Simon & Schuster.
**Football at the Olympics** D Wallechinsky, J Loucky. 2008. *The complete book of the Olympics* . London: Aurum Press.
**The universal language** R Goode, M Bottanelli, K Javier. 2010. *Football Muti*. Johannesburg: Jacana Media.
**The USA – Football's final frontier**
American Sports Data, Inc. 2008. See under AMERICAN FOOTBALL.
AS Markovits, SL Hellerman. 2001. *Offside: Soccer and American exceptionalism*. Princeton and Oxford: Princeton University Press.
T Miller. Soccer Conquers the World. 2010 May 30. *The Chronicle Review: The chronicle of higher educat*R Blum. World Cup Final draws record U.S. TV audience. 2010 July 12. http://nbcsports.msnbc.com
**Women's football**
FIFA Women's World Cup. www.fifa.com
Women footballers blast Blatter. 2004 Jan 16. http://news.bbc.co.uk
**Women's World Cup winners** FIFA Women's World Cup. op. cit.

## 52–53 FOOTBALL – EUROPEAN
S Hamil, S Chadwick (eds). 2010. *Managing football: An international perspective*. Oxford: Elsevier.
D Runciman. They can play, but they can never win. 2006 May 29. www.newstatesman.com
A Tomlinson. Something for the weekend: The Champions League Final moves to a weekend. 2010 July. *When Saturday comes*. 281.
**Leagues of their own**
T Mason. 1980. *Association football and English society 1863-1915*. Sussex: The Harvester Press.
D Goldblatt. 2008. *The ball is round: A global history of soccer*. New York: Riverhead Books.
**Lionel Messi caption** The 50 highest salaries of football players 2009/2010. 2009 Feb 15. www.futebolfinance.com
**Finances of top clubs**
PJ Schwartz, P Maidment, MK Ozanian. Most valuable soccer teams. 2010 Apr 21. www.forbes.com
**UEFA** Member Associations. www.uefa.com [Acc. 2010 July 20]
**UEFA Champions League TV audience**
ViewerTrack – The most watched TV sporting events of 2009. 2010. London: Initiative, futures sport + entertainment. www.futuressport.com
A King. 2004. The new symbols of European football. *International Review for the Sociology of Sport* 39/3: p323-36.
UEFA documentation and databases, in possession of the author (including 2006-07 UEFA Champions League Television Coverage & Audience Report, with Sponsorship Intelligence).
**"...nothing unites..."** Gazetto dello Sport. 2005. (cited in UEFA documentation).
**€310m...**S Chadwick. 2009. *The MasterCard heart of sports commerce report*. Commissioned by UCL sponsor MasterCard.
**European Cup/UCL winners *1956-2010*** History – Football's premier club competition. www.uefa.com

## 54–55 GOLF – AMATEUR
Golf and the economic downturn. 2010. Budapest: KPMG Advisory Ltd. www.golfbenchmark.com
*The value of golf to Europe, Middle East and Africa. 2008.* Budapest: KPMG Advisory Ltd. www.golfbenchmark.com
*Public Golf Courses Industry Report. 2010.* Michigan: The Gale Group.
*NGF reports number of core golfer in US higher than expected. 2007 May 22.* www.worldgolf.com
*J Hays. Recreational golf in Japan.* http://factsanddetails.com [Acc. 2010 Nov 19]
*GolfNow.* www.golfchannelsolutions.com
*The golf business community.* http://golfbusinesscommunity.com
**Origins of the modern game**
J Lowerson. 1993. *Sport and the English middle classes 1870-1914*. Manchester and New York: Manchester University Press.
J Lowerson. 1989. Golf. In T Mason (ed) *Sport in Britain: A social history*. Cambridge: Cambridge University Press.
**Golfing terms** B Kelley. Golf history FAQ. http://golf.about.com
**US golfers; Number of golfers**
Public golf courses industry report op. cit.
G D'Amato. Number of golfers continues to decline in US. 2009 May 13. www.jsonline.com
**Ethnicity of golfers; Percentage of ethnic population**
National Golf Foundation. 2003. Minority golf participation in the US – African-American, Asian-American, Hispanic-American. www.golf2020.com
**The cost of golf** Golf Link. www.golflink.com [Acc. 2010 Mar 16]
**Golf in the USA** Golf Course Directory. www.golflink.com [Acc. 2010 Mar 16]
**Green fees** Golf Benchmark Survey 2007. Budapest: KPMG Advisory Ltd. www.golfbenchmark.com
**Course upkeep** L Alyward. By the numbers. 2003 Sept 1. www.golfdom.com

## 56–57 GOLF – PROFESSIONAL
Agence-France Presse. Obama on Tiger: still a 'terrific golfer'. 2010 Mar 18. http://sports.sg.msn.com
J Azpiri. 2009 British Open prize money: Stewart Cink takes home £750,000. 2009 July 19. www.nowpublic.com
Armchair supporters. Is the Super Bowl the most popular sports event in the world? 2010 Feb 9. www.economist.com
**The Tiger factor**
K Badenhausen. *Sports' first billion-dollar man*. 2008 Sept 29. www.forbes.com
B Elliott. Before and after Tiger Woods. 2009 Dec 13. www.guardian.co.uk
Tiger Woods sex scandal won't derail PGA Tour, Commissioner Tim Finchem says. 2009 Dec 17. http//:www.leighvalleylive.com
**National pride**
The history of the Ryder Cup. www.rydercup.com
Past results of the Ryder Cup. www.rydercup.com
The Ryder Cup 2010. www.rydercupwales2010.com
**Professional tours**
US PGA Tour. www.pgatour.com [Acc. 2010 Nov 19]
PGA European Tour. www.europeantour.com [Acc. 2010 Nov 19]
LPGA. www.lpga.com [Acc. 2010 Nov 19]
Ladies European Tour. www.ladieseuropeantour.com [Acc. 2010 Nov 19]

## 58–59 GYMNASTICS AND EXERCISE
Artistic gymnastics equipment and history. www.olympic.org
**Politicized bodies** A Tomlinson. 2010. *A dictionary of sports studies*. Oxford: Oxford University Press.
**The fitness boom**
Resilience in the fitness sector. www.theleisuredatabase.com
Gym, health and fitness clubs – US Industry Report. www.ibisworld.com
L Mansfield. 2011. Sexercise: Working out heterosexuality in Jane Fonda's Fitness Books. *Leisure Studies*. Forthcoming.
**Elfins of the bars: East to West**
A Guttmann. 1996. *Sports spectators*. New York: Columbia University Press.
Olga today. www.olgakorbut.com
**Five gymnastic disciplines**
Fédération Internationale de Gymnastique. www.fig-gymnastics.com
D Wallechinsky, J Loucky. 2008. *The complete book of the Olympics*. London: Aurum Press.
**Gymnastics for all** Fédération Internationale de Gymnastique op. cit.
**Artistic gymnastics medals** www.olympic.org [Acc. 2010 July 28]
**9 The number of Olympic golds...** Larissa Latynina. www.olympic.org

## 60–61 HANDBALL
A Fraser. Handball is big business across Europe. 2009 Dec 11. www.sportspromedia.com
Ranking table. www.ihf.info [Acc. 2010 Aug 13]
A Tomlinson. 2010. *A dictionary of sports studies*. Oxford: Oxford University Press.
ViewerTrack – The most watched TV sporting events of 2009. 2010. London: Initiative, futures sport + entertainment. www.futuressport.com www.coachinghandball.com
**Konrad Koch** A Tomlinson. 2010. *A dictionary of sports studies*. Oxford: Oxford University Press.
**17m TV viewers** ViewerTrack op. cit.
**Beach handball** www.ihf.info [Acc. 2010 Aug 13]
**International handball; Marcus Wislander** Ranking table op. cit.
**Olympic handball; Olympic gold;** www.olympic.org [Acc. 2010 Aug 12]

## 62–63 HOCKEY
**Origins of field hockey**
Hockey Equipment and History. www.olympic.org
Sport England. 2006 Dec 7. *Active people survey*. London: Sport England.
**Field hockey**
Directory – National Associations 2010. www.fihockey.org www.olympic.org [Acc. 2010 May 29]
**Ice Hockey**
R Gruneau, D Whitson. 1994. *Hockey night in Canada: Sport, identities and cultural politics*. Toronto: Garamond Press.
*Sport market place directory*. 2008. Millerton, NY: Grey House Publishing.
International Ice Hockey Federation. www.iihf.com
IIHF Member National Associations. www.iihf.com [Acc. 2010 July 23]
*NFHS participation survey: Participation statistics*. 2010. National Federation of High School Associations.
**IIHF member national associations**
www.iihf.com [Acc. 2010 July 23]
www.iihf.com [Acc. 2010 May 29]
**Top 10 NHL Teams**
K Badenhausen, MK Ozanian, C Settimi. The business of hockey, 2009. 2009 Nov 11. www.forbes.com
**Photo** J Soares. 2011. East Beats West – Ice-hockey and the Cold War. In A Tomlinson et al (eds). *Sport and the transformation of modern Europe*. London: Routledge. Forthcoming.

## 64–65 HORSE RACING
C Milmo. How the sport of Kings became everyone's favourite pastime. 2008 Jan 3. www.independent.co.uk
G Plumptree. 1985. *The fast set: The world of Edwardian racing*. London: Andre Deutsch.
W Vamplew. 1989. Horse-Racing. In T Mason (ed). *Sport in Britain: A social history*. Cambridge: Cambridge University Press.
**Seabiscuit** L Hillenbrand. 2001. *Seabiscuit: The true story of three men and a racehorse*. London: Fourth Estate.
**Gambling** Betting statistics in Euro 2008. www.horseracingintfed.com [Acc. 2010 June 20]

£15m…Bindaree wins Grand National. 2009 Apr 8.
www.dailymail.co.uk
**Racing purses** Race fixtures & results.
www.horseracingintfed.com [Acc. 2010 June 20]
**World's top ten equine earners** M Farrell. The world's
top earning horses. 2009 Jan 5. www.forbes.com

**66–67 ICE SKATING**
American Sports Data, Inc. 2008. See under AMERICAN
FOOTBALL.
Sport England. 2006 Dec 7. *Active people survey headline
results. Sport by sport fact sheet.*
www.sportengland.org
D Wallechinsky. 1993. *The complete book of the Winter
Olympics.* London: Aurum Press.
**Sonja Henie**
A Tomlinson. 2010. *A dictionary of sports studies.* Oxford:
Oxford University Press.
Wallechinsky op. cit.
**The expansion of ice skating** International Skating
Union. www.isu.org [Acc. 2010 Aug 23]
**Going for gold; Top gold-medal winning countries
to 2010** www.olympic.org [Acc. 2010 Aug 6]
www.olympic.it [Acc. 2010 Aug 6]
**Class wars on the ice** S Stoloff. 2000. Tonya Harding,
Nancy Kerrigan, and the bodily figuration of social
class. In S Birrell, MG McDonald (eds) *Reading sport:
Critical essays on power and representation.* Boston:
Northeastern University Press.

**68–69 LIFESTYLE AND EXTREME SPORTS**
A Tomlinson et al. 2005. *Lifestyle sports and national sport
policy: An agenda for research.* London: Sport England.
B Wheaton. 2004. Introduction: Mapping the lifestyle
sport-scape. *Understanding lifestyle sports:
Consumption, identity and difference.* London:
Routledge.
Sport England. 2006 Dec 7. Active people survey headline
results. Sport by sport fact sheet.
www.sportengland.org
H Thorpe, B Wheaton. The Olympic movement, action
sports, and the search for generation Y. In J Sugden,
A Tomlinson (eds) *Watching the Olympics: Politics,
power and representation.* London: Routledge.
Forthcoming 2011.
**Characteristics of lifestyle sports** Wheaton op. cit.
**Pay for display; Highest-earning action sports stars**
K Badenhausen. The highest paid action sports stars.
2009 Feb 18. www.forbes.com
**X Games**
ESPN X Games 16: Increased attendance and record on-
line activity. www.espnmediazone3.com
[Acc. 2010 Sept 23]
ESPN personal communication, email: 2010 Aug 23.
X Games 16 best whip comp HD. www.youtube.com
[Acc. 2010 Sept 25]
**Snowboard superstars; 30m US viewers…**
R Kim. Tony Hawk, Shaun White top Forbes' list of richest
action sports athletes. 2009 Feb 20.
http://outdoors.fanhouse.com
C Settimi. Top-earning athletes of the 2010 Winter
Olympics. 2010 Feb 9. www.forbes.com
J Gomez. Shaun White, Kim Yu-Na are 2010 Winter
Games' highest-paid athletes with $8M earnings each
in 2009. 2010 Feb 11. http://thenextreporter.com

**70–71 MARATHON**
J Bryant. 2006. *The London Marathon: The history of the
greatest race on earth.* London: Random House.
M Polley. Brasher, Christopher William (1928–2003).
www.oxforddnb.com
D Wallechinsky, J Loucky. 2008. *The complete book of the
Olympics .* London: Aurum Press.
**Origins of the marathon**
JJ MacAloon. 1981. *This great symbol: Pierre de Coubertin
and the origins of the Modern Olympic Games.*
Chicago: Chicago University Press.
JP Verinis. 2005. Spiridon Loues, the modern *Foustanéla,*
and the symbolic power of *Pallikariá* at the 1896
Olympic Games. *Journal of Modern Greek Studies* 23.

**$1m WMM jackpot…**2009 Berlin Marathon media pack.
www.berlin-marathon.com
**In for the long run** D Wallechinsky, J Loucky op. cit.
**The Big Five; Country of origin of winners of World
Marathon Majors**
2009 Berlin Marathon media pack.
www.berlin-marathon.com
Berlin Marathon 2010. www.berlin-marathon.com
[Acc. 2010 Oct 26]
Boston Marathon. www.baa.org [Acc. 2010 Aug 9]
Chicago Marathon 2010 website and media pack.
www.chicagomarathon.com [Acc. 2010 Oct 26]
London Marathon website and media guide.
www.virginlondonmarathon.com [Acc. 2010 Aug 9]
New York Marathon. www.ingnycmarathon.org
[Acc. 2010 Nov 20]
**London 2010 logistics** London media guide op. cit.
**New York 2009 logistics** Official facts and stats via email
from event organisers. 2010 July 31.
**Olympic gold** www.olympic.org [Acc. 2010 Aug 13]
**African domination** A Tomlinson. 2010. *A dictionary of
sports studies.* Oxford. Oxford University Press.

**72–73 MARTIAL ARTS**
American Sports Data, Inc. 2008. See under AMERICAN
FOOTBALL.
Sport England. 2006 Dec 7. *Active people survey headline
results. Sport by sport fact sheet.* London: Sport
England.
D Wallechinsky, J Loucky. 2008. *The complete book of the
Olympics .* London: Aurum Press.
Martial Arts Clubs United Kingdom.
www.martialartsclubs.co.uk
National Federation of State High School Associations.
Participation statistics: sports statistics. www.nfhs.org
[Acc. 2010 Aug 26]
**Principles for karate practitioners** International Karate
Federation. www.ikfhawaii.com
**Karate**
World Karate Federation. www.wkf-handicapped.com
Martial Arts Clubs United Kingdom op. cit.
A Tomlinson. 2010. *A dictionary of sports studies.* Oxford:
Oxford University Press.
**Taekwondo**
Sport England. op .cit.
A Tomlinson. 2005. The making of the global sports
economy: ISL, Adidas and the rise of the corporate
player in world sport. In ML Silk et al (eds) *Sport and
corporate nationalisms.* Oxford: Berg.
Andrew Jennings (with Clare Sambrook). 1996. *The New
Lords of the Rings: Olympic corruption and how to buy
gold medals.* London: Simon & Schuster.
World Taekwondo Federation. www.wtf.org
[Acc. 2010 Aug 19]
www.olympic.org [Acc. 2010 Aug 12]
**Judo**
International Judo Federation World ranking list updated
12 July 2010. http://intjudo.eu [Acc. 2010 Aug 23]
www.olympic.org [Acc. 2010 Aug 12]

**74–75 MOTOR RACING**
C Sylt, C Reid. 2009. *Formulamoney: Formula One's
financial performance guide.* Money Sport Media Ltd
with publishing partner CNC-Communications and
Network Consulting.
C Sylt, C Reid. Mid season sponsor boost for F1 teams,
but cash is still short. 2010 May 9.
www.independent.co.uk
ViewerTrack – The most watched TV sporting events
of 2009. 2010. Initiative, futures sport +
entertainment. www.futuresport.com
**Top 10; $4.6bn…; Ferrari car caption** Sylt, Reid. 2009
op cit.
**The Magic of Fangio** A Tomlinson. 2010. *A dictionary of
sports studies.* Oxford: Oxford University Press.
**Racing USA**
JI Newman. 2007. A Detour through NASCAR Nation:
Ethnographic articulations of a neoliberal sporting
spectacle. *International Review for the Sociology of
Sport,* 42/3: pp289-308.

Indianapolis 500. www.indianapolismotorspeedway.com
*Dario Franchitti. www.franchitti.com*
*Helio Castroneves. http://heliocastroneves.com*
Danica Patrick NASCAR 2010 deal likely soon.
2009 Nov 6. www.dancewithshadows.com
Danica Patrick at the SI Swimsuit Party. www.youtube.com
[Acc. 2010 Aug 13]
**Formula 1**
FIA Member Clubs. www.fia.com [Acc. 2010 Aug 10]
Formula 1 2010 – world venue map and circuit guide.
http://news.bbc.co.uk [Acc. 2010 June 16]

**76–77 MULTI-SPORTS**
**The greatest athlete; Multisports at the Summer
Olympics**
A Tomlinson. 2010. *A dictionary of sports studies.* Oxford:
Oxford University Press.
D Wallechinsky, J Loucky. 2008. *The complete book of the
Olympics .* London: Aurum Press.
International Triathlon Union. www.triathlon.org
**Main events** Wallechinsky, Loucky op. cit.
**Olympic gold medals** www.olympic.org
[Acc. 2010 Aug 6]

**78–79 RUGBY**
E Dunning, K Sheard. 1979. *Barbarians, gentlemen and
players: A sociological study of the development of
rugby football.* New York: New York University Press.
**Rugby sevens** Emirates Airline Dubai Rugby Sevens.
www.dubairugby7s.com
**28lbs…**JH Brooks et al. 2005. Epidemiology of injuries in
English professional rugby union: part 1 match injuries.
*British Journal of Sports Medicine,* 39/10. pp757-66.
**The class divide**
T Collins. 1998. *Rugby's great split: Class, culture and the
origins of Rugby League football.* London: Frank Cass.
Super League. www.superleague.co.uk
**Jonah Lomu caption** C Hewett. On the wing and a
prayer: Profile: Jonah Lomu. 1999 Oct 9.
www.independent.co.uk
**International Rugby Board**
World Rankings. www.irb.com [Acc. 2010 May]
IRB World Cup. www.rugbyworldcup.com
[Acc. 2010 Nov 20]
**Rugby World Cup winners** Rugby World Cup History.
www.rugbyfootballhistory.com
**Global reach of Rugby World Cup** Financing the Global
Game. Dublin: Rugby World Cup Limited.
www.irb.com

**80–81 SAILING**
P Bourdieu. 1986. *Distinction: A social critique of the
judgement of taste.* London: Routledge.
ISAF Sailing World Championships. www.sailing.org
ISAF Sailing World Cup. www.sailing.org
Classes and equipment. www.sailing.org
The Vendée Globe. www.vendeeglobe.org
The Volvo Ocean Race. www.volvooceanrace.com
**Peter Blake**
T Bruce, B Wheaton. 2009. Rethinking global sports
migration and forms of transnational, cosmopolitan
and diasporic belonging: A case study of international
yachtsman Sir Peter Blake. *Social Identities: Journal for
the Study of Race, Nation and Culture,* 15/5: 585-608.
**The America's Cup**
Victory USA! 2010 Feb 14. http://33rd.americascup.com
BMW Oracle Racing's America's Cup: A victory for
database technology. 2010 Apr. www.oracle.com
**ISAF Map** ISAF member national authorities.
www.sailing.org [Acc. 2010 July 7]
**First world first**
Olympic sailing medal table. www.sailing.org
[Acc. 2010 July 3]
The history of Olympic sailing. www.sailing.org
[Acc. 2010 July 7]
**Windsurfing**
Sport England. 2006 Dec 7. *Active people survey
headline results. Sport by sport fact sheet.* London:
Sport England.

# SOURCES

B Wheaton. 2004. *Understanding lifestyle sports: Consumption, identity and difference*. London: Routledge.

## 82–83 SKIING AND SNOWBOARDING

S Hudson. 2000. *Snow business: A study of the international ski industry*. London: Cassell.

TF Burns. Lunn, Sir Arnold Henry Moore (1888–1974). www.oxforddnb.com

International Ski Federation. www.fis-ski.com

**Piste pioneer** In search of… Conan Doyle in the Swiss Alps. 2003 Nov 2. www.independent.co.uk

**High earners**

C Settimi. Top-earning athletes of the 2010 Winter Olympics. 2010 Feb 9. www.forbes.com

J Gomez. Shaun White, Kim Yu-Na are 2010 Winter Games' highest-paid athletes with $8M earnings each in 2009. 2010 Feb 11. http://thenextreporter.com

**Ski disciplines and boarder tensions**

A Tomlinson. *A dictionary of sports studies*. Oxford: Oxford University Press.

D Wallechinsky, J Loucky. 2008. *The complete book of the Olympics* . London: Aurum Press.

Alpine Skiing. www.fis-ski.com

**Olympic gold medals**

www.olympic.org [Acc. 2010 Aug 13]

Alpine skiing medals. www.vancouver2010.com [Acc. 2010 Aug 13]

## 84–85 SWIMMING AND DIVING

D Wallechinsky, J Loucky. 2008. *The complete book of the Olympics*. London: Aurum Press.

K Juba. 2008. *The Story of LEN*. Luxembourg: HNI International and Ligue Europpènne de Natation.

G Chambers, AAP. Cathy Freeman's golden memory still shines. 2010 Sept 15. www.dailytelegraph.com.au

S Linacre. Article: Participation in sports and physical recreation. 2007 Aug 7. Canberra: Australian Bureau of Statistics. www.ausstats.abs.gov.au

Sport England. 2006 Dec 7. *Active people survey headline results. Sport by sport fact sheet*. London: Sport England.

*Sports market place directory*. 2008. Millerton, New York: Grey House Publishing.

C Sprawson. 1993. *Haunts of the Black masseur: Swimmer as hero*. New York: Pantheon.

Ligue Européenne de Natation. www.len.eu

The Fédération Internationale de Natation. www.fina.org

On the scene: Cliff diving for the Olympics. Around the Rings. 2010 Sept 28. http://aroundtherings.com

**Ahead of the game**

S Hart. Swimwear giant Speedo hit back at 'unfair advantage' claims. 2010 Feb 19. www.telegraph.co.uk

Wallechinsky, Loucky op. cit.

**Channel swimming**

C Sprawson. Webb, Matthew [Captain Webb] (1848–1883). www.oxforddnb.com

A Tomlinson. 2010. *A dictionary of sports studies*. Oxford: Oxford University Press.

**Olympic success**

D Rovell. Phelps' Kellogg deal won't be renewed. 2009 Feb 5. www.cnbc.com

V Michaelis. Michael Phelps hits reset with new suit at US championships. 2010 Aug 3. www.usatoday.com

**Swimming gold medals** www.olympic.org [Acc. 2010 Aug 31 & Sept 1]

**Diving for China** Wallechinsky, Loucky op. cit.

**Diving gold medals** www.olympic.org [Acc. 2010 Aug 31 & Sept 1]

## 86–87 TENNIS

J Feinstein. 1991. *Hard courts*. London: Bloomsbury.

Barclays ATP World Tour Finals. www.barclaysatpworldtourfinals.com

J Macur. Serbian players emerge from a broken country. 2007 June 3. www.nytimes.com

National Federation of State High School Associations. Participation statistics: sports statistics. www.nfhs.org [Acc. 2010 June 30]

Sport England. 2006 Dec 7. *Active people survey*

headline results. Sport by sport fact sheet. London: Sport England.

**A sporting gem**

G Clerici. 1976. *Tennis*. London: Octopus.

A Rowley. Gem, Thomas Henry (1819–1881). www.oxforddnb.com

**The tennis models; Top 8** K Badenhausen. Top earning tennis players. 2009 Sept 4. www.forbes.com

**Davis Cup ranks and wins** Davis Cup Groups. www.daviscup.com [Acc. 2010 Sept 30]

**The greatest prizes**

Tournaments: ATP World Tour Season. www.atpworldtour.com [Acc. 2010 June 12]

Tournaments: 2010 WTA Tournament Calendar. www.wtatour.com [Acc. 2010 June 12]

## 88–89 TRACK AND FIELD

N Müller (Editing director). 2000. *Pierre de Coubertin 1863-1937, Olympism – Selected writings*. Lausanne: International Olympic Committee.

Samsung Diamond League. http://diamondleague.com

International Amateur Athletics Federation. www.iaaf.org [Acc. 2010 Sept 26]

**The sub-four-minute mile**

Special Issue: The sporting barrier: historical and cultural interpretations of the four-minute mile. 2006. *Sport in History*, 26/2.

J Bryant. 2004. *3.59.4: The quest to break the four-minute mile*. London: Hutchinson.

**Isinbayeva caption**

J McAsey. Princess of the pole vault a class above the rest. 2008 Nov 25. www.theaustralian.com.au

Yelena Isinbayeva. www.yelenaisinbaeva.com

**100 metres**

Pages 546–47 and 640 of partial document uploaded on International Association of Athletics Federation's website in honour of Berlin 2009. www.iaaf.org

Cited in Wikipedia articles: Men's 100 metres world record progression. Women's 100 metres world record progression. www.wikipedia.org [Acc. 2010 Oct 12]

**World Athletics Championships** Track and field intro. www.iaaf.org [Acc. 2010 Sept 28]

**Top 10** IAAF World Championships in Athletics. www.wikipedia.org [Acc. 2010 Sept 28]

**Berlin 2009** Placing table. http://berlin.iaaf.org [Acc. 2010 Sept 28]

## 90–91 VOLLEYBALL AND BEACH VOLLEYBALL

D Wallechinsky, J Loucky. 1996. *The complete book of the Olympics 1996 Edition*. London: Aurum Press.

Fédération Internationale de Volleyball. www.fivb.org

**Old folks at play** The volleyball story. www.fivb.org

**404,000 girls…**National Federation of State High School Associations. Participation statistics: sports statistics. www.nfhs.org [Acc. 2010 Aug 16]

**Sex appeal; FIVB Regulations quote…**FIVB. Beach volleyball. Players' uniforms guidelines for Olympic Games. 2004. www.fivb.org

**Volleyball** FIVB Volleyball World Ranking. www.fivb.org [Acc. 2010 Aug 19]

**Olympic medals** www.olympic.org [Acc. 2010 Aug 16]

**Beach volleyball**

Swatch FIVB World Tour 2010 Media Guide. Lausanne: FIVB. www.fivb.org

Swatch FIVB World Tour. www.fivb.org [Acc. 2010 Aug 16]

## 92–93 WRESTLING

National Federation of State High School Associations. Participation statistics: sports statistics. www.nfhs.org [Acc. 2010 Aug 26]

Fédération Internationale des Luttes Associées. www.fila-wrestling.com

R Dilley. Fighting over the scraps. 2000 Mar 7. http://news.bbc.co.uk

GC Boase. Cann, Abraham (*bap.* 1794, *d.* 1864), rev. Dennis Brailsford. www.oxforddnb.com

J Huntington-Whiteley, compiled by. 1998. *The book of British sporting heroes*. London: National Portrait Gallery Publications.

D Wallechinsky, J Loucky. 2008. *The complete book of the Olympics* . London: Aurum Press.

**To the death** A Tomlinson. *A dictionary of sports studies*. 2010. Oxford: Oxford University Press.

**267,000 boys…**National Federation of State High School Associations op. cit.

**Men in tights**

A Tomlinson. 1990. Introduction: Consumer culture and the aura of the commodity. In *Consumption, identity and style: Marketing, meanings and the packaging of pleasure*. London: Routledge.

Strength in Numbers: World Wrestling Entertainment 2009 annual report. Stamford, CT: World Wrestling Entertainment. http://corporate.wwe.com

Frozen in time - June 1981, Wembley. 2000 Nov 5. http://observer.guardian.co.uk

**Sumo**

PL Cuyler. 1979. *Sumo: From rite to sport*. New York and Tokyo: John Weatherhill.

L Watson. 1988. *Sumo*. London: Sidgwick and Jackson.

S WuDunn. Sumo wrestlers (they're BIG) facing a hard fall. 1996 June 28. www.nytimes.com

J McCurry. Sumo threatened by scandal and crime. 2010 July 4. www.guardian.co.uk

60% of sumo fans skeptical over end of ties between JSA, gangsters. 2010 July 19. www.japantoday.com

**International Sumo Federation** International Sumo Federation. http://AmateurSumo.com [Acc. 2010 Aug 28]

**Olympic wrestling** www.olympic.org [Acc. 2010 Aug 17]

## 96–97 INTERNATIONAL FEDERATIONS

**The growth of the federations**

V Simson, A Jennings. 1992. *The Lords of the Rings: Power, money and drugs in the modern Olympics*. London: Simon & Schuster.

J Sugden, A Tomlinson. 2004. Not for the good of the game: Crisis and credibility in the governance of world football. In L Allison (ed). *The global politics of sport: The role of global institutions in sport*. London: Routledge.

SportAccord. www.sportaccord.com

J-L Chappelet, B Kübler-Mabbott. 2008. *The International Olympic Committee and the Olympic system: The governance of world sport*. London: Routledge.

A Jennings, C Sambrook. 2000. *The great Olympic swindle: When the world wanted its Games back*. London: Simon & Schuster.

P Dietschy. French sport: Caught between universalism and exceptionalism. In A Tomlinson, C Young (eds). Special Issue/Forum of *European Review*. Forthcoming, 2011.

A Tomlinson. *A dictionary of sports studies*. 2010. Oxford: Oxford University Press.

**Where the power lies** Members. www.sportaccord.com [Acc. 2010 June 2]

**International Olympic Committee**

Chappelet, Kübler-Mabbott op. cit.

Jennings, Sambrook op. cit.

**Lack of accountability**

R Lloyd, J Oatham, M Hammer. *2007 global accountability report*. London: One World Trust. www.oneworldtrust.org

R Lloyd, S Warren, M Hammer. *2008 global accountability report*. London: One World Trust. www.oneworldtrust.org

## 98–99 MEDIA

Sports Illustrated Sales and Marketing Information Centre. http://sportsillustrated.cnn.com

M Sweney. Premier League goals app. 2010 Aug 12. www.guardian.co.uk

R Milliken. Sport is Murdoch's 'battering ram' for pay TV. 1996 Oct 16. www.independent.co.uk

R Boyle. 2006. *Sports journalism. Contexts and issues*. London: Sage.

O Gibson. ESPN Undaunted by prospect of challenging season on half rations. 2010 Aug 19. www.guardian.co.uk

J Horne. 1992. General sports magazines and "Cap'n

Bob": The rise and fall of *Sportsweek*. *Sociology of Sport Journal* 9/2: pp179-191.

T Mason. 1988. *Sport in Britain*. London: Faber and Faber.

J Sugden, A Tomlinson. 2010. What Beckham had for breakfast: The rolling menu of 24/7 sports news. In S Cushion, J Lewis (eds). *The Rise of 24-hour news television: Global perspectives*. New York: Peter Lang.

LA Wenner (ed). 1998. MediaSport. London and New York: Routledge.

G Whannel. 1992. *Television sport and cultural transformation*. London and New York: Routledge.

**The rising price of Olympic coverage** Olympic marketing fact file 2010 edition. Lausanne: International Olympic Committee. www.olympic.org [Acc. 2010 Aug 24]

**Top media events; Where events were watched** ViewerTrack – The most watched TV sporting events of 2009. 2010. London: Initiative, futures sport + entertainment. www.futuressport.com

**$908m...** Sony and World Sports Group bag IPL television rights. 2008 Jan 14. www.espncricinfo.com

## 100–01 SPONSORSHIP

J Sugden, A Tomlinson. 1998. *FIFA and the contest for world football: Who rules the peoples' game?* Cambridge: Polity Press.

B Smit. 2007. *Pitch invasion: Adidas, Puma and the making of modern sport*. London: Penguin.

**Olympic sponsorship** *Olympic marketing fact file, 2010 edition*. Lausanne: IOC. www.olympic.org

**The golden triangle** Sugden, Tomlinson op. cit.

**An un-free market** A Serrao, G Gifford, A Lewis. Ambush at Soccer City: Police quiz 36 women after FIFA gets in froth over Bavaria beer dress. 2010 June 15. www.thestar.co.za

**Value of sponsorship** *Hyundai 2006 FIFA World Cup™ sponsorship report*. 2006 Sept. Seoul, Korea: Hyundai Motor Company.

## 102–03 CONSUMING SPORT

D Sabo, PM Gray, L Moore. 2000. Domestic violence and televised athletic events: "It's a man thing". In J McKay et al (eds). *Masculinities, gender relations and sport*. London: Sage.

E Friedenberg. 1980. The changing role of homoerotic fantasy in spectator sports. In DF Sabo, R Runfola (eds). *Jock: Sports and male identity*. Englewood Cliffs, NJ: Prentice-Hall.

H-U Gumbrecht. 2006. *In praise of athletic beauty*. Cambridge: Harvard/Belknap (for the concept of "focused intensity").

A Guttmann. 1986. *Sports spectators*. New York: Columbia University Press.

S Redhead. 2007. Those absent from the stadium are always right: Accelerated culture, sport media, and theory at the speed of light. *Journal of Sport & Social Issues* 31/3. pp226-41.

J Sugden, A Tomlinson. 2010. What Beckham had for breakfast: *See* 98–99 MEDIA.

**Sport subculture** P Donnelly. 1981. Toward a definition of sport subcultures. In M Hart, S Birrell (eds). *Sport in the sociocultural process*. Dubuque, Iowa: Wm C Brown Company Publishers.

**Fan types** R Giulianotti. 2002. Supporters, followers, fans and flâneurs: A taxonomy of spectator identities in football. *Journal of Sport & Social Issues* 26/1: p25-46.

**Cheerleading**

L Grindstaff, E West. 2006. Cheerleading and the gendered politics of sport. *Social Problems* 53/4. pp500-18

K Torgovnik. 2008. *Cheer! Inside the secret world of college cheerleading*. Touchstone Books.

**Virtual sports; Fantasy Football** G Crawford. 2005. Sensible soccer: Sport fandom and the rise of digital gaming. In J Magee et al (eds). *The bountiful game? Football identities and finances*. Oxford: Meyer & Meyer.

## Computer games

EA Celebrates 2010 FIFA World Cup South Africa with exclusive release of officially licensed videogame. 2010 Jan 27. www.ea.com

Sales and Genre Data. www.theesa.com [Acc. 2010 Sept 17]

About Us. http://aboutus.ea.com [Acc. 2010 Sept 16]

M Walton. FIFA 10 Europe's fastest selling sports game ever. 2009 Oct 7. http://uk.gamespot.com

Games. http://fifa.easports.com [Acc. 2010 Sept 16]

**$97m...** Author calculation based on data supplied on: Sales and genre data. www.theesa.com [Acc. 2010 Sept 17]

**8 of the 20...** Top-selling video games of 2009: family-friendly titles most popular. 2010 June 19. www.independent.co.uk

## Wii

Top-selling video games. op. cit.

Nintendo consolidated financial highlights. 2010 July 29. www.nintendo.co.jp

Nintendo annual report 2010. www.nintendo.co.jp

Financial results briefing for the nine-month period ended Dec 2009 (Briefing date: 2010 Jan 29) – supplementary information. www.nintendo.co.jp

## 104–05 MERCHANDISING

**20m, 6.5m** 2010 FIFA World Cup™ already sales success for Adidas. 2010 June 21. www.adidas-group.com

**Popular pressure – Honduras** Students and workers beat industry giant. 2010 July 26. www.commondreams.org

**Three steps to heaven** N Klein. 2000. *No logo – Taking aim at the brand bullies*. New York: Alfred Knopf.

**Stitched up in India**

Child labour in football stitching activity in India: A case study of Meerut District in Uttar Pradesh. 2008 Oct 6. New Delhi: Bachan Bachao Andolan. www.laborrights.org

They make footballs, score nothing. 2006 June 27. www.hindu.com

**Pakistan** World Cup: Pakistan football makers have a ball. 2010 June 30. http://timesofindia.indiatimes.com

**West Java, Indonesia** Hamdani's story. www.playfair2012.org.uk ; Hamdani's Adidas story. www.youtube.com

**Vietnam** S Greenhouse. Nike shoe plant in Vietnam is called unsafe for workers. 1997 Nov 8. www.mindfully.org

## 106–07 GAMBLING

Report of the Sports Betting Integrity Panel. 2010 Feb. www.culture.gov.uk

*National Gambling Impact Study Commission final report. Chapter 3: Gambling regulation*. 1999 June 18. http://govinfo.library.unt.edu

S Briggs. How sleaze has brought sport to its knees. 2010 Sept 6. www.telegraph.co.uk

*Soccer Investor News Bulletin*. No. 2678. Poland: Another referee arrest. p3. 2009 Mar 27. www.soccerinvestor.com

*Soccer Investor Weekly Issue*. No. 282. CFA establish anti-corruption task force. p4. 2006 Oct 13. www.soccerinvestor.com

7 2009. London and Brussels: RGA. www.rga.eu.com.

C Geertz. 1972. Deep play: notes on the Balinese cockfight. *Daedalus*. p1-37.

M Neal. 1998. "You lucky punters!" A study of gambling in betting shops. *Sociology*. 32/4. pp581-600.

O Newman. 1968. The sociology of the betting shop. *The British Journal of Sociology*. 19/1. pp17-33.

Sports betting in South Africa. www.gamblingsa.com

Gambling. Australian Government Productivity Commission Inquiry Report Vols 1&2. no. 50. 2010 Feb 26. www.pc.gov.au

**Global gambling market** J Fasman. Shuffle up and deal. 2010 July 8. www.economist.com

**Sports betting; Most globally successful** Sports Betting: Legal, Commercial and Integrity Issues op. cit. Figure 5.25.

**Gross winnings; Global online sports betting** ibid. Figs 2.4, 2.5.

**Value of advertising; Status of advertising** ibid. Figs 5.10, 5.17.

**UK National Lottery Funding** Sport England. www.sportengland.org

**€4.5bn...** Where the money goes. www.national-lottery.co.uk

## 108–09 SPORTS TOURISM

G Richards. 1995. The UK ski market: Determinants of destination choice and skilled consumption. In D Leslie (ed). *Tourism and leisure – Culture, heritage and participation*. Eastbourne: Leisure Studies Association Publication No. 51.

J Standeven, P de Knop. 1999. *Sport tourism*. Champaign, IL: Human Kinetics.

Sports in Dubai. www.dubaitourism.ae

L Roberts. Winter brings closure to Snowdon summit café. 2009 Nov 11. www.grough.co.uk

Lac du Salagou. www.saint-guilhem-vallee-herault.com

**Types of sports tourism** M Weed, C Bull. 2009. *Sports tourism: Participants, policy and providers*. London: Elsevier/Butterworth-Heinemann.

**Pros and cons of sport tourism**

M Weed (ed). 2008. *Sport & tourism: A reader*. London: Routledge.

Standeven, Knop op. cit.

**60m...**

US Ski industry reports second best season on record. 2010 May 4. www.nsaa.org

Final Report: 57.4 million skier visits in 2008/09. 2009 Aug 1. www.nsaa.org

**Striking a delicate balance**

J Higham (ed). 2005. *Sport tourism destinations: Issues, opportunities and analysis*. Oxford: Elsevier/Butterworth-Heinemann.

S Hudson. 2000. *Snow business: A study of the international ski industry*. London: Cassell.

G Jennings (ed). 2007. *Water-based tourism, sport, leisure, and recreation experiences*. Oxford: Elsevier/Butterworth-Heinemann.

JG Winter, PJ Dillon. 2004. Effects of golf course construction and operation on water chemistry of headwater streams on the Precambrian Shield. *Environmental pollution* 133/2: p243-53.

Ski lift price report - worldwide lift pass prices. 2008 Jan 22. www.j2ski.com

US ski industry reports second best season on record op. cit.

Final report: 57.4 million skier visits in 2008/09. 2009 Aug 1. www.nsaa.org

Everest clean-up mounted. 2001 Apr 1. http://news.bbc.co.uk

Kilimanjaro Ecotourism Project. www.kilimanjaroproject.com

History of Kilimanjaro: Kilimanjaro today. www.climbmountkilimanjaro.com

B Skoloff. 'Complete collapse' of coral possible. 2010 Mar 25. www.msnbc.msn.com

Tennis holidays. www.markwarner.co.uk

Golf in Wisconsin: US$2.4 billion impact. www.golfbusinesscommunity.com

Golf Travel Insights 2010. Budapest: KPMG Advisory Ltd. www.golfbenchmark.com

Majorca Cycling. www.majorcacycling.com

# INDEX